Contents

Acknowledgments

We would like to thank Ralph Page, Lindsay Fitzclarence, Jeanne Brady Giroux, and Richard Quantz for having read substantial sections of this book and for providing invaluable criticisms. We are grateful to Jan Fulton and Fran Shaloe for their patience and skill in typing much of this manuscript. We would also like to thank Dean Jan Kettlewell and Professor Nelda Cameron-McCabe of Miami University for the time, support, and professional encouragement they provided for Henry Giroux after his exodus from Boston University. Of course, we are solely responsible for the book in its final form.

Some of the chapters in this book appeared in slightly or substantially altered form in the following journals: *Harvard Educational Review, College English, Curriculum Inquiry, Journal of Education, Educational Theory, Issues in Education, New Education* (Australia). An altered version of Chapter 2 was written for a colloquium at Suffolk University on "Creativity and the Implementation of Change: Liberal Learning in the Practical World," February 20–21, 1985. For the past fourteen years, the two of us have been involved in a collaboration over the relationship between pedagogy and politics and the evolving vision of emancipatory and transformative education. During that time, some of the articles in this book initially were written and published under separate authorship, though they had almost always been mutually discussed and influenced by our joint work. In writing the book itself, we jointly authored a number of chapters, and in other instances rewrote and edited work that we incorporated, but, in all cases, each chapter was the final product of an editing and writing process that allows us to view the book in its published form as a strictly collaborative effort. It is an effort characterized by a warmly held friendship as well as a deeply shared belief in the need to struggle for a better world for all human beings.

Introduction: Beyond the Melting Pot—Schooling in the Twenty-first Century

During the twelve years of the Reagan/Bush administrations the educational system in the United States was the object of a massive reform movement, led mainly by conservatives. During these years, the meaning and purpose of schooling at all levels of education were refashioned around the principles of the marketplace and the logic of rampant individualism. Ideologically, this meant abstracting schools from the language of democracy and equity while simultaneously organizing educational reform around the discourse of choice, reprivatization, and individual competition. Consistent with a broader attack on all notions of democratic public life, schools became a prime battleground for removing the language of ethics, history, and community from public discourse. Within this approach, schools became the quintessential institutions of bureaucratic individualism. Under the incentive of school choice, market relations asserted themselves with a vengeance on public schools and higher education. Devastated by the recession, diminished local tax bases, and drastic cutbacks in federal expenditures, school systems around the country were forced to increase class size and decrease teaching staffs, while using fewer resources.

On a policy level, the conservative reform movement of the Reagan/Bush era resulted in instituting state legislation that increasingly promoted standardized curricula, increased testing for entry-level teachers, and removed equity considerations from the discourse of excellence. Lacking any social strategy for addressing the crisis of public schooling, the Reagan/Bush administrations essentially attempted to dismantle public schooling by turning it over to the imperatives of choice, business, and reprivatization.

Politically, the Reagan/Bush attack on public schools manifested itself in further reproducing a two-tier system of schooling designed to privilege upper middle-class whites, on the one hand, while containing the working class, the poor, and students of color, on the other. The policy of racialized, class containment had devastating consequences for public education and the social problems that both informed and were exacerbated by the attack on public schooling. In the midst of a growing division between rich and poor, the dropout rate for nonwhite children in major cities such as New York exceeded 70 percent during the 1980s. Buttressed by policies that refused to adequately fund programs such as Head Start and Chapter I, schools increasingly were unable to address a growing population of students from poverty-stricken families. This failure is especially relevant in light of the fact that 25 percent of all children under the age of 18 lived in poverty during the Reagan/Bush years.

At the same time, the working conditions of teachers became worse during those twelve years. Teachers have become increasingly deskilled through an emphasis on accountability schemes, teaching to the tests, and management by objective approaches that reduce their work to reductionist, instrumental, and demeaning procedures. Demoralized by their working conditions, increasingly alienated by the heavy-handed imposition of reforms initiated through the growing corporatization of the schools, and left out of the dynamics of educational reform, teachers were reduced to clerks of the empire under the reform movement of the Reagan/Bush administrations.

Of course, it was during this decade, too, that conservatives and neoliberals launched a major assault on the democratization of the curriculum spurned by the new social movements of the 1970s and 1980s. Whereas various interest groups that are organized around racial, class, gender, and sexual orientation have demanded curricula responsive to their histories, experiences, and voices, conservatives have attempted to transform the schools into cultural beachheads for imposing not simply corporate ideologies but also the Eurocentric imperatives of a narrowly defined nationalism. Under the Reagan/Bush administrations, schools became institutions for moral regulation and character education in which family values, moral fundamentalism, and a Great Books ethic reasserted a nostalgic and mythic view of what it meant to be a citizen in the New World Order. The language of selfishness, competition, consumption, and success spawned a meanspiritedness toward those who were victimized in the Reagan/Bush world order. The sentiment was elitist and racist. Within this discourse, nationalism and Eurocentrism combined as part of a broader attempt to promote and legitimate a "common culture" in which cultural diversity rather than intolerance was seen as the "enemy" of democracy. The result was a notion of schooling that was at odds with educating all students to learn how to govern rather than be governed.

The great waves of immigration to our shores since 1980 provide a startling case study of the failure of social and educational policy. We are in the midst of a veritable sea change in the demographic, social, and cultural composition of the United States. In brief, the nation is experiencing a new wave of immigration which, by the end of this century, may exceed in volume and importance the last wave at the turn of the twentieth century. Key geographic areas within the country—chiefly large metropolitan regions of the Northeast and Southwest, including California—and major public institutions, especially those of social welfare and education, are grappling with entirely new populations that are bringing with them new needs.

From 1985 to 1990 some 5 million immigrants came to the United States, exceeding the annual rate in the great second wave of immigration that took place between 1880 and 1910 when 20 million people, primarily from southern Italy and Eastern Europe, came to this country. In this, the third great wave, migrants from Central America, the Caribbean, South America, and Asia—especially Korea, Vietnam, Taiwan, and China—are the most prevalent, although important immigrant cohorts from Eastern and Southern Europe continue to arrive. Given the worldwide movement of populations from the peripheral, rural regions to the metropolitan centers, this trend is bound to accelerate, especially in the cities.

While there are similarities between the current immigrant cohorts and those of the last great wave, particularly their preponderant rural origins, the striking differences between them have barely been confronted. Perhaps the most important of these differences is that the earlier migration occurred in the context of a dramatic, long-wave economic expansion in the United States. Immigrants were recruited in the millions for the burgeoning mines and mills, the garment and shoe factories, and performed the bulk of the unskilled labor in the growing transportation and construction industries. Pay was low, hours were long, and working conditions were abominable. Yet, many of this generation of newly arrived workers shared the tacit belief that, even if they themselves were destined to economic insecurity, if not abject poverty, their children were certain to do better. And many actually moved up the social and economic ladder within their own lifetimes.

Certainly, the American dream of material well-being and social mobility lives today in the hearts and minds of many immigrants. But they have come to this country in large numbers in two decades (1970–present) when the American economy has entered a prolonged era of stagnation, punctuated by short-term growth spurts. Since 1970, millions of jobs were lost to capital flight, and technological change wiped out millions more. From 1970 to 1990 the U.S. economy lost more than 5 million jobs in the manufacturing sector. In this period, it gained more than 10 million service and clerical jobs, but these were, in the main, unavailable to workers who were undocumented and whose mastery of English was still evolving. Moreover, on the average they paid only 60 percent of the wages and salaries in the manufacturing sector. After 1987, growth in the service sector ended, and the number of jobs, especially in retail and clerical trades, is declining rapidly.

More to the point, among the greatest losses were precisely those in industries where immigrants have traditionally found entry-level jobs: the needle trades, textiles, shoes, and, more recently, plastics. For example, in the 1980s the needle trades and textiles lost half a million jobs; the shoe industry was virtually wiped out to imports; and the auto industry, an important source of employment for African-Americans, lost 300,000 jobs, mostly among assemblers and machine operators. General Motors' recent announcement of layoffs for 70,000 additional employees and IBM's aggregate reduction of its labor force by 65,000 in 1992 have accelerated the trend toward the elimination of highly paid jobs. In the next decade, native-born workers who would have taken these jobs will be competing with immigrants, women, and native-born minorities for lower wage work.

Many immigrants have remained unemployed, have become low-wage workers in the legal economy, or have been condemned to casual and seasonal labor. But others are helping to create an entire new sector of the U.S. economy. The new immigrants have become the core workers for a growing "underground" or informal economy. Today, in New York, Philadelphia, Los Angeles, and other large cities, tens of thousands make garments, shoes, plastic novelties, toys, and other products. Others drive non-medallion, extralegal cabs and unlicensed trucks, many of which serve their own community. Those who enjoy legal status may work in the informal or above-ground economy, but they usually earn income at or below the minimum wage. In communities such as the Williamsburg section of Brooklyn and south central Los Angeles, it is not unusual to find entire extended families, including grandparents and young children, working long hours, making garments or toys in their homes or in dimly lit lofts.

In the face of extremely limited prospects for economic growth over the next period of U.S. history and, perhaps equally saliently, the rapid decline of well-paying jobs, even in the technical and professional spheres, schools are facing an identity crisis. The long-held assumption that school credentials provide the best route to economic security and class mobility may prove to have been a truth confined to the industrializing era, and, at that, available to perhaps half the population. The labor market is becoming increasingly bifurcated: organizational and technical changes are producing a limited number of jobs for highly educated and trained people-managers, scientific and technological experts, and researchers. On the other hand, we are witnessing the disappearance of many middle-level white-collar subprofessions. Teaching and technical and professional categories in the health industry remain reasonably viable options, but, since the fiscal crisis of the late 1980s, budget cuts have restricted new hiring in many cities and towns. Even employment in computer programming has become subject to its own technology. Computer-aided software programming, not yet widely disseminated, threatens to eliminate programmers. And in the face of sharpening competition, employers typically hire a growing number of low-paid, part-time workers; in this connection, temporary substitutes are becoming more common in teaching. Even some professionals have become free-lance workers with few, if any, fringe benefits. These developments call into question the efficacy of mass schooling for providing the "well-trained" labor force that employers still claim they require. Educators must reexamine the mission of the schools in the light of these shattering shifts. While the two major teacher organizations claim some 2.5 million members and now represent more than 75 percent of the profession, there is little evidence, beyond their general support for multiculturalism as a *supplement* to the standard curriculum, that the National Education Association and the American Federation of Teachers have come to grips with these issues.

Although most immigrant groups have settled in the large cities of the East and West coasts, in the past five years new immigrant populations have increased markedly in the Midwest and the Southeast as well. Twenty-four percent of New York City's population is foreign born. By the year 2000 more than a third of the city's residents will have been born in another part of the globe. Even more dramatic figures may be adduced for Los Angeles, and somewhat smaller, but significant, proportions of the residents of Chicago, Detroit, San Diego, and San Jose are recent immigrants. Characteristically, most are under 25, and a heavy proportion is of school age. Indeed, New York's schools—both at the elementary and secondary levels and higher education—are struggling to understand the implications of the entrance of large numbers of Latino and Asian immigrants for their curricula, for the provision of support services, and for the management of schools.

Most school systems lack basic information about students of migrant (students from other parts of the United States and Puerto Rico) and immigrant backgrounds: they have little organized knowledge of their countries of origin, their families' socioeconomic position, the specific features of their native culture(s), and their expectations of schooling. While the new multicultural curricula have made some impact and some change has taken place in the culture of some urban secondary schools to take account of the changes in the school population, still strong counterpressures exist at the highest levels to retain and strengthen the uniform curriculum. The idea that equality of opportunity means the expectation that students may master a definite Eurocentrically based body of knowledge by the completion of high school is based on the assimilation assumptions that guided the early twentieth-century school reforms and still dominate the thinking of many "progressives" in education. For example, the education program of the Governors Conference in 1989, of which President Clinton was then a leader, favored strengthening the standardized curriculum and national testing. Similar views have been expressed by President Albert Shanker of the American Federation of Teachers.

Moreover, most multicultural reforms such as English as a Second Language (ESL) and "rainbow" curricula provide, at best, a template whose applications are often too mechanically conceived. Few efforts are being made to rethink the *entire* curriculum in the light of the new migration and immigration, much less develop entirely different pedagogies. In secondary schools and community colleges, for example, students still study "subjects"—social studies, math, science, English, and "foreign" languages. Some schools have "added" courses in the history and culture of Asian, Latin American, and Caribbean societies, but they have little thought of transforming the entire humanities and social studies curricula in the light of the cultural transformations of the school. Nor are serious efforts being made to integrate the sciences with social studies and the humanities; hence, science and math are still being deployed as sorting devices in most schools rather than as crucial markers of a genuinely innovative approach to learning.

In short, multiculturalism has severe limits. In order for it to be a real help in educational transformation, concrete social, cultural, and, equally important, intellectual contexts must inform innovation. These not only are subject-centered, but they also refer to the specific conditions of school life—the administrations, teacher abilities and background, the socioeconomic profile of students and their already acquired knowledge.

The multicultural curriculum should seek to develop a context-dependent series of learnings that will take account of student experiences. But, on the whole, the currency of this approach seems to be limited to elementary education. By the time most students reach junior high school and certainly high school, context-dependent education is rarely practiced. Of course, some teachers try to make their classrooms places that build on the cultural knowledge that students already possess and is woven into learning. But in most places teaching remains articulated with performance tests, most of which is tied to standardized curricula. Despite the growing diversity of college students, we can cite few examples of sensitivity by administrators and teachers outside language arts to the multiplicity of economic, social, and cultural factors that bear on a student's educational life in higher education. At best, some urban colleges and universities created ethnic studies programs in the 1970s that recognized diversity, but they strictly separated these programs from the traditional academic disciplines which, overwhelmingly, today remain bound to the old assumptions. As a result, there is a surprising paucity of courses and programs that integrate new student populations and their needs into the curriculum, counseling, and placement activities.

As the evidence is increasingly showing, the historic assumption of immigrant "meltability" no longer obtains because many, if not all, immigrant groups hold fast to important elements of their native cultures while the prevailing economic situation gives them little reason to accept the standard curriculum as the key to a better life. The crucial culture war today is between, on the one hand, education institutions that do not meet the needs of a massively shifting student population and, on the other, students and their families who perceive schools as merely one more instrument of repression.

Occupying the front line of the education crisis are teachers and administrators. Even when school authorities and teachers understand the importance of change, most still experience everyday life in the school as an uphill battle to achieve minimum order. In 1991 one New York City principal proudly told an in-service trainer that the halls in "his" school were finally quiet enough to permit classroom teaching and learning. But he acknowledged that, despite gestures of change such as a small pre-professional program that had effected a significant turnaround among a small group of students, the course offerings and the pedagogic practices for the vast majority were, for the most part, conventional. In this school, where the student population is, overwhelmingly, of Caribbean origin—particularly Haitian and Dominican—average daily attendance was about 70 percent of the enrolled students, and the principal reported this statistic as a sign of progress!

In areas of high-immigrant African-American and Latino populations in major cities, daily attendance of 50 percent of enrolled students is far more typical and dropout rates are similarly high. Although some school authorities and politicians recognize that the "problem" is complex and that responsibility must be placed squarely on the shoulders of the institutions of governance, education, and the economy, there is still a strong tendency to blame the victims of the centrifugal forces that account for school failure.

Next to the students and their families, perhaps teachers are the most severe casualties of the crisis. In many of these schools, when not bewildered or in despair, many have grown cynical about the chance that anything can be done to reverse the situation in their schools. We have spoken to teachers who experience fear that they will be attacked or caught in the crossfire of gang warfare every day of their working lives. Others admit that they do not expect to do much "teaching" in the classroom but have settled for maintaining order most of the time. They have remade themselves, against their own social and political beliefs, into harsh disciplinarians—rule makers without an ultimate goal—as a strategy of self-defense.

Some of the more hopeful and enterprising teachers and administrators beat the bushes for funds to start special programs, often in conjunction with corporations and public agencies willing to work in schools. These are usually language, culture, and occupational programs that invariably report high-retention, graduation, and college admission rates, largely because they are small, run by dedicated teachers, and often produce jobs or educational advancement for students. Typically, the director and teachers in these alternative programs—both within and outside large schools—are able to address many of the social, cultural, and curricular needs of students. Staff usually works long hours, have tacit understandings of the students' life-situation, and are willing to devote attention to individual educational and personal needs.

But the alternative schools and special programs, while providing some hope that high schools and community colleges may reverse the reproduction of school failure, succeed precisely because they involve a relatively tiny proportion of the school population. They give corporations and other outside organizations the opportunity to take some social responsibility without, at the same time, obliging them to address the larger student population. The point is, that as long as alternative education remains just that—programs geared to a tiny minority of either upper class kids or dropouts, their two major constituencies—school systems that are otherwise failing the vast majority can proudly wrap themselves in the mantle of innovation and change without altering the larger context of schooling.

In this perspective, high dropout rates, low reading scores, absenteeism, drugs, boredom, and student resistance have become categories that serve as cultural markers to let Americans know that students who are poor, black, ethnic, or the "devalued other" do not count for much. School failure in the neo-conservative era was defined as a matter of poor character, stigmatized as a poverty of values rather than understood through the widespread poverty of resources and human compassion. Equity was disarticulated from the notion of social justice and was transformed into a radical scheme to cheat rich white kids out of an opportunity to get into an Ivy League school. Pedagogical authority was invoked as a major policy consideration when the Reagan/Bush administrations talked about troubled schools in urban areas.

During the last decade, schools became the new scapegoat for the American economy's increasing failure to compete in the new global marketplace. They were reimagined by the neo-conservatives as the new launching pad for injecting into the school curricula the kind of patriotic and commercial fervor that would serve up future generations of adults who would shut up and serve in the new army of service sector workers or simply disappear into the ranks of the unemployed and homeless.

Under the Reagan/Bush administrations, the notion of schooling as a vehicle for social justice and public responsibility was trashed for the glitter of the marketplace and the logic of the spirited entrepreneur. Making it in schools became a marriage between trying hard (real individual effort) and being in the right place at the most opportune time (the suburbs). For Reagan/Bush conservatives, the construction of a New World Order in foreign policy was to be matched by the emergence of a New School Order driven by the ideology of corporate capitalism and the structuring principles of institutionalized racism. The discourse of a multicultural and multiracial democracy had no place in the educational reforms of the Reagan/ Bush era. Instead, its guiding reform principles were respect, order, and submission. One of the most ominous results of the conservative reform effort was the emergence of an educational reform movement that viewed democracy as a political liability and public schooling as an obstacle to the demands of the marketplace. In this instance, the historic but unfulfilled relationship between schooling, democracy, and public life was junked in the interest of a world order in which public values became a burden rather than a condition for democratic public life.

With the election of Bill Clinton as president of the United States in 1992, many have assumed that the concerted attack on public education and other spheres of democratic public life will be replaced by a new language of possibility grounded in the imperatives of social responsibility, compassion, and critical citizenship. It is hoped that the new administration will not view the problems of schooling as merely procedural, but will reformulate them as a crisis of citizenship and ethics. It is in the spirit of such hope that we would like to suggest some general guidelines for rethinking the language of educational reform and possibility for the rest of the 1990s.

As we stated in the preface to the first edition of this book, we believe that any viable educational reform program must return schools to their primary task: to serve as places of critical education in order to create a public sphere of citizens who are able to exercise power over their own lives and especially over the conditions of knowledge acquisition. Central to any such reform effort is the recognition that democracy is not a set of formal rules of participation, but the lived experience of empowerment for the vast majority. At one level this means that the Clinton administration needs to reinsert the language of moral, political, and civic conscience into the discourse of educational reform. We are not merely interested in equality, but in empowerment for the vast majority of students in the United States who need to be educated in the spirit of a critical democracy. Equality is essential but inadequate as a basis for educational reform. The Clinton administration needs to extend the principles of social justice to all spheres of economic, political, and cultural life. Within this context, the experiences that constitute the production of knowledge, identities, and social values in the schools will be inextricably linked to the quality of moral and political life within the wider society. Hence, the reform of schooling must be seen as part of a wider revitalization of public life.

Accordingly, the Clinton administration must link the reform of schools to the reform of other social spheres. For instance, any viable policy of educational reform must be matched by the guarantee of full employment for our nation's youth. The skills of critical citizenship must be addressed and extended within a set of policies that enable people to have decent work, food, shelter, and sense of hope in the future. Thus, if schools are to become a bastion for experiencing and living out the dictates of democratic community, they must be defined and integrated with other social agencies, so that the primary physical and psychological needs of students can be understood and addressed as part of their development as critical agents. One concrete expression of this policy might be to provide immediate and full funding to Head Start and other programs designed to ensure that all students start school ready to learn. Of course, this would also mean funding programs that provide day care, literacy programs, and opportunities to work and study in the schools.

Central here is not the issue of turning schools into massive and overburdened welfare agencies, but of redefining the relationship between the school and community in terms that provide dialogue, trust, resources, and mutual forms of empowerment. Democracy in the schools does not begin with forcing kids to say the Pledge of Allegiance; it begins with a commitment to exhibit respect for the communities, families, and neighborhoods in which students live out their identities and sense of collective self. Schools commit forms of symbolic violence when they deny the voices and legacies of the communities that give meaning to the students who inhabit their classrooms. Returning schools to their public function means making families and communities co-owners in the schools. It means making democracy work through the process of sharing power, providing a democratic vision, and working collectively to create a multicultural and multiracial democracy. Schools abstracted from their communities diminish rather than enhance the public and civic functions of schooling.

During the twelve Reagan/Bush years, conservatives argued that money doesn't count as a viable factor in promoting school reform. While money doesn't guarantee school success, it does provide the conditions for setting the parameters necessary for any viable school reform policy. As Jonathan Kozol has eloquently demonstrated in *Savage Inequalities,* underpaid teachers, overcrowded classrooms, a crumbling infrastructure, and a massive shortage of basic resources have condemned large numbers of teachers and students in urban cities to forms of schooling that parallel educational systems in the poorest of underdeveloped, colonial countries.[1] It is a travesty when some schools in one of the richest countries of the world ask students to bring toilet paper from home because their schools cannot afford it; it is a moral affront when poor, working-class students are forced to learn in schools with broken-down heating systems, to use the corridor as a makeshift classroom, or to work in science labs with no equipment.

The Clinton administration needs to implement a federal program that commits adequate funding for educational reforms. This means eliminating the property tax system as the basis for funding public schools. It means shifting resources from the defense budget to the budget for educational reform. It means drastically increasing federal expenditures for public schooling as a basic investment in the future of this country. But beyond refinancing public education, the Clinton administration needs to immediately provide a program in which the highest financial salaries would go to the best teachers willing to teach in the poorest schools in this country. It means mobilizing a federal employment-construction bill to provide jobs as part of a large-scale effort to tear down many of the uninhabitable buildings that now pass for schools. It also means simultaneously rebuilding and refurbishing those schools worth saving, repairing buildings, providing decent classrooms, constructing new schools, and making schools safe and enjoyable places in which to teach and learn. Central to such an effort is the need to build smaller schools, hire more teachers, and maintain smaller class size. At issue here is addressing the space of power. That is, any viable educational reform must create the spatial and structural conditions for learning to take place.

The Clinton administration also needs to provide massive aid in the form of scholarships, grants, and loans to entice minorities into the field of teaching. This could take the form of a program that would offer not only financial aid, but also incentives to those institutions of higher education that would be willing to create programs that address the needs of minorities and urban education.

In addition to linking schooling to the imperatives of democracy and providing adequate funding and resources for establishing the material conditions necessary for decent teaching and learning, the Clinton administration must reverse the top-to-down policies of the last twelve years in which teachers were both deskilled and reduced to the role of technicians. In this book we argue that teachers need to gain some control over their work conditions. In part, this means giving teachers rather than the state more power to regulate the conditions of their work. It means suspending the drive for national testing, standardized curriculum, and management-based pedagogy. Pedagogy must be attentive to the content and context of the sites in which it takes place. This is not meant to suggest that a national debate should not be waged over the meaning of education or that the federal government should remove itself from all ideological aspects of schooling. On the contrary, we believe that the federal government has a responsibility to ensure the civil rights of all students, teachers, and parents. It should also provide a large part of the financial investments and opportunities for teachers to receive a decent salary, organize the conditions of their workplace, and interact in government-sponsored seminars and conferences with other teachers and educators from around the country.

Finally, if the purpose and meaning of schooling is to be linked to the creation of a multiracial and multicultural democracy, the issue of cultural difference must become a defining principle of curriculum development and research. In an age of shifting demographics, large-scale immigration, and multiracial communities, the Clinton administration must make a firm commitment to cultural difference as central to the meaning of schooling and citizenship. First, this means dismantling and deconstructing the legacy of nativism and racial chauvinism that has defined the rhetoric of school reform for the last decade. The Reagan and Bush era witnessed a full-fledged attack on the rights of minorities, civil rights legislation, affirmative action, and the legitimation of curriculum reforms pandering to Eurocentric interests. The Clinton administration needs to reverse these policies through legislation and ideological support for making schools more attentive to the cultural resources that students bring to the public schools.

Second, the Clinton administration must take the lead in encouraging programs that open school curricula to the narratives of cultural difference, without falling into the trap of merely romanticizing the experience of Otherness. At stake here is the development of an educational policy that asserts public education as part of a broader ethical and political discourse, and that both challenges and transforms those curricula reforms of the last decade that are profoundly Eurocentric in context and content. In part, this suggests changing the terms of the debate regarding the relationship between schooling and national identity. It also suggests providing federal funding for programs that encourage teachers and students to rely less on standardized textbooks and more on creating curricula materials that are, in part, responsive to the rich and disparate legacies that give this country a diverse national identity. It means funding public school programs that view teaching and learning as a dialogue in which cultural differences become the new borderlands where democratic identities are fashioned. As part of a pedagogy of possibility, cultural differences are not asserted and privileged through the specificity of dominant notions of race, gender, and class, but through a commitment to expanding dialogue and exchange across lines of cultural difference as part of a wider attempt to deepen and develop democratic public life.

NOTE

1. Jonathan Kozol, *Savage Inequalities* (New York: Crown Publishing, 1991).

Chapter One

Rethinking the Nature of Educational Reform

For the last twelve years, schools have been the subject of an intense national debate. In the recent past, discussion has centered on three issues: whether schools can be the central institution for achieving racial and sexual equality; in higher education, whether the traditional liberal arts curricula are still "relevant" to a changing labor market; and whether the authoritarian classroom stifles the creativity of young children or, conversely, how permissiveness has resulted in a general lowering of educational achievement. All of these issues are still with us, but they have been subsumed under a much larger question: how to make schools adequate to a changing economic, political and ideological environment.

As has been the case with most public issues in American society, the conservatives have seized the initiative and put liberals and progressives on the defensive. Their arguments have force not only because conservatism has become dominant in the ideological realm, but also because their critique seems to correspond to the actual situation. In the first place, conservatives have joined radical critics in announcing that the schools have failed to educate, a perception shared by most parents, teachers and administrators. And, second, they have coupled their point with a clear analysis of the causes and a program for curing the affliction. To be sure, their analysis is by no means original or intellectually challenging. They have taken their cue from some radical critics who claim that schooling is merely an adjunct to the labor market. But, unlike the left, conservatives criticize the schools for failing to fulfill this function. With some exceptions, they are happy to jettison the traditional liberal vision that schools must be responsible for transmitting Western cultural and intellectual traditions. Instead, they have repeated the 1960s radical attack that schools are not relevant to students' lives. However, at a time when nearly everyone is anxious about his/her place in a rapidly shifting job market, relevance has come to mean little else than job preparation. While many jobs require applicants to know how to read and write and to possess skills for specialized employment, few employers require mastery or even familiarity with the literary canon, the arts, and music, much less a secure command of history and the social sciences. Conservatives demand "excellence," by which they usually mean that schools should offer more rigorous science and math curriculum—a notion in keeping with the conservative idea that the mastery of techniques is equivalent to progress. Their language of "achievement," "excellence," "discipline," and "goal orientation" really means vocational education or, in their most traditional mode, a return to the authoritarian classroom armed with the three Rs curriculum.

The ascendancy of the conservative critique and program was prepared unintentionally by the success of the educational movements of the 1960s. These movements were aimed at both preparing black and other minority students for the job market and changing the relations of power within the schools by transferring curriculum determination and administrative authority, in part, from teachers and administrators to parents and students. In the 1960s the traditional liberal arts curriculum was attacked for being culturally biased. Since intelligence and achievement tests were based on knowledge that presupposed "middle-class" culture, grades and testing were scrapped by some elementary and secondary schools, and, more importantly, were severely reduced as a measure of achievement, even when these practices survived the reform onslaught.

In the halcyon days of apparently unlimited expansion, the fundamental impulse motivating educational reform was how to help the excluded get a piece of the economic action. The widespread assumption among school critics was that their "leveling" function remained unfulfilled as long as minorities and women were excluded from the mobility routes that seemed to be available to white men. The "levelers" tried to change the restrictive policies of unions and corporations as well as transform schools. However, their focus on education was based on the perception, largely correct, that because social welfare institutions were public, they were somewhat less intractable than the economic behemoth. Those who concentrated on unions were interested in bringing minorities and women into the working class. Those who fought to make schools instruments of social and class mobility were fighting a different battle: they wanted the opportunity to become professionals and managers and believed that credentials were the most appropriate weapon. In neither case, except for the criticism of the school curricula as class-, gender-, and race-oriented, did most reformers ask the question about the external and internal orientation of school knowledge since they already assumed that curriculum should be articulated with the labor market. Thus, these reformers saw their task as accurate forecasting. For the minority who cared about political power in schools, the main issue was who could hire and fire the administrators and teachers. In 1968, the conflict between radical nationalists, school authorities, the unions and liberal "politicos" came to a head in a teachers strike over whether and to what extent the "community" (read blacks and Puerto Ricans) should exercise power within the system. Community control advocates assumed that if they had power over employment in the schools, the rest would follow. They made no profound critique of the existing curriculum, just who would implement it.

Among the most dramatic victories of the 1960s was "open admission" of minorities to colleges and universities. The right of any high school graduate to attend postsecondary schools regardless of his/her grades or test scores did not signify full democratization of higher education because reformers did not demand integration at all levels of the academic system. It did signify, though, a sharp rise in college enrollments in vocational programs, particularly in community colleges, and the wholesale creation of an entirely new level of higher education, that is, the second-tier public liberal arts colleges. But the Carnegie Foundation and other major institutional leaders in higher education made sure that open admissions did not jeopardize the elite schools. New York's City University Chancellor William Bowker, later president of the University of California at Berkeley, took care that open admissions would not mean weakening academic standards at Queens, Hunter, and other top-level city colleges, but, instead, would require organizing new campuses as "open enrollment" institutions. Open admissions meant a new era for those historically left out of college, but also reinforced the hierarchical character of higher education.

As we will show, the new education debate has little to do with fulfilling the American dream of social equality; justice is quite beside the point for the new conservative reformers. Their major concern is the changing world economy and the new international division of labor. Schools, appropriately, are considered producers of human capital. After a century of underground existence in economic doctrine, recent neo-conservative wisdom has rediscovered labor. Supply side economics blames the relative decline of U.S. manufacturing on lowered productivity in the new, more competitive environment. In turn, part of the productivity picture is ascribed to declining school effectiveness. Industry has rediscovered education because it has lost its once secure markets. Supply side economics argues that government should get out of the way of investment by reducing taxes and thereby increasing business incentives to enlarge and modernize our decrepit productive plant. On the other side, education conservatives advocate reducing federal aid to education in the form of categorical programs, but have intensified their ideological intervention by insisting that schools upgrade themselves through changed curriculum and new management systems rather than massive financial inputs. "Human capital" theorists articulate "back to basics," increased salaries for math and science teachers, and reducing the cultural and recreational curricula to a bare minimum, as responses to the leaner economic environment. School conservatives have attributed the multiple sins of the schools to the education reforms of the 1960s. If students have failed to perform in the workplace as well as the classroom, this condition is due to the loss of power over curriculum and discipline by teachers and administrators. Chester Finn has succinctly stated the case:

> The sad fact is that for close to two decades now we have neglected educational quality in the name of equality. Trying to insure that every child would have access to as much education as every other child, we have failed to attend to the content of that education. Seeking to mediate conflict and forestall controversy over the substance of education, we begin to find ourselves with very little substance needed. Striving to avoid invidious comparisons among youngsters we have stopped gauging individual progress by testing. . . . Hesitant to pass judgment on lifestyles, cultures and forms of behavior we have invited relativism into the curriculum and pedagogy.[1]

Although Finn does not explicitly reject the goal of equality, his emphasis on "quality" is framed in the discourse of absolute standards which can constitute some kind of objective measure of individual and group progress. These measures are needed to insure "the kind of society we want to inhabit, the kinds of people we want our children to become, the productivity and competitiveness of our national economy," and "our sense of national security and national purpose."[2] What follow from these objectives are a dozen prescriptions that combine the neo-conservative slogan to "get the federal government off the backs of the schools" with the demand that we "throw the special interests out of the schoolhouse," by which he means any "greedy/single-minded group" such as the handicapped and linguistic minorities whose demands, however abstractly valid, prevent schools from marshalling "enough resources to pay for solid instruction in the basics."[3]

Finn's no frills educational program does indeed signify the kind of society and people the neo-conservatives want: workers who can willingly perform the specialized tasks required by an economy facing increased competition from abroad. Of course, Finn enters the obligatory caveat for pluralism in education, which means, among other things, the free choice of even poor students to attend nonpublic schools if they could receive vouchers from the government to pay for it. And, of course, "basics" signify student subordination to school authority. Finn wants no more of this "student-centered" curriculum in which courses are designed collaboratively by students and teachers rather than being left to administrators and teachers. After all, teenagers cannot be expected to know what's good for them.

To those trained in the varieties of progressive education movements, the platonism inherent in this program will seem arcane and even ridiculous. Finn's rejection of educational relativism and his assertion (nowhere argued) that "standards" exist and are, moreover, knowable, have the ring of falsehood for anyone aware of the chaotic state of our moral life. However, to dismiss neo-conservatives as reactionary utopians or to discount their program as, in any case, a measure of the degree to which they are wedded to the past, would be a grievous error. The neo-conservatives' strength lies in their bold invocation of morality in education, their hubris that declares they know what truth and the good life really are, and their ability to speak the language of possibility even as they appropriate the left's critique of contemporary schooling.

In contrast, radical critics remain mired in the language of critique even as its own constituency, much less the majority of teachers, parents, and students have, at least for now, tired of this discourse. The impressive corpus of radical and Marxist analysis of American, Canadian, and British education has accumulated evidence, from many angles, against the liberal vision of schooling as a broad preparation for life, as an effective means to reproduce the kind of society and individual consistent with Western humanist traditions. As we shall show in another chapter, left discourse demonstrates that schools are something other than transmitters of humanist values. Instead, as Bowles and Gintis, Willis, Carnoy, Whitty, Apple and many others have argued, school knowledge is instrumental for the reproduction of capitalist social relations, which are not confined to preparation for hierarchically arranged occupational and class structures, but also transmit the discourse of domination. According to left theory, tests serve to blame the victim for school failure. Students are prepared for subordination because they view themselves as possessors of "free will." As Willis shows, those who leave school march out in rebellion against middle-class cultural capital and knowledge forms and thereby "condemn" themselves to working-class existence.[4] However positive such resistance may be, it generally contributes in the long run to a form of school failure that is the mechanism through which the working class reproduces itself culturally.

The agony of Marxist and radical social theory, including educational theory, is that its anti-reformist ethos prevents programmatic discourse *within* institutions. According to left education theory, schools cannot truly serve workers and other subordinate groups because they are, in the last instance (and increasingly in the first as well), reproducers of the dominant relations of production. Consequently, Marxism has found its critique and even its language appropriated by the right which, as we have argued, is entirely sympathetic to an economic interpretation of the function of schools, including their role as reproducers of prevailing social relations. Furthermore, since left morality prevents a serious consideration of alternatives under nonrevolutionary circumstances, it appears to be devoid of possibility and often presents itself in scientific garb that, by definition, even disguises its ethical foundation. For Marxism claims that history replaces ethics, that class analysis precludes reform, and that the language of possibility must address only the project of global social transformation. Lacking an immediate prospect for the latter, Marxist education theorists are constrained, at a certain point, to shut up.

A second, and equally debilitating problem is the orthodox Marxist conception of ideology, which it shares with many radical populists. According to this view, ideology is a kind of false consciousness, a set of ideas and beliefs that distort social reality. Marxists take seriously Marx's statement that the ruling ideas of any society are the ideas of the ruling class and that the task of the left is to demystify them through relentless critique. In turn, the left regards school knowledge as an instance of bourgeois ideology. Ideas such as freedom and equality are far from the objectives of school authorities who are, perhaps unwittingly, clerks not only of the state, but also of the class that dominates it. Thus, school knowledge within capitalist society is an instrument of ruling class power, because it reproduces the ideology that in this society individuals possess not only rights, such as school attendance, but also equal opportunity to advance on the social ladder. School knowledge is viewed negatively as an instrument of domination; therefore, given the structural limits imposed by bourgeois hegemony, the chance for genuine education through schooling is virtually nil. Almost nowhere in Marxist educational theory and critique can one find a discussion of *counterhegemony* as a category for enabling students, parents, and teachers to wage political struggle within schools. Marxist education theorists have spent little time discovering the internal contradictions within prevailing school knowledge, disruptions that could provide a basis for a real educational movement. The discourse of demystification prevents the question of internal, counterhegemonic moments within school knowledge from being asked. Furthermore, the power/knowledge antinomy is rarely, if ever, explored as *possibility*. That is, the left ignores the degree to which popular forces might appropriate the democratic ideology of schools, elements of existing school knowledge, and on the basis of these, find the possibility of accumulating power within the schools. Instead, the left has worked itself into a theoretical cul de sac. For if school knowledge, governance, and finances are, for all practical purposes, subsumed under the capitalist state and the state is an instrument for ruling class domination, what possible perspectives for political struggle are there within the education sector? What are the points of intervention of a putative social movement aimed at countering neo-conservative hegemony? Unless we posit the existence of internal contradictions and a positive relationship of knowledge and power rather than posing them as antinomies, theory remains abstract and critique sterile.

Before suggesting some paths out of the dead end that currently afflicts left educational theory, we must return to the original culprit against which both radicals and conservatives have inveighed—liberal humanism. We will argue that far from constituting a linchpin of bourgeois mystification, progressive education—the core American doctrine of liberal educational humanism—contains a language of possibility for fruitful intervention into contemporary educational battles, because it poses the relationship of power and knowledge in a positive as well as critical way. To begin with, we want to make a distinction between the progressive education movement as it evolved in the early decades of the century, reemerged later in the 1960s, and the ideas of its leading theorists John Dewey and the Columbia School (Kirkpatrick, Rugg, Hook, and Mike Hohn). The movement never achieved hegemony within school ideology but was appropriated, piecemeal, into a hybrid discourse of liberal reform that has dominated our schools since the turn of the century. Moreover, in its latter incarnation, radical school reform of the 1960s adopted an anti-intellectual stance that helped prepare the victory of the right. They surrendered the concept of systematic knowledge acquisition and uncritically privileged an anti-intellectual concept of student experience. This ideology constituted merely the mirror image of the cognitive orientation of school officials which prescribed a set of learnings prior to any possible experience. Thus, the radical reformers were prey to the charge that they had betrayed the interests of the poor and minorities who desperately needed to learn how to read, write, and calculate. We want to make clear that, while recognizing the achievement of radical school movements, particularly their program to empower students, parents, and the community, we distance ourselves from their refusal to grapple with the specific intellectual and political issues entailed by the reproduction and dissemination of school knowledge and social practices.

It is hard to imagine how far we have come from the philosophy and program of early progressive education theorists. The movement is now eighty years old and has had several incarnations. Each successive resuscitation of radical school reform has added new dimensions to the ideology, but lost some too. The 1960s demand for relevance in school curriculum appropriated John Dewey's philosophy of experience in such manner as to misconstrue and even discredit his arguments. When Dewey placed experience at the center of the educational process, his view was not to adjust school knowledge to the vicissitudes of the labor market:

Gardening, for example, need not be taught for the sake of preparing future gardeners, or as an agreeable way of passing time. It affords an avenue of approach to knowledge of the place farming and horticulture have had in the history of the race and which they occupy in present social organization. Carried on in an environment educationally controlled, they are means for making a study of the facts of growth, the chemistry of soil, the role of light, air and moisture.[5]

For Dewey, the point of occupationally and recreationally based education was not to prepare students for jobs, but for the broad requirements of citizenship in a democratic society. He held to Jefferson's belief that an informed citizenry was the best assurance that democracy would not degenerate into dictatorship or authoritarian regimes. Contrary to many of his followers, "learning by doing" did not signify a devaluation of theoretical knowledge in favor of the practical. Dewey's claim was that transmitting theory apart from practice reduced the student to that side of experience he called "undergoing," that is, a passive object of education. Instead, he wanted to stress the active side. Experience was not merely the undergoing of a particular event, such as when a child puts her hand in a flame. The child must *understand* the consequences of what has been undergone for reflective experience to come into play. For Dewey, the aim of education is to help the student gain conscious direction and control of the learning process. Work and play make concrete the social and cognitive function of theoretical knowledge, and are the means by which the student achieves control.

Here Dewey makes a distinction between habit and knowledge:

> Habit means that an individual undergoes a modification through an experience, which forms a predisposition to easier and more effective action in a like direction in the future. Thus, it also has the function of making one experience available to subsequent experiences. . . . But habit apart from knowledge does not make allowance for change of conditions, for novelty. Prevision of change is not part of its scope, for habit assumes the likeness of the new situation with the old. Consequently, it often leads astray, or comes between a person and the successful performance of his task, just as skill based on habit alone, of the mechanic will desert him when something unexpected occurs in the running of the machine. But a man who understands the machine is the man who knows what he is about. . . . In other words, knowledge is a perception of those connections of an object which determine its applicability in a given situation.[6]

As we argue in the last section of this book, the program of neo-conservative school theorists is to introduce habit into the curriculum, to program students in a certain direction so that they will behave in set ways, responding to predetermined situations. Neo-conservatives have renounced the critical intent of education, which begins, according to Dewey, with "knowing" what we are about and being able to make connections between our formal knowledge and the changed conditions under which activity takes place. Thus, Dewey's philosophy of education is to direct schools to devise curricula that are oriented around critical thinking. Self-knowledge is seen as the key to one's knowledge of the world and, specifically, to the ability to connect contemporary experience to the received information that others have gained through their generalized experience which he calls theory.

The object of theoretical knowledge, so defined as making available to the individual "former experiences for subsequent ones, is: (1) increased power of control, and (2) it also increases the meaning, the experienced significance attached to an experience." Here Dewey wants to avoid "merely reacting physically to new circumstances. There is no mental reward in such responses."[7] Rather, knowledge is prospective if it permits us to "experience a meaning" in situations, even if we have not succeeded in enlarging our control over it.

We may fault Dewey for not bringing his theory of education into the context of problems of state and institutional life. Although he has a clear idea of what schools *ought to be,* he carefully avoids making a social and political analysis of what schools actually *are.* He argues that schools should be a community, in effect a small society in which "intercourse, communication and cooperation" take place. He wants to break down the conventional separation of theory and practice, schooling, and education so that learning can take place both within and outside the school walls. Yet he does not come to grips with the concrete obstacles to his objective of linking knowledge and power, by which he means enlarging the student's capacity to control his own social destiny by consciously shaping experience. Thus, implicit in Dewey's philosophy is the notion of schools as vessels waiting to be filled with enlightened, democratic, and critical learning modes.

Radical theorists have generally ignored Dewey because of his lack of sociological and political insight. They have concluded that, under capitalism, schools could never fulfill the goal of social empowerment. As a result, Dewey's best ideas are all but lost to American educational practice. Humanists and progressives have been discursively defeated by both orthodox left and conservative critics who have labeled these ideas either as bad *ideology* or destructive *utopian fantasies.* As we detail in chapters four and five, the left argues that schools habituate individuals to the real world of domination, while the right argues that the ideology of student-centered education has destroyed the ability of schools to help the economy as well as its workers to survive and perform in an ever-changing market economy.

The failure of the progressive humanists was not the inadequacy of their ideas. It can be shown that Dewey's educational thought closely approximates the best of Marxist and radical education theory, little of which stems from contemporary American sources. For example, we may compare Dewey's work with the education writings of the Italian Marxist Antonio Gramsci. "Every relationship of 'hegemony' is necessarily an educational relationship," writes Gramsci. In order to receive the active or passive assent of the general population, nations, dominant classes and ruling groups must generate a "common sense" that is broadly disseminated in what Gramsci calls "civil society," by which he means everyday or private life as distinct from either economic or political life. Gramsci, like Dewey, distinguishes between specific school knowledge and knowledge acquired in the ensemble of social life, and thereby broadens the concept of education from its narrow bureaucratic construction as merely instruction. Nevertheless, his prescriptive discussion of school knowledge draws strikingly similar conclusions with those of Dewey. In the first place, he separates habitual from critical knowledge. Because of the need to inculcate study discipline in children, he relegates habitual knowledge to the early years of the common school. Although he favors vocational and specialized education directed to specific career goals, Gramsci's idea of the secondary school corresponds to an institution that not only instructs pupils in "dead" knowledge (although he makes an eloquent case for this kind of learning) and prepares them for the world of work, but also develops in them "the element of independent responsibility." Gramsci's concept of the two stages of schooling culminates in the "creative" school where "learning takes place especially through a spontaneous and autonomous effort of the pupil, with the teacher only exercising a function of friendly guide. . . . To discover a truth oneself, without external suggestions or assistance, is to create—even if the truth is an old one." [8]

Gramsci's Marxism did not prevent him from undertaking prescriptive work even under conditions of fascist Italy and while in prison. The originality of his Marxism consists in this—that he was capable of speaking the language of possibility even under the most objectively onerous circumstances. The reason Gramsci entered into the discourse of institutional reform was based on his theory of hegemony as education. For Gramsci, unlike orthodox Marxists, the revolution did not consist in some kind of big bang theory, for example, the insurrectionary seizure of state power by a radicalized working class and peasantry. Having experienced both the abortive radicalization of the Italian workers immediately following the First World War and the painful course of the Bolshevik revolution, he came to understand the crucial importance of those aspects of the social sphere called civil society—the ideological, cultural, religious sphere (the so-called superstructural relations) where humans live by ingrained concepts of justice, morality, and truth. Gramsci believed the left could not contest merely the political and state sphere or remain locked in factory struggles as it had previously. His program was tantamount to what became known in the 1960s as the long march through institutions: to contest the moral and intellectual leadership of society by entering the public sphere of both institutional and political life where people debated their "truths" about education, morality, and law as well as struggled over their

immediate and antagonistic interests. Put another way, Gramsci understood the necessity of making the political more pedagogical.

Gramsci's concept of education presupposes the reality of Italian capitalism in the 1930s: industrially incomplete with a weak professional and
technical cadre, gaping regions of underdevelopment, and a relatively weak
national identity. Thus, we may expect him to have a different idea of the
need for vocational education than his counterparts in more developed
societies. Yet, for him, the task before left educators was to appropriate
critically those best features of traditional educational practice, which constituted the pedagogy of the ruling and "mandarin" classes. Although
Gramsci was pessimistic about the chances of maintaining Latin and Greek
as centerpieces of the elementary and secondary school curricula, he was
concerned to find the moral and intellectual equivalent provided to the
elites' children: "to understand the historical movement of the whole language," the entire philosophical and logical basis of Western thought and
civilization and to inculcate the habit of scholarship among ordinary people.[9]

Gramsci wanted to find a "school form" that would enable children of
the "subaltern" classes to achieve not only what ruling class students learned
in earlier times, but also to appropriate critically the best dimensions of
their own histories, experiences, and culture. For him, that form would be
an institution that breaks down the wall between vocational and academic
education, bringing students to the threshold of the world of work with a
broadly based education in both aspects of school knowledge. He rejects
the traditional vocational school because it "tends to perpetuate traditional social differences," just as Dewey was opposed to schools that "try
to educate individuals with an eye to only one line of activity." Although
Dewey was fairly blind to class analysis, his concern for the free development of independent and critical individuals, able to gain meaning from
their experience, including educational experiences, forced him to oppose
the dominant tendency of his time.

Working under radically different circumstances, Paulo Freire drew conclusions that are by no means far from the educational philosophies of
Dewey and Gramsci.[10] His overriding goal of empowerment for oppressed
Brazilian peasants entailed distinct but closely related steps: the validation
of the "voices" of people who are traditionally deprived of legitimate participation in political as well as civil society. Thus, Freire's pedagogy is
dialogic: learning occurs within conversation, and not as top-to-down instruction between the teacher and student. Dewey's still unrefined idea of
communication and cooperation in schools is made into a detailed method,
but the foundation is the history, experience, and culture of the learner
herself. Freire's reflexive concept of knowledge is compatible with Dewey's
notion that experience is not reactive but a creative and meaningful relationship between the individual and her historical and contemporary situ-

ation where changed circumstances produce new and transformed knowledges. Similarly, Freire inserts education directly into the political sphere by arguing that education represents both a struggle for meaning and a struggle over power relations. Thus, education becomes a central terrain where power and politics operate out of a dialectical relation between individuals and groups who live out their lives within specific historical conditions and structural constraints as well as within cultural forms and ideologies that are the basis for contradictions and struggles.

Of course, Gramsci and Freire formed their educational theory in the framework of a historical and social understanding of the collective fates of classes within modern society. Their objective is not to empower the individual to take a secure place within democratic society as Dewey seems to hold, but to transform society itself to meet the collective needs of individuals. Education becomes a radical project for economic, political, and cultural change in which relations of power are transformed. Yet, what unites these writers is their understanding that the core of popular democratic power resides in the appropriation, by the vast majority, of past knowledge as well as knowledge of one's own creative powers. In all three positions, the dialectic between education as the transmission of cultural values and knowledge and the new knowledge produced by the creative acts of the people themselves is the guiding educational principle.

We are not claiming that Dewey is a revolutionary thinker in the socialist or Marxist sense. But the penchant of radical and humanist thinkers to ignore his contribution or, worse, to dismiss his work as idealist, utopian, reactionary, and so on, is informed by the profound pessimism to which critical educational scholarship has descended. We invent a language of possibility that proposes extensive philosophic and programmatic changes in education only if we can imagine a public sphere within which alternatives are seriously considered. Epistemologically, the language of critique turns in on itself and loses its emancipatory character when political imagination has disappeared. The theorist becomes overwhelmed by the immediate circumstances which, admittedly, since the early 1970s have become unfavorable to such proposals. On the other hand, the failure of the theorist to find a field to "test" such proposals simply strengthens the hegemony of conservatives who today have the field to themselves. Part of the job is to establish links with parents, students, and progressive teachers who are obliged, by necessity as well as their ideological proclivities, to engage in the debate.

Here we might draw a contrast between the Frankfurt School whose fate in prewar Germany was sealed by the rise of Nazism, on the one hand, and Gramsci and Freire on the other. The leading figures of the Frankfurt School draw the rational conclusion that all "positive" discourse had been foreclosed by fascism, and went further to assert that the language of possibility within the framework of repressive societies was a kind of crackpot positivism that could do nothing but strengthen the existing regimes. Thus, in their view, the task of theory was to deconstruct the link between liberalism and fascism. The Frankfurt School justly objected to the tendency of nearly all other Marxists to make a radical break between fascism and liberal capitalism. They insisted that the absolutist state, the command economy, and cultural "barbarism" characteristic of fascist regimes were all prepared by the one-dimensional thought modes of advanced industrial societies in which technological domination prevailed. Their critique, which stemmed from a close reading of the darker side of the enlightenment, particularly the elevation of the domination of nature and of humans to the status of a new quasi-religious creed, constituted the heart of theory.[11] Lacking a practice with which to oppose this development, the Frankfurt School gloried in its marginality and tended to elevate intellectual work and art to the status of subversive activity. The Frankfurt School was always too realistic to imagine that its theoretical and critical works were engaged in some kind of struggle for hegemony: to them such illusions were immature at best, dangerous at worst. They were upholding that rare commodity, *reason,* whose existence became more precarious with each passing consumerist fad.

History played a cruel trick on the Frankfurt self-image of towering loneliness. For a brief instant, the famous society of total administration disaggregated in the 1960s and Marcuse and Adorno, if not the others, became instant "organic" intellectuals to a youth and student movement that became visible and sometimes powerful in all Western democracies. Along with Henri Lefebvre, C. Wright Mills, and a few others, the Frankfurt School's knowledge was linked with oppositional power.[12] Although its weight in the political institutions was always problematic, the new left succeeded in exerting considerable influence among intellectuals, even if something short of hegemony in the Gramscian sense. Its work in all countries might well be described as pedagogical, and at times its critique of the cultural forms of capitalism reached deeply into other social classes and strata. Ideas such as grassroots democracy to replace the oppressive structures of representative government, the critique of consumer society, the demands for community control and individual freedom in major institutions such as schools became commonplace public issues. While no set of ideas can be traced to the work of intellectuals exclusively, insofar as they played an important role in transforming the experience and the power of an entire generation of youth, the Frankfurt School's influence proved exactly the opposite of what their critical theory had suggested. Technological domination was not complete; in some places, resistance and imagination were still possible, and, in limited spheres, it had come to power.

Adorno and Horkheimer never acknowledged that their own critique contained a hidden discourse of possibility. When they attacked the domination of nature as a mask for human domination, some of their readers began to question the efficacy of scientific rationality that subordinated all environmental consequences of technology to profit and consumption; others interpreted the normal processes of bureaucratic institutions as assaults on individuality and freedom and proceeded to organize popular movements for civil rights and against the apparently unstoppable war machine. In short, while Dewey, Gramsci, and Freire are intellectuals who made the political more pedagogical, the Frankfurt School denied the possibility of genuine politics in technological societies, yet each has contributed to engendering the language of possibility in the late twentieth century.

Still, Marcuse's darkest prognostications cannot be so easily dismissed. For, even though feminism, and the ecological, peace, and black movements serve to remind us of the ineluctability of oppositional politics, the post-sixties years have been marked by a resurgence of the technological rationality that Marcuse feared. Its most ubiquitous current form is the so-called computer revolution. Since the energy crisis reminded Americans of their economic vulnerability, a perception strengthened by the economic decline of the early 1980s, the computer has been touted as the solution to (almost) all of our economic problems. This wondrous machine, once used exclusively for payrolls and as a tool for storing information, has now been elevated to a savior, the embodiment of technologically based culture, a way of life for millions of Americans. For us, the rise of scientific culture finds its most ambiguous expression in the rise of computer technology. Our call for the pedagogical to become more political gains reactionary expression in the almost strident call of liberals, conservatives, and others to establish technocratic rationality as the basis for all school knowledge. We do not mean to dismiss scientific culture and technocratic rationality as much as to subject it to the dialectical interrogation it deserves.

The computer's functions have been dramatically expanded to include industrial design, manufacturing, and, important for our discussion, computer-aided education. Writers, researchers, and kids who play games with them have taken computers into the home. For some, they have replaced television as the constant companion that has been missing since personal interaction went the way of the horse and buggy. Computers have mediated work, leisure, and virtually all communications—and in this sense have become a form of culture.

The pervasiveness of computer technology has evoked two distinct and contradictory responses. Critics such as David Noble regard computerization of the workplace as a political as well as an economic arm of capitalism.[13] Drawing on the results of the industrial revolution, Noble sees computers as merely the latest stage of capital's offensive against labor, a means to subordinate workers by both degrading their labor and eliminating them from the workplace. Noble's new luddism despairs that workers could gain a measure of freedom from onerous, boring labor through the technology of the computer. Furthermore, the computer facilitates centralization of control over the workplace. The warp and woof of computerization is that information has become the foundation of production and administration. But information, although it can aid in the production of things, also replaces corporeal objects and makes many industrial functions, once anchored in geographic space and a large quantity of living labor, subject to radical decentralization of execution while facilitating centralized control. Machine operators, designers, as well as data processors can work from their own homes, or in rural communities, or in suburbs far from control centers which may or may not be located in large cities. The traditional basis of workers' power, the factory and the industrial center of which it was a part, seem destined to follow the typewriter and the belt-driven lathe into the museum.

For Noble as well as his progenitor, Harry Braverman, technology embodies social relations.[14] Far from being a "tool" of a neutral production process, the computer is value-laden. It embodies, for Noble, elements of economic and social domination because, like Marcuse, Braverman and Noble regard rationalization, that is, the division of labor according to productivity norms, as ideological. There is no question of resituating the computer in a democratic workplace where workers participate in decision-making. They view the machine as the reified form of social relations of domination. And, following Marcuse's critique of technological thought, the computer represents the apogee of this development because it reduces things to processes, the concrete to the abstract, and quality to quantity.

The most sophisticated critics of contemporary technology are merely extending Marx and Weber's critique of capitalist rationality to processes of production and administration. Like Georg Lukacs, they find the key to understanding the modern world in Marx's analysis of the transformation of value into exchange values through the permutations of the commodity form; and concomitantly, Weber's argument that our epoch is marked by the disenchantment of the world through administration, especially the formation of industrial and state bureaucracies.[15]

The underlying presupposition of the computer's fervent advocates is that science and technology, one of the crucial moments in disenchantment, and its accompanying rationality, constitute the basis of unshackling humans from the religious world view. Although mostly unstated, for these advocates the computer is viewed as the latest step in our progressive domination of nature which follows from the unleashing of rational thought from mystical constraints. Thus, even when celebrants declare the computer to be nothing more than a tool wielded for human purposes and subject only to the constraints of manmade social context, this neutralization of technology reveals complete support for the scientific ideology of objectivity through experimental method and value-free research. Consequently, computer scientist Seymour Papert wants to harness this tool to help solve the education crisis.[16]

Papert has invented a new computer language called Logo in order to assist students to learn mathematics and science. Students could master a new language, learn elementary logical processes, and most important of all, acquire a sense of mastery of the external world, especially a significant machine of our industrial and commercial system. Apart from those like Herbert Simon for whom humans are merely ants with information-processing apparati, Papert is a humanist for whom education is a way to empowerment through knowledge.[17] He sees the computer as an instrument for these ends precisely because it embodies nothing but the intentions of its user.

But Edmund Sullivan's critique of this perspective is worth reviewing because he regards Papert as an advocate, but his objection is not made from the standpoint of those for whom computers are inimical to social freedom.[18] Sullivan believes the computer has both positive and negative features, but its value depends on the "human intentions" that guide its use. Papert's book is interesting not only because it tries to devise a program for computer-aided instruction, but also because it adopts a strategy that enables the child to program the computer and consequently acquire a sense of mastery as well as intellectual adventure. Sullivan praises this goal and other aspects of Papert's viewpoint. Far from "programming the child to work with computers," his position is to place the child at the center of the process. Moreover, he sees the computer as a part of culture and not merely a tool. It is, of course, consistent with scientific culture of which we are the heirs.

But Sullivan faults Papert's conception that the computer enables education to become a "private act," removing the child from the competitive environment of schools that has suppressed learning by subordinating the child to grades and the approval of elders, particularly teachers. Papert's vision of private interaction between the learner and her machine may be attractive to those who are repelled by the authoritarianism of the classroom, but for Sullivan this view suffers from an essential flaw. Learning is neither a purely cognitive act nor a private one. Sullivan insists that machines cannot truly replicate the I-Thou interactive relation between two or more persons since it is not genuinely *other* by Papert's own admission. (The machine, for Papert, is subordinate to human mastery.) Hence, it cannot provide the moral side of sociability. Moreover, it does not even satisfy the cognitive requirements, because human interaction is really two-way communication and person-machine interaction is not. At the same time, Sullivan approves of the use of computer-based learning for the limited purposes of helping the child to understand that "knowledge is a system" which is ordered according to abstract logical principles and is "not arbitrary." Second, Sullivan agrees that Papert's "systematic use of error" to enhance education "has revolutionary import for contemporary education" since most schools discourage error.

Sullivan's and Papert's return to experimentalism is a breath of fresh air in an educational environment suffused with conformity, fear, and hierarchy. At the same time Sullivan is justly critical of Papert's reliance on Piagetian psychology and epistemology because Papert places this perspective within the framework of artificial intelligence. As Joseph Weizenbaum has argued, artificial intelligence does not give us the opportunity to transfer mental processes, particularly activities such as judgment and value, to machines.[19] Sullivan concludes that Papert's mind/body split—his reliance on a purely cognitive model of learning—results in distorting the education objectives he so fervently desires. Sullivan goes on to review the split-brain literature with a view to correcting Papert's rationalism by pointing out that the affective side (the left side of the brain) remains underdeveloped in all computer-aided educational models.

Sullivan argues for a dialectical approach to the learning process in which the cognitive and the creative sides are accorded equal weight. But, by using split-brain research, he has succeeded in reproducing the dichotomous existence of the two modes of learning. Now, for Sullivan, the split-brain is a heurism, a device for showing that the brain is not a computer but is also endowed with artistic features that should not be subject to rationalization, particularly quantitative abstraction.

While it may be that the creative and analytic aspects of the brain can be located physically in different sides, we object to the use of a biological metaphor to refute the abstract, cognitive orientation of artificial intelligence and other computer-mediated theories of human interaction and intelligence. One need not resort to theories of human nature to argue that the brain is not a machine. Rather, we approach this question in an historical framework: the doctrine of "man the machine" is deeply rooted in pre-Freudian psychology and French materialism of the late eighteenth and early nineteenth centuries. It corresponded to the fallacy of all analogical thinking of the period that derived its world view from Newtonian physics and Cartesian metaphysics. According to this doctrine, humans were endowed biologically with cognitive capacities that were abetted or retarded by the socialization processes. In effect, biologism was the other side of environmentalism. In the twentieth century, these views have been echoed in the behaviorisms of B. F. Skinner and organizational and information theorists from Shannon to Simon.[20]

We do not need "scientific" support to see that these mechanistic views of the world ignored the "active" side of human understanding—production, social interaction, intentionality, interpretation. For it is not only that we make the world according to the limits placed on our action by prior conditions (Marx), but education as opposed to training is the process by which we assimilate our environment in relation to our desires. We are not only needy organisms, but desiring ones as well. And desire cannot be limited to goal-oriented behavior directed at achieving ends that are dictated by our social/biological "needs." We learn as much by assimilating the world to the dictates of the sphere we call "imaginary" (which cannot always be adjusted to practical tasks) as we do in the so-called socialization process, one that is increasingly technologically directed. By imaginary we mean the proclivities toward creating an alternative world, not representing that which is. The imaginary is the foundation of play; it is the way we make a new world as well as achieve selfhood. Play can be understood as the interaction of two imaginaries, especially among children where the activity itself is directed to creating not only the social self, but also a self that "goes beyond" the givens of existing social structures. The relationship between education as socialization, which is directed toward suppressing the imaginary, and learning as a means by which the imaginary takes command over the ego is inevitable in any society that wishes to insure the adaptation of its young to prevailing norms. The point of technological domination is to make the imaginary into an instrument of the prevailing order. This struggle has been theorized in various ways: Reich posited liberated sexuality as the subversive element in repressive society; Deleuze and Guattari have called this "desire," which capitalism transforms into a machine, the desiring machine, along with the surplus that remains unharnessed by the environment; Habermas speaks the utopian language of undistorted communication, but retains a rationalistic framework within which more perfect interaction may take place.[21]

This is not the place to enter the important debate about alternative theoretical formulations to the instrumentalization of everyday life, the repressive character of social relations, and the loss of civic courage that accompanies it. Suffice to remark here that we firmly reject the notion that computers or any other machine address the crisis in education. We do not hold that machines are, themselves, responsible either for historical progress (whatever that may be) or our present malaise. On the other hand, they do embody social relations; science and technology, far from being saviors of our distressed public sphere, have been subordinated to the interests of domination. We agree with the critics of scientific and technological culture insofar as we are persuaded that machines are by no means separate from ideology. Social relations constitute the invisible content of many things including science. Yet, with Sullivan only the most backward-looking position could maintain that scientific and technological developments are unmixed evils. Here we only wish to emphasize the point that educational alternatives require more than tools of administration. Schools as a *democratic public sphere,* a concept that corresponds to the way many advocates of public schools at the turn of the century understood them, cannot be created unless learning itself is a democratic process. While we do not offer here an algorithm for achieving this end, some of what follows suggests a different way to think about schooling and education.

Among the first steps is to specify what we as a community want education to be. This means acknowledging both the importance and the limits of the language of critique. It means moving beyond analyses of the ideological and material conditions of public schooling to the language of possibility. In this case, we move to the terrain of hope and agency, to the sphere of struggle and action, one steeped in a vision that chooses life and offers constructive alternatives.

Second, rethinking the purpose of education also means reformulating the social and ideological role of educators. We believe that educators at all levels of schooling have to be seen as intellectuals, who as mediators, legitimators, and producers of ideas and social practices, perform a pedagogical function that is eminently political in nature. By viewing educators as intellectuals, we want to expand the theoretical insights provided by Freire and Gramsci on the role of the intellectual in modern society and, specifically, of the role of educators in public schools and in higher education. In effect, we want to offer a set of categories that will allow for a better understanding of intellectual work, the preconditions for its existence, and the political role it does and can serve. We also want to illuminate the way in which teaching as a labor process has been governed by a notion of industrial ideology that separates conception from execution. We want to transform that model of the labor process and redefine the nature of intellectual work in schools so as to join conception and execution. We make a detailed attempt at this task in chapter two.

If we are to fight for schools as democratic spheres, it is imperative to understand the contradictory roles that educators occupy within the various levels of schooling. It is also important to understand who educators are in order to build alliances and who we have to attack and oppose on all fronts. Clearly, if we are going to face the task of developing the ideological and material conditions from which radical educators can rethink the project of schooling and human emancipation, then surely we cannot accept either the near hysterical description of education as providing human capital to commerce or socialization models that speak to the limited task of transmitting dominant culture to succeeding generations. If we want a creative citizenry that is capable of constituting itself as a democratic public sphere, then curriculum and school organizations must address the imaginary, and refrain from finding techniques to displace it by fear to the prevailing order. Of course, we do not expect this hope to become a majority movement in the near future. There are political and cultural limits to such aspirations. But this book may stimulate some who would organize a social movement in schools and outside them to restore education to an honorable and autonomous place in our culture. To these educators, parents, students, and citizens we address ourselves.

NOTES

1. Chester Finn, "A Call for Quality Education," *American Education* (January–February 1982), p. 32.

2. Ibid., p. 33.

3. Ibid., pp. 33–36.

4. Paul Willis, *Learning to Labor* (New York: Columbia University Press, 1981).

5. John Dewey, *Democracy and Education* (New York: Free Press, 1966), p. 200.

6. Ibid., pp. 339–340.

7. Ibid., pp. 340–341.

8. Antonio Gramsci, *Selections from Prison Notebooks.* ed. and trans. Quinten Hoare and Geoffrey Smith (New York: International Publishers, 1971), p. 33.

9. Ibid., p. 37.

10. Paulo Freire, *Pedagogy of the Oppressed* (New York: Seabury Press, 1973); also see *The Politics of Education* (South Hadley, Mass.: Bergin and Garvey, 1984).

11. Theodor Adorno and Max Horkheimer, *Dialectic of the Enlightenment* (New York: Seabury Press, 1972); Herbert Marcuse, *One Dimensional Man* (Boston: Beacon Press, 1964).

12. Henri Lefebvre, *Everyday Life in the Modern World* (New York: Harper and Row Publishers, 1968); C. Wright Mills, *The Sociological Imagination* (London: Oxford University Press, 1959).

13. David Noble, *America by Design* (New York: Alfred A. Knopf, 1977).

14. Harry Braverman, *Labor and Monopoly Capital* (New York: Monthly Review Press, 1974).

15. George Lukacs, *History and Class Consciousness* (Cambridge, Mass.: MIT Press, 1968).

16. Seymour Papert, *Mind Storms* (New York: Basic Books, 1980).

17. H. A. Simon, *The Science of the Artificial* (Cambridge, Mass.: MIT Press, 1969).

18. Edmund Sullivan, "Computers, Culture and Educational Futures," Ontario Institute for Studies in Education, Unpublished paper, 1984.

19. Joseph Weizenbaum, *Computers and Human Reason* (New York: W. H. Freeman Co., 1976).

20. B. F. Skinner, *About Behaviorism* (New York: Alfred A. Knopf, 1974); C. Shannon, *Mathematical Theory of Communication* (Urbana: University of Illinois, 1975); Simon, op. cit.

21. W. Reich, *Sex-Pol,* ed. Lee Baxandall (New York: Vintage Books, 1972); Gilles Deleuze and Felix Guattare, *Anti Oedipus: Capitalism and Schizophrenia* (New York: Viking Press, 1977); Jürgen Habermas, *Communication and the Evolution of Society,* trans. by Thomas McCarthy (Boston: Beacon Press, 1979).

Chapter Two

Teaching and the Role of the Transformative Intellectual

A strange paradox haunts the discourse regarding the crisis facing public education in the United States.[1] On the one hand, this crisis is characterized as a failure of the schools to prepare students adequately for the ever changing demands of a sophisticated technological economy. It is also described by less vocal critics as the growing failure of schools to prepare students to think critically and creatively with regard to developing the sophisticated literacy skills necessary to make informed and effective choices about the worlds of work, politics, culture, personal relationships, and the economy. Underlying both sets of criticisms is the notion that schools have failed to take the issues of excellence and creativity seriously and in doing so have undermined the economic and academic possibilities that could be conferred on both students and the larger society.

On the other hand, educational reformers have responded to the crises in public education by primarily offering solutions that either ignore the roles of teachers in preparing learners to be active and critical citizens, or they suggest reforms that ignore the intelligence, judgment, and experience that teachers might bring to bear on such issues. The call for excellence and improved student creativity has been accompanied by policy suggestions that further erode the power teachers have over the conditions of their work, while simultaneously proposing that administrators and teachers look outside of their schools for improvements and needed reforms. The result is that many of the educational reforms appear to reduce teachers to the status of low-level employees or civil servants whose main function is to implement reforms decided by experts in the upper levels of state and educational bureaucracies. Furthermore, such reforms embrace technological solutions that undermine the historical and cultural specificity of school life and further weaken the possibilities for school administrators and teachers to work with parents and local groups to improve schools. Underlying the paradox at work in the discourse of school reform is a dual failure: first, there is the growing public failure to recognize the central role that teachers must play in any viable attempt to revitalize the public schools; second, the failure to recognize that the ideological and political interests underlying the dominant thrusts in school reform are at odds with the traditional role of organizing public education around the need to educate students for the maintenance and defense of the traditions and principles necessary for a democratic society.

We want to argue that part of the growing crisis in public education centers around the declining competence of students and others to effectively interrogate and communicate ideational content. In other words, in jeopardy is not merely the ability of students to be creative, but the very capacity for conceptual thought itself. Moreover, since democratic social, cultural, and political forms depend on a self-motivated and autonomous public, the precondition for which is critical thinking, the crisis at hand may be the very survival of democracy itself.

Our main point will be that the crisis in creativity and critical learning has in large part to do with the developing trend toward the disempowerment of teachers at all levels of education. This involves not only a growing loss of power among teachers around the basic conditions of their work, but also a changing perception of their role as reflective practitioners. In effect, we will argue that teacher work is being increasingly situated within a technical and social division of labor that either reduces teachers to the dictates of experts removed from the context of the classroom, or serves to widen the political gap between those who control the schools and those who actually deal with curricula and students on a day-to-day basis. In the first instance, teachers are relegated to instrumental tasks that limit the possibilities for oppositional discourse and social practices. Pedagogy, in this case, is reduced to the implementation of taxonomies that subordinate knowledge to forms of methodological reification, while theories of teaching are increasingly technicized and standardized in the interest of efficiency and the management and control of discrete forms of knowledge.[2]

Teachers are not simply being proletarianized; the changing nature of their roles and function signifies the disappearance of a form of intellectual labor central to the nature of critical pedagogy itself. Moreover, the tendency to reduce teachers to either high-level clerks implementing the orders of others within the school bureaucracy or to specialized technicians is part of a much larger problem within Western societies, a problem marked by the increasing division of intellectual and social labor and the increasing trend toward the oppressive management and administration of everyday life. The current tendency to reformulate the status and nature of teacher work is evident in a number of historical and sociological tendencies that

,need to be mentioned briefly before we argue for an alternative view of how teacher work should be interpreted.

TOWARD A PROLETARIANIZATION OF TEACHER WORK

Historically, the relationship between the role of educators and the larger society has been mediated by the image of the school teacher as a dedicated public servant reproducing the dominant culture in the interest of the common good, and the university community as a body of social scientists who in their capacity as experts "were to educate the masses and provide direction for moral and social progress."[3] With the advent of the twentieth century, the administration and organization of public schools were increasingly brought under the influence of the instrumental ideologies of corporate business interests. Moreover, the growing professionalization of academics and their respective disciplines resulted in a redefinition of the theoretical nature of the social sciences. Increasingly, university social scientists shifted from the terrain of social reform to the role of expert as policy advisor. Within this context, the relationship between knowledge and power took on a new dimension as the development of social science became closely linked to supporting the ideological and social practices of a business society. In charting the rise and success of the academic social sciences, Silva and Slaughter ably document that in the United States between 1865 and 1910 the emerging professional associations of the developing social sciences lent their skills and knowledge to the economic and social problems faced by corporate liberal interests. In commenting on the rise of the American Economic Association, they provide an insight into the general political direction in which the professional associations and the social sciences in general were moving:

> As economists were more routinely called to expert service and initiated in the politics of power, they refined their notion of constituency. Although using the rhetoric of objective science and the public welfare, their clientele was the Progressive wing of corporate capital and other professionals. . . . Claiming to be impartial and scientific arbiters of social questions, they used the ideology of expertise in the interests of social control and developed pragmatic, technical mechanisms to consolidate and finance colonial fiscal policy, federal industrial relations commissions, and the income tax. Thus, social science experts became advocates for the existing order, hegemonic intellectuals serving the emerging national corporate elite.[4]

The theoretical tenets of the natural sciences began to provide the model for dominant academic discourse and inquiry in the social sciences. This move tended to reduce critical thought and reason to its merely technical dimensions. Within this positivistically oriented discourse, research techniques became increasingly freed from value judgments, useful knowledge was measured next to its managerial capabilities, and science became synonymous with the search for trans-historical laws. Theory was required to explain rather than constitute or determine the object under analysis.[5]

It is important to stress that the primacy of technical and economic rationality did more than devalue the importance of moral and religious reason in everyday life; it also strengthened relations of dependency and powerlessness for ever widening groups of people through the social practices of an industrial ideology and psychology that reached far into the culture industry and other spheres of public life.[6] Underlying this technical rationality and its accompanying rationalization of reason and nature was a call for the separation of conception from execution, the standardization of knowledge in the interest of managing and controlling it, and the devaluation of critical intellectual work for the primacy of practical considerations. The history of this emerging technocratic rationality in both the schools and public life has been amply documented, and it need not be reinvented here, but its effects took on a special significance in the 1980s and can be seen in a number of areas.[7]

One area in which the dominance of technocratic rationality becomes manifest is in the training of prospective teachers. As Kliebard,[8] Zeichner,[9] and others[10] have pointed out, teacher education programs in the United States have long been dominated by their behavioristic orientation towards issues of mastery and methodological refinement as the basis for developing teacher competence. The normative and political implications of this approach are made clear by Zeichner.

> Underlying this orientation to teacher education is a metaphor of "production," a view of teaching as an "applied science" and a view of the teacher as primarily an "executor" of the laws and principles of effective teaching. Prospective teachers may or may not proceed through the curriculum at their own pace and may participate in varied or standardized learning activities, but that which they are to master is limited in scope (e.g., to a body of professional content knowledge and teaching skills) and is fully determined in advance by others often on the basis of research on teacher effectiveness. The prospective teacher is viewed primarily as a passive recipient of this professional knowledge and plays little part in determining the substance and direction of his or her preparation program.[11]

Within this behavioristic model of education, teachers are viewed less as creative and imaginative thinkers who can transcend the ideology of methods and means in order to critically evaluate the purpose of educational discourse and practice than as obedient civil servants dutifully carrying out the dictates of others. All too often teacher-education programs lose sight of the need to educate students to be teacher-scholars by developing edu-

cational courses that focus on the immediacy of school problems and substitute the discourse of management and efficiency for a critical analysis of
the underlying conditions that structure school life. Instead of helping students to think about who they are and what they should do in classrooms,
what their responsibility might be in interrogating the means and ends of
specific school policy, students are often trained to share techniques on
how to control student discipline, teach a given subject effectively, and
organize a day's activities as efficiently as possible. The emphasis of teacher-
education curricula is on finding out what works. The technical rationality
that underlies this type of educational training is not confined to undergraduate programs; its logic exercises a strong influence on graduate programs as well, which are often intended to promote what is often euphe-
mistically called "educational leadership." For instance, it was noted in a
recent study of doctoral programs in education that "Research in education is preoccupied with techniques, rather than with the inquiry into the
nature and course of events—with 'how to' rather than 'what,' with form
rather than substance. . . . Too often students in education . . . have
difficulty even finding serious questions worth addressing." [12]

If prospective teachers are often trained to be specialized technicians,
future school administrators are trained in the image of the social science
expert. Richard Bates [13] and William Foster [14] have pointed out that much
of the training for school administrators, principals, and superintendents
is narrowly technical, concerned primarily with producing a marriage between organization theory and the principles of "sound" business management. Inherent in such training is the notion that complex language systems, management controls, and systems of accountability are beyond the
grasp of either teachers or the average layperson. The technocratic consciousness embodied in this view is not only at odds with the notion of
decentralized control and the principles of participatory democracy, but it
also presents an ahistorical and depoliticized view of school governance
and policy. Schools are not seen as sites of struggle over different orders
of representation, or as sites that embody particular configurations of power
that shape and structure activities of classroom life. On the contrary, schools
become reduced to the sterile logic of flow charts, a growing separation
between teachers and administrators, and an increasing tendency toward
bureaucratization. The overriding message here is that the logic of technocratic rationality serves to remove teachers from participating in a critical way in the production and evaluation of school curricula. For example, the form that school knowledge takes and the pedagogy used to
legitimate it become subordinated to the principles of efficiency, hierarchy,
and control. One consequence is that decisions and questions over what
counts as knowledge, what is worth teaching, how one judges the purpose
and nature of instruction, how one views the role of school in society, and
what the latter implies for understanding how specific social and cultural

interests shape all levels of school life, is removed from the collective influence of teachers themselves. The relationship between the bureaucratization of schools and the specific structuring of knowledge is illuminated in the following:

> The major demands placed upon the structures of knowledge by bureaucratized schools are: that the knowledge be divided into components or relatively discrete components; that the units of knowledge be ordered in sequences; that the knowledge be communicable from one person to another using conventional media of communication; that success in acquisition of part, if not most of the knowledge is recordable in quantifiable form; that the knowledge be objectified in the sense of having an existence independent of its human origins; that the knowledge is stratified into various levels of status or prestige; that knowledge based upon concrete experience be treated as low status, but that knowledge expressed in abstract and generalized principles be regarded as having high status.[15]

The increasing tendency to reduce teacher autonomy in the development and planning of curricula is also evident in the production of prepackaged curriculum materials that contribute to a form of deskilling among teachers. For instance, Apple has pointed to elementary school science curricula packages that orient teachers to simply carrying out predetermined content and instructional procedures.[16] Similarly, the principles at work in this rationality are also found in many school textbooks and what we call management pedagogies. In many school textbooks knowledge is broken down into discrete parts, standardized for easier management and consumption, and published with the intent of being marketed for large general student audiences.[17] Furthermore, schools increasingly adopt forms of pedagogy that routinize and standardize classroom instruction. This is evident in the proliferation of instructional-based curricula and management schemes, competency-based learning systems, and similar approaches such as mastery learning. These are basically management pedagogies because the central question regarding learning is reduced to the problem of management, that is, "how to allocate resources (teachers, students, and materials) to produce the maximum number of certified . . . students within a designated time."[18]

The principles underlying management pedagogies are at odds with the notion that teachers should be actively involved in producing curricula materials suited to the cultural and social contexts in which they teach. These pedagogies ignore questions regarding cultural specificity, teacher judgment, and how student experiences and histories relate to the learning process itself. The issues embodied in such questions represent a mode of teacher autonomy and control that are a positive hindrance to those school administrators who believe that excellence is a quality displayed primarily in higher reading, math, and college board scores. This becomes more obvious in light of the major assumption underlying management pedagogy: that the behavior of teachers needs to be controlled and made consistent and predictable for different schools and student populations. The payoff for schools systems is not merely the touting of more manageable forms of pedagogy; this type of school policy also makes for good public relations in that school administrators can provide technical solutions to the complex social, political, and economic problems that plague their schools. Simultaneously, they invoke the tenets of accountability as indicators of success. In other words, if the problem can be measured, it can be solved. The following statement by some Chicago school administrators enamored of management pedagogy points to the ideology behind the growing proletarianization and deskilling of teacher work.

> Providing materials that were centrally developed and successfully field tested would: 1) reduce greatly the time needed to prepare and organize materials; 2) require little inservice time; 3) be economical for schools in Chicago and elsewhere to implement; 4) standardize the definition, sequencing, and quality of instruction necessary for mastery of each objective; 5) reduce greatly the time needed for developing lesson plans; and 6) be easy for substitutes to use.[19]

Underlying this approach to educational reform is a mode of technocratic rationality that restricts curricula and student diversity and simultaneously refuses to address seriously the issue of how to deal pedagogically with less privileged learners. In the first instance, the narrowing of curricula choices to a back-to-basics format, and the introduction of lock-step, time-on-task pedagogies operates from the pedagogically erroneous assumption that all students can learn from the same materials, pedagogies, and modes of evaluation. The notion that students come from different histories, embodying different experiences, linguistic practices, cultures, and talents, is ignored. Similarly, the current drive among school reformers to deny a high school diploma to students who don't pass a comprehensive graduating exam, or deny entrance to undergraduate and graduate schools to students who don't measure up to the call for higher scores on any one of a number of tests, represents a technological solution to a highly charged political and social problem. The central issue is how public schools and institutions of higher education might be systematically failing certain groups of students, or how they might reevaluate their own approaches to teaching and learning so as to take seriously their obligation to educate all students to be productive citizens. K. Patricia Cross sums the problem up well in her comment:

> Clearly, we cannot afford to "improve" educational institutions at the expense of society. But it is distressing to see how many well-meaning but

short-sighted legislators and educators are taking advantage of the current mandates for excellence by supporting proposals that can have the effect of eliminating from local high schools and colleges the very students who need them most.[20]

RETHINKING THE NATURE OF THE INTELLECTUAL

What we have tried to do in the previous section is point to the various ideological and material forces at work in the United States that currently undermine the role and conditions of work necessary for teachers to assume the posture of thoughtful, critical educational leaders. In what follows, we want to argue that one way to rethink and restructure the nature of teacher work is to view teachers as intellectuals. The category of intellectual is helpful in a number of ways. First, it provides a theoretical basis for examining teacher work as a form of intellectual labor. Second, it clarifies the ideological and material conditions necessary for intellectual work. Third, it helps to illuminate the various modes of intelligibility, ideologies, and interests that are produced and legitimated by teacher work.

By viewing teachers as intellectuals, we can illuminate and recover the rather general notion that all human activity involves some form of thinking. That is, no activity, regardless of how routinized it may become is abstracted from the functioning of the mind in some capacity. This is a crucial issue because by arguing that the use of the mind is a general part of all human activity, we dignify the human capacity for integrating thinking and practice, and in doing so we highlight the core of what it means to view teachers as reflective practitioners. Within this discourse, teachers can be seen not merely as "performers professionally equipped to realize effectively any goals that may be set for them. Rather, [they should] be viewed as free men and women with a special dedication to the values of the intellect and the enhancement of the critical powers of the young."[21]

Furthermore, viewing teachers as intellectuals provides a strong critique of those ideologies that legitimate social practices which separate conceptualization, planning, and designing from the processes of implementation and execution. It is important to stress that teachers must take active responsibility for raising serious questions about what they teach, how they are to teach it, and what the larger goals are for which they are striving. This means that they must take a responsible role in shaping the purposes and conditions of schooling. Such a task is impossible within a division of labor where teachers have little influence over the ideological and economic conditions of their work. There is also a growing political and ideological tendency as expressed in the current debates on educational reform, to remove teachers and students from their histories and cultural experiences in the name of pedagogical approaches that will make schooling more instrumental. These approaches generally mean that teachers and students alike are "situated" within curricula approaches and instructional management schemes that reduce their roles to either implementing or receiving the goals and objectives of publishers, outside experts, and others far removed from the specificities of daily classroom life. This issue becomes all the more important when seen as part of the growing objectification of human life in general. The concept of teacher as intellectual provides the theoretical posture to fight against this type of ideological and pedagogical imposition.

Moreover, the concept of intellectual provides the theoretical groundwork for interrogating the specific ideological and economic conditions under which intellectuals as a social group need to work in order to function as critical, thinking, creative human beings. This suggests being critical not only of the relationship between knowledge and power in the interest of dominating social forms, but also being critical of the politics and partiality of their own location as intellectuals. This last point takes on a normative and political dimension and seems especially relevant for teachers. For if we believe that the role of teaching cannot be reduced to merely training in the practical skills, but involves, instead, the education of a class of intellectuals vital to the development of a democratic society, then the category of intellectual becomes a way of linking the purpose of teacher education, public schooling, and in-service training to the very principles necessary for the development of a democratic order and society.

Neither teaching training institutions nor the public schools have viewed themselves historically as important sites for educating teachers as intellectuals. In part, this has been due to the pervasiveness of a growing technocratic rationality that separates theory from practice and contributes to the development of modes of pedagogy that ignore teacher creativity and insight. It is also due to the predominance of theories and forms of school leadership and organization that give teachers little control over the nature of their work. The latter not only shape the structure and experiences of what teachers do in schools, but also the way in which they are prepared in teacher training institutions. The general overriding principle in most teacher education programs is the emphasis on having prospective educators master pedagogical techniques that eschew questions of purpose and the discourse of critique and possibility.

We have argued that by viewing teachers as intellectuals we can begin to rethink and reformulate those historical traditions and conditions that have prevented schools and teachers from assuming their full potential as active, reflective scholars and practitioners. We want both to qualify this point and extend it further. We believe that it is imperative not only to view teachers as intellectuals, but also to contextualize in political and normative terms the concrete social functions that teachers perform. In this way, we can be more specific about the different relationships that teachers have to both their work and to the society in which such work takes place.

Any attempt to reformulate the role of teachers as intellectuals has also to include the broader issue of how to view educational theory in general. If we view educational theory as a form of social theory, the discourse of educational theory can be understood as a form of knowledge that legitimates and reproduces forms of social life. Educational theory in this case is not viewed as merely the application of objective scientific principles to the concrete study of schooling and learning. Instead, it is seen as an eminently political discourse that emerges from and characterizes an expression of struggle over what forms of authority, orders of representation, forms of moral regulation, and versions of the past and future should be legitimated, passed on, and debated within specific pedagogical sites. All educational theories and discourse are ideologies that have an intimate relation to questions of power. This is evident in the way such discourses arise out of and structure the distinctions between high- and low-status knowledge, legitimate cultural forms that reproduce specific class, racial, and patriarchal interests, and help to sustain specific organizational patterns and classroom social relations.

We see educational theory as having a deep commitment to developing schools as sites that prepare students to participate in and struggle to develop democratic public life. This means that the value of educational theory and practice should be linked to providing the conditions for teachers and students to understand schools as public spheres dedicated to forms of self- and social empowerment. It also means defining teacher work against the imperative to develop knowledge and skills that provide students with the tools they will need to be leaders rather than simply managers or skilled civil servants. Similarly, it means fighting against those ideological and material practices that reproduce privileges for the few and social and economic inequality for the many.

By politicizing the notion of schooling and revealing the ideological nature of educational theory and practice, it becomes possible to be more specific in defining the meaning of the category of intellectual and to interrogate the political and pedagogical function of the intellectual as a social category. There are two related but separate points by which to venture a definition of the intellectual. The more general definition is rooted in a quality of mind that is characterized as having a creative, critical, and contemplative relationship to the world of ideas. Richard Hofstadter epitomizes this position in his distinction between the meaning of intellect and the meaning of intelligence. Intelligence, for him, is "an excellence of mind that is employed within a fairly narrow, immediate predictable range; it is a manipulative, adjustive, unfailingly practical quality. . . . Intellect, on the other hand is the critical, creative, and contemplative side of mind. Whereas intelligence seeks to grasp, manipulate, reorder, adjust, intellect examines, ponders, wonders, theorizes, criticizes, imagines."[22]

Paul Piccone provides a similar distinction but places it within a larger social context.

> Unless one fudges the definition of intellectuals in terms of purely formal and statistical educational criteria, it is fairly clear that what modern society produces is an army of alienated, privatized, and uncultured experts who are knowledgeable only within very narrowly defined areas. This technical intelligentsia, rather than intellectuals in the traditional sense of thinkers concerned with the totality, is growing by leaps and bounds to run the increasingly complex bureaucratic and industrial apparatus. Its rationality, however, is only instrumental in character, and thus suitable mainly to perform partial tasks rather than tackling substantial questions of social organization and political direction.[23]

Herb Kohl is more specific and provides a definition of the intellectual that relates directly to teachers. He writes:

> An intellectual is someone who knows about his or her field, has a wide breadth of knowledge about other aspects of the world, who uses experience to develop theory and questions theory on the basis of further experience. An intellectual is also someone who has the courage to question authority and who refuses to act counter to his or her own experience and judgment.[24]

In our view all of these positions make distinctions that are important but also problematic by suggesting that intellectual inquiry is either the repository of specific groups of people, or that the quality of intellectual inquiry is only operative within specific social functions. We do not mean to suggest that the question of what qualities of mind constitute intellectual inquiry is not an important one. These positions are informative because they suggest that intellectual inquiry is characterized by someone who has a breadth of knowledge about the world, who views ideas in more than instrumental terms, and who harbors a spirit of inquiry that is critical and oppositional, one that is true to its own impulses and judgments. But we want to make a distinction between those characteristics of intellectual inquiry as they exist in various degrees and proportions among different individuals and the social function of intellectual work itself. In his attempt to turn the issue of the nature and role of the intellectual into a political question, Antonio Gramsci provides a more helpful theoretical elaboration on this issue. For Gramsci, all men and women are intellectuals, but not all of them function in society as intellectuals. Gramsci is worth quoting on this issue.

> When one distinguishes between intellectuals and nonintellectuals, one is referring in reality only to the immediate social function of the professional

category of the intellectuals, that is, one has in mind the direction in which their specific professional activity is weighted, whether towards intellectual elaboration or towards muscular-nervous effort. This means that, although one can speak of intellectuals, one cannot speak of nonintellectuals, because non-intellectuals do not exist. But even the relationship between efforts of intellectual-cerebral elaboration and muscular-nervous effort is not always the same, so that there are varying degrees of specific intellectual activity. There is no human activity from which every form of intellectual participation can be excluded: *homo faber* cannot be separated from *homo sapiens*. Each man (sic), finally, outside his professional activity, carries on some form of intellectual activity, that is, he is a "philosopher," an artist, a man of taste, he participates in a particular conception of the world, has a conscious line of moral conduct, and therefore contributes to sustain a conception of the world or to modify it, that is, to bring into being new modes of thought.[25]

For Gramsci, all people are intellectuals in that they think, mediate, and adhere to a specific view of the world. The point here, as mentioned previously, is that varying degrees of critical and common sense thought is endemic to what it means to be human. The significance of this insight is that it gives pedagogical activity an inherently political quality. For instance, Gramsci's view of political activity was deeply rooted in the task of raising the quality of thought of the working class. At the same time, by arguing that all people do not function in their social capacity as intellectuals, Gramsci provides the theoretical groundwork for analyzing the political role of those intellectuals who had to be considered in terms of the organizational and directive functions they performed in a given society.

In the broadest sense, Gramsci attempts to locate the political and social function of intellectuals through his analyses of the role of conservative and radical organic intellectuals. For Gramsci, conservative organic intellectuals provide the dominant class with forms of moral and intellectual leadership. As agents of the status quo, such intellectuals identify with the dominant relations of power and become the propagators of its ideologies and values. This group represents a stratum of intellectuals that gives ruling classes a homogeneity and awareness of their economic, political, and social functions. In the advanced industrial countries organic intellectuals can be found in all strata of society and include specialists in industrial organizations, professors in universities, journalists in the culture industry, and various levels of executives in middle management positions.[26]

Gramsci's categories illuminate the political nature of intellectual work within specific social functions. Moreover, Gramsci's analysis helps to shatter the myth that the nature of intellectual work is determined by one's class location. On the contrary, there is no immediate correspondence between class location and consciousness; but there is a correspondence between the social function of one intellectual's work and the particular relationship it has to modifying, challenging, or reproducing the dominant society. In other words, it is the *political nature* of intellectual work that is the issue at hand. This is a major theoretical advance over the ongoing debate among Marxists and others as to whether intellectuals constitute a specific class or culture.[27] Furthermore, by politicizing the nature of intellectual work, Gramsci strongly challenges dominant theoretical traditions that have decontexulized the role that intellectuals play in education and the larger society. In other words, he criticizes those theorists who decontextualized the intellectual by suggesting that he or she exists independently of issues of class, culture, power, and politics. Inherent in such a view is the notion that the intellectual is obligated to engage in a value-free discourse, one that necessitates that he or she refuse to make a commitment to specific views of the world, refuse to take sides on different issues, or refuse to link knowledge with the fundamental principles of emancipation. Such a view reinforces the idea that intellectuals are free floating and detached in the sense that they perform a type of labor that is objective and apolitical.

Similarly, Gramsci's notion that intellectuals represent a social category and not a class raises interesting questions as to how educators might be viewed at different levels of schooling in terms of their politics, the nature of their discourse, and the pedagogical functions they perform. But Gramsci's terms need to be expanded in order to grasp the changing nature and social function of intellectuals in their capacities as educators. The categories around which we want to analyze the social function of educators as intellectuals are: (a) transformative intellectuals, (b) critical intellectuals, (c) accommodating intellectuals, and (d) hegemonic intellectuals. It is imperative to note that these are somewhat exaggerated, ideal-typical categories whose purpose is to bring into bold relief the cluster of integrated elements that indicate the interests and tendencies to which they point. Needless to say, there are teachers who move in and out between these categories and defy placement in any one of them; moreover, it is conceivable that teachers under different circumstances may opt out of one tendency and move into another category. Finally, these categories are irreducible to any one specific political doctrine. They point to forms of ideology and social practice that could be taken up by any number of diverse political positions or world views.

Transformative Intellectuals

Transformative intellectuals is a category which suggests that teachers as intellectuals can emerge from and work with any number of groups, other than and including the working class, that advance emancipatory traditions and cultures within and without alternative public spheres.[28] Utilizing the language of critique, these intellectuals employ the discourse of self-criticism so as to make the foundations for a critical pedagogy explicit while simultaneously illuminating the relevance of the latter for both students and the larger society. Central to the category of transformative intellectuals is the task of making the pedagogical more political and the political more pedagogical. In the first instance, this means inserting education directly into the political sphere by arguing that schooling represents both a struggle for meaning *and* a struggle over power relations. Thus, schooling becomes a central terrain where power and politics operate out of a dialectical relationship between individuals and groups, who function within specific historical conditions and structural constraints as well as within cultural forms and ideologies that are the basis for contradictions and struggles. Within this view of schooling, critical reflection and action become part of a fundamental social project to help students develop a deep and abiding faith in the struggle to overcome injustices and to change themselves. Knowledge and power are inextricably linked in this case to the presupposition that to choose life, so as to make it possible, is to understand the preconditions necessary to struggle for it.

In the second instance, making the political more pedagogical means utilizing forms of pedagogy that treat students as critical agents, problematizes knowledge, utilizes dialogue, and makes knowledge meaningful, critical, and ultimately emancipatory. In part, this suggests that transformative intellectuals take seriously the need to provide the conditions for students to be able to speak, write, and assert critically their own histories, voices, and learning experiences. It means developing a critical vernacular that is attentive to problems experienced at the level of everyday life, particularly as these are related to pedagogical experiences connected to classroom practice. As such, the starting point pedagogically for such intellectuals is not with the isolated student but with collective actors in their various cultural, class, racial, historical, and gendered settings, along with the particularity of their diverse problems, hopes, and dreams. It is at this point that the language of critique unites with the language of possibility. That is, transformative intellectuals must take seriously the need to come to grips with those ideological and material aspects of the dominant society that attempt to separate the issues of power and knowledge. This means working to create the ideological and material conditions in both schools and the larger society that give students the opportunity to become agents of civic courage, and therefore citizens who have the knowledge and courage to take seriously the need to make despair unconvincing and hope practical. In short, the language of critique unites with the language of possibility when it points to the conditions necessary for new forms of culture, alternative social practices, new modes of communication, and a practical vision for the future.

Critical Intellectuals

Critical intellectuals are ideologically alternative to existing institutions and modes of thought, but they do not see themselves as connected either to a specific social formation or as performing a general social function that is expressively political in nature. Their protests constitute a critical function, which they see as part of their professional status or obligation as intellectuals. In most cases, the posture of critical intellectuals is self-consciously apolitical, and they try to define their relationship to the rest of society as free-floating. As individuals they are critical of inequality and injustice, but they often refuse or are unable to move beyond their isolated posture to the terrain of collective solidarity and struggle. Often this retreat from politics is justified on the basis of arguments that posit the impossibility of politics for reasons as ideologically diverse as the claim that we live in a totally administered society, or that history is in the hands of a technology out of control, or the simple refusal to believe that human agencies exist that have any effect on history.

Of course, the most celebrated effort to establish the status of intellectuals as a "free-floating" critical social layer was that of Karl Mannheim.[29] He argued that genuine intellectuals could not be situated in any particular social class even if, in their origins, they identified with one. To the extent that the "man of knowledge" was engaged in the critical appropriation of truth, he was free of the interests which, if he were situated within a particular class, transformed knowledge into ideology. For Mannheim, any ideology was understood as inquiry subject to the contamination of social interest. It was by its nature partial knowledge. Mannheim wrestled with the Kantian question of how to achieve knowledge of the social totality and concluded that this could not be achieved within the framework of partisan research. When the intellectual is freed from particular interests, "he" can achieve the distance required to grasp the truth.

Recent attempts to continue this discourse about knowledge, such as those of Jürgen Habermas, argue the same point from a somewhat different premise.[30] Habermas tries to counter Marxism's claim that truth can be arrived at by the proletariat: as the rising class their interests are universal by virtue of their partial exclusion from society. This claim has failed in the twentieth century to the degree that the workers have been integrated within, and are no longer excluded from, the benefits of the social order. Although there is much to commend in Habermas's critique of Marxism's conception of the relation between knowledge and human interest, we do not share his faith in objective reason as the goal to which intellectual labor strives. Rather, we hold that the conception of rationality which believes in the possibility of separating science from ideology to be another form of ideology. Habermas wishes to free the emancipatory human interest from the limits imposed by history on the capacity of social class to make their particular interests universal. Yet by positing the autonomy of reason and the possibility of freeing knowledge from its ideological presuppositions, he has merely reasserted the ideology of modernity in which science as a value of neutral discourse is possible and depends for its realization on such categories as undistorted communication, reflexive understanding, and autocritique. Certainly, we agree with the proposition that reflexive understanding and critical discourse are necessary to overcome the limitations imposed by common sense on human emancipation. Yet, this is not the same as arguing that intellectuals must remain on the fringes, refusing to link with social movements whose world view condemns them to partial knowledge. That social movements are bound to influence the intellectuals as much as be influenced by them is part of the contradictory, but necessary, result of the formation of the transforming intellectual. We cannot discuss in detail here our assertion that the enlightenment conceptions of truth, objective reason, and so on, are themselves part of the partial discourses of historical actors, situated in specific times and places. Suffice it to say that science itself has become aware of the limits of its own aspirations for totalization, that the discovery of the ineluctability of difference is among the most important achievements of physics and biology of the twentieth century. To claim, as Habermas does, that intersubjective understanding can clear away the tangled web of discourse is a retreat from Sartre's admonition that only the committed intellectual can arrive at assertions that serve human emancipation. In other words, critical intellectuals forget that emancipation cannot be delivered from the outside.

Accommodating Intellectuals

Accommodating intellectuals generally stand firm within an ideological posture and set of material practices that support the dominant society and its ruling groups. Such intellectuals are generally not aware of this process in that they do not define themselves as self-conscious agents of the status quo, even though their politics further the interests of the dominant classes. This category of intellectuals also defines themselves in terms that suggest they are free-floating, removed from the vagaries of class conflicts and partisan politics. But in spite of such rationalizations, they function primarily to mediate uncritically ideas and social practices that serve to reproduce the status quo. These are the intellectuals who decry politics while simultaneously refusing to take risks. Another more subtle variation is the intellectual who disdains politics by proclaiming professionalism as a value system, one that often entails the spurious concept of scientific objectivity.

Hegemonic Intellectuals

Hegemonic intellectuals do more than surrender to forms of academic and political incorporation, or hide behind spurious claims to objectivism;

they self-consciously define themselves through the forms of moral and intellectual leadership they provide for dominant groups and classes. This stratum of intellectuals provides various factions of the dominant classes with a homogeneity and awareness of their economic, political, and ethical functions. The interests that define the conditions as well as the nature of their work are tied to the preservation of the existing order. Such intellectuals are to be found on the consulting lists of major foundations, on the faculties of major universities, as managers of the culture industry, and in spirit, at least, in teaching and administrative positions at various levels of schooling.

For fear of these categories appearing to be too rigid, it is important to stress more specifically that the teachers who occupy them cannot be viewed merely from the perspective of the ideological interests they represent. For instance, as Erik Olin Wright has pointed out, the positions that teachers hold must also be analyzed in terms of the objective antagonisms they experience as intellectuals who occupy contradictory class locations.[31] That is, like workers they have to sell their labor power and have no control over the educational apparatus as a whole. On the other hand, unlike most workers they do have some control over the nature of their labor process, that is, what to teach, how to teach, what kind of research to do, and so on. Needless to say, the relative autonomy that teachers have at different levels of schooling differs, with those in some tiers of higher education, particularly the elite universities, having the most autonomy. Moreover, regardless of the ideological interests such teachers represent there is always the possibility for real tensions and antagonisms between their lack of control over the goals and purposes of schooling and the relative autonomy they enjoy. For example, in a time of economic crisis, teachers have been laid off, given increased course loads, denied tenure, and forced to implement administratively dictated pedagogies. It is within these tensions and objective contradictions that the possibilities exist for shifting alliances and movement among teachers from one category to the next.

THE DISCOURSE AND ROLE OF EDUCATORS AS TRANSFORMATIVE INTELLECTUALS

In order to fight for schools as democratic spheres, it is imperative to understand the contradictory roles that transformative intellectuals occupy within the various levels of schooling. In the most immediate sense, the notion of transformative intellectual makes visible the paradoxical position that radical educators face in the public schools and in the universities. On the one hand, such intellectuals earn a living within institutions that play a fundamental role in producing the dominant culture. On the other hand, they define their political terrain by offering to students forms of alternative discourse and critical social practices whose interests are often at odds with the overall hegemonic role of the school and the society it supports.

The paradox is not easy to resolve, and often represents a struggle against incorporation by the university or school system which reward those educators willing either to remove critical scholarship from their teaching or remove it from any relation to concrete political movements. At the university level, for example, there is enormous pressure for radical educators to peddle their academic wares merely as viable commodities for academic journals and conferences. Under the banner of accountability, teachers at all levels of schooling are subtly and sometimes not so subtly pressured to respond to the issues, modes of research, discourse, and social practices deemed legitimate by the dominant culture. Erik Olin Wright is worth quoting on this issue:

> [Radical] theorists within . . . universities are under tremendous pressure to ask questions structured by bourgeois problems, bourgeois ideological and political practices. Such pressures are often extremely direct, taking the form of tenure criteria, blacklisting, harassment, etc. But often the pressures are quite subtle, played out through the intellectual debates within professional conferences and journals. To publish in the proper journals one has to ask questions which those journals see as relevant, and such relevance is dictated not by the centrality of the questions to [radical social theory and practice], but to the dilemmas and problems within bourgeois social science.[32]

Rather than surrender to this form of academic and political incorporation, it is essential to define the role of the transformative intellectual in a way that points to forms of counterhegemonic practice that can both avoid and challenge such incorporation. One essential starting point is for transformative intellectuals to form alliances among themselves, struggle to win over critical intellectuals when possible, and join and work with oppositional social movements outside of the schools.

In the first instance, teachers and academics who function as transformative intellectuals can collectively organize in order to engage in projects designed to understand the critical role that educators play at all levels of schooling in producing and legitimating existing social relations. This might take the form of educators establishing social projects in which they critically interrogate existing school curricula, the hidden curricula, policy formation at the local and state levels, the form and content of school texts, their own ideologies and the working conditions under which teachers operate. Not only would such projects provide a theoretical and political service by critically engaging the nature of school life, it would also give radical and critical educators the opportunity to begin to communicate to each other about their common concerns. Moreover, such alliances provide the possibility for university and public school people to redefine the traditional theory-practice relationship within the context of their alliances with each other. That is, in order to overcome the social division of labor between theoretical production and practical knowledge (read as theory and practice), particularly as it defines the university-public school relationship, transformative intellectuals from these different spheres can forge alliances around common social and political projects in which they share their theoretical concerns and practical talents. The point here is that we recognize that these different educational sites give rise to various forms of theoretical production, and that such sites cannot be seen as respectively representative for the development of theory and practice.

Such projects also have value not only because they promote political unity and are necessary to fight against accommodating and hegemonic intellectuals, but also because they open the possibility for transformative intellectuals to develop and work with movements outside of the limiting contours of the academic disciplines, symposiums, and reward systems that have become the traditional referents for intellectual activity. In effect, we are arguing that teachers as transformative intellectuals need to become a movement marked by an active involvement in oppositional public spheres in which the primacy of the political is asserted anew. Transformative intellectuals can join with any number of social groups engaged in emancipatory struggle. By linking up with ecology, feminist, peace, trade union, and neighborhood groups, transformative intellectuals can bring their skills and talents to bear on vital forms of resistance at the local level, for example, locally based efforts against toxic waste dumping, nuclear power, consumer fraud, racial and sexual discrimination. Within this context, the political becomes pedagogical. Intellectuals learn from and with others engaged in similar political struggles.[33]

Such alliances are absolutely necessary if teachers, particularly within the public schools, are to be able to bring outside forces to bear on fighting for ideological and material conditions within the schools that will allow them to function as intellectuals—that is, conditions that will allow them to reflect, read, share their work with others, produce curriculum materials, publish their achievements for teachers and others outside of their local schools, and so on. At the present time, teachers labor in the public schools under organizational constraints and ideological conditions that leave them little room for collective work and critical pursuits. Their teaching hours are too long, they are generally isolated in cellular structures and have few opportunities to teach with others, and they have little say over the selection, organization, and distribution of teaching materials. Moreover, they operate under class loads and numerous noncurricular tasks such as bus duty, cafeteria duty, and playground duty that needlessly constrain their time and teaching abilities. Their salaries in the United States are a scandal that is only now being fully recognized by the American public. Intellectual work needs to be supported by practical conditions buttressed by concomitant democratic ideologies. If teachers are to fight for conditions that support joint teaching, collective writing and research, and democratic planning, they will also have to struggle simultaneously against the ingrained values of competition, individualism, patriarchy, racism, and ageism that permeate all levels of schooling.

It is within conditions marked by popular control over bureaucratization that new spaces will open for creative and reflective discourse and action. Such a discourse will be able to relate language and power, take popular experience seriously as part of the learning process, combat mystification, and help students to reorder the raw experiences of their lives through the perspectives opened up by history, philosophy, sociology, and other related disciplines. The discourse of the transformative intellectual takes the issues of community and liberation seriously, and in doing so, gives new meaning to the pedagogical and political necessity of creating the conditions for emancipatory forms of self and social empowerment among both educators and students. It is a struggle worth waging.

NOTES

1. The discourse of crisis in public education has been dealt with in a series of reports and books, including the following: The National Commission on Excellence, *A Nation at Risk: The Imperative for Educational Reform* (Washington, D.C., 1983); Task Force on Education for Economic Growth, *Action for Excellence: A Comprehensive Plan to Improve Our Nation's Schools* (Denver: Education Commission of the States, 1983); College Entrance Examination Board, *Academic Preparation for College* (New York: College Entrance Examination Board, 1983); Twentieth Century Fund Task Force on Federal Elementary and Secondary Education Policy, *Making the Grade* (New York: Twentieth Century Fund, 1983); Carnegie Corporation of New York, *Education and Economic Progress: Toward a National Educational Policy* (New York: Carnegie Corp., 1983); John Goodlad, *A Place Called School: Promise for the Future* (New York: McGraw-Hill, 1984); Ernest L. Boyer, *High School: A Report on American Secondary Education* (New York: Harper and Row, 1983). One of the few analyses that takes the role of teachers seriously is: Theodore Sizer, *Horace's Compromise: The Dilemma of the High School* (Boston: Houghton Mifflin, 1984).

2. An example of this trend in the teaching of reading through a mastery learning approach can be found in Patrick Shannon, "Mastery Learning in Reading and the Control of Teachers and Students," *Language Arts* 61:5 (September 1984), pp. 484–493.

3. Thomas S. Popkewitz, *Paradigm and Ideology in Educational Research* (Philadelphia and London: Falmer Press, 1984), p. 108.

4. E. T. Sliva and S. Slaughter, "Prometheus/Bound: Knowledge, Power, and the Transformation of American Social Science, 1865–1920." Unpublished manuscript, University of Toronto, 1981, chapter 5, p. 2.

5. For a general critique of positivism, see Max Horkheimer, *Critique of Instrumental Reason* (New York: Seabury Press, 1974); see also Jürgen Habermas, *Theory and Practice* (Boston: Beacon Press, 1973), especially chapter 7. For a specific critique of the legacy of positivist thought and its influence on educational

theory and practice, see Henry Giroux, *Ideology, Culture and the Process of Schooling* (Philadelphia: Temple University Press, 1984).

6. Herbert Marcuse, *One Dimensional Man* (Boston: Beacon Press, 1964); Stuart Ewen, *Captains of Consciousness* (New York: McGraw-Hill, 1975).

7. See Joel Spring, *Education and the Rise of the Corporate State* (Boston: Beacon Press, 1972); David Tyack, *The One Best System* (Cambridge, Mass.: Harvard University Press, 1974); Theodor Adorno and Max Horkheimer, *The Dialectic of Enlightenment* (New York: Herder and Herder, 1972).

8. Herbert Kleibard, "The Question of Teacher Education," *New Perspectives on Teacher Education,* ed. D. McCarty (San Francisco: Jossey-Bass, 1973).

9. Kenneth M. Zeichner, "Alternative Paradigms on Teacher Education," *Journal of Teacher Education* 34:3 (May–June 1983), pp. 3–9.

10. Henry A. Giroux, *Ideology, Culture and the Process of Schooling,* op. cit.

11. Zeichner, op. cit., p. 4.

12. Karen J. Winkler, "Research Focus of Education Doctorate Is Too Ill-Defined, Officials Say," *The Chronicle of Higher Education* 29:11 (November 7, 1984), p. 11.

13. Richard Bates, "Bureaucracy, Professionalism and Knowledge: Structures of Authority and Structures of Control," *Educational Research and Perspectives* 7:2 (1980), pp. 66–76.

14. William S. Foster, "The Changing Administrator: Developing Managerial Praxis," *Educational Theory* 30:1 (Winter 1980), pp. 11–23.

15. Andrew Wake, "School Knowledge and the Structure of Bureaucracy," Paper presented at the conference of the Sociological Association of Australia and New Zealand, Canberra, July 1979, p. 16.

16. Michael Apple, *Education and Power* (Boston: Routledge and Kegan Paul, Ltd, 1982).

17. Michael Apple, "The Political Economy of Text Publishing," *Educational Theory* 43:4 (Fall 1984), pp. 307–319.

18. Patrick Shannon, op. cit., p. 488.

19. M. Katims and B. F. Jones, "Chicago Mastery Learning Reading: Mastery Learning Instruction and Assessment in Inner City Schools," Paper presented at the Annual Meeting of the International Reading Association, New Orleans, 1981, p. 7.

20. K. Patricia Cross, "The Rising Tide of School Reform Reports," *Phi Delta Kappan* 66:3 (November 1984), p. 11.

21. Israel Scheffler, "University Scholarship and the Education of Teachers," *Teachers College Record* 70:1 (1968), p. 11.

22. Richard Hofstadter, *Anti-Intellectualism in American Life* (New York: Random House, 1963).

23. Paul Piccone, "Symposium on the Role of the Intellectual in the 1980s," *Telos,* No. 50 (Winter 1981–82), 116.

24. Herbert Kohl, "Examining Closely What We Do," *Learning* (August 1983), p. 29.

25. Antonio Gramsci, *Selections from the Prison Notebooks,* ed. and trans. Q. Hoare and G. Smith (New York: International Publishers, 1971).

26. For Gramsci, radical intellectuals also attempt to provide the moral and intellectual leadership of a specific class, in this case, the working class. More spe-

cifically, radical organic intellectuals provide the pedagogical and political skills that are necessary to raise political awareness in the working class in order to help the members of that class to develop leadership skills and to engage in collective struggle.

27. For an overview of this debate, see Carl Boggs, "Marxism and the Role of Intellectuals," *New Political Science* 1:2/3 (1979), pp. 7–23.

28. Gramsci, op. cit.; Paulo Freire, *The Politics of Education* (South Hadley, Mass.: Bergin and Garvey Publishers, 1984).

29. Karl Mannheim, *Ideology and Utopia* (New York: Harvest Book, 1936).

30. Jürgen Habermas, *Knowledge and Human Interests* (Boston: Beacon Press, 1968); *The Theory of Communicative Action, Volume 1: Reason and the Rationalization of Society* (Boston: Beacon Press, 1984).

31. Erik Olin Wright, "Intellectuals and the Working Class," *The Insurgent Sociologist* 8:1 (Winter 1978), pp. 5–18.

32. Ibid., p. 16.

33. The problems that confront the making of such alliances are analyzed in: Ferenc Feher and Agnes Heller, "From Red to Green," *Telos* 59 (Spring 1984), pp. 35–44.

Chapter Three

The Literacy Crisis:
A Critique and Alternative

Two decades ago, American education seemed on the verge of a renaissance commensurate to the era of progressivism of the 1920s and 1930s. Practical innovations dotted the landscape; experimentalism from Montessori to free schools, often student controlled, succeeded in forcing a modicum of school reform in the public sector from the outside. At the beginning of the 1970s, education officials in cities and towns throughout the country had decided that it was necessary to create alternative elementary and secondary schools *within* the established order. The motivating power for starting these programs was by no means altruistic or a far-sightedness by educational professionals. They were simply persuaded, either by the example of successful projects outside the system or the eloquence of educational planners and critics, that certain problems of the schools could at least be ameliorated, if not solved by educational innovations.

Building on the example of the community-controlled districts in New York elementary and junior high schools, big city Boards of Education moved into the new decade with plans to encourage neighborhoods and educators to begin experiments in alternative high schools as well. In most cities, the conservative Boards felt their backs to the wall: enrollments were exploding, but school attendance was dropping among many segments of the cities' high school population. The metaphor of *siege* was widely employed to describe the atmosphere in the schools, with teachers steadily losing ground to more confident young guerrilla warriors. Employers and colleges complained that applicants lacked the needed skills to perform jobs or do "college" work. These skills deficits were defined as literacy as well as good work habits.

The legitimacy of schools as *educational* institutions was challenged by low attendance and plummeting test scores, an all too familiar theme in the 1990s. Parents, especially those from minority communities and the remaining white middle classes in the cities, began demanding educational changes, the content of which remained unspecified. Neil Postman, George Dennison, Jonathan Kozol, and other "radical" writers may not have become gurus for the establishment, but their ideas were seriously considered in the quest for stability in schools.

In March 1970, Stanley Aronowitz joined a small staff of educational planners, parents, and liberal reformers on New York's upper east side and East Harlem who managed to extract a mandate from the Board to start an experimental public high school. The nature of the experiment was not clear at the outset and, indeed, was never clarified beyond a few well-worn clichés: this was to be a "community"-controlled school within the limits set by state and city laws governing such issues as credentials for teachers, minimum requirements expected of students, and, importantly, the requirement that the head of the school be qualified by Board licensure. Each of these boundaries presented difficulties for the Committee for a Comprehensive Education (the group endowed with the essential power to organize the school). But it was not bureaucratic restrictions that played the major role in transforming the school from a promising experiment into a slightly more gentle version of a New York City public high school. The story of Park East High School, which opened for students in February 1971, is the story of the demise of the new progressivism that accompanied the beginning of the 1970s. Although the political climate of rebellion and reform that marked the 1960s was responsible for the impulse for change, it was not only a changed political climate that ultimately undermined the forward march of educational reform. As the decade wore on, the rise of the new conservatism in educational policy reflected a pervasive retreat among progressive forces. It was a combination of wrongheaded concepts among most educational innovators that were easily refuted or at least repudiated by the opposition. An effective counterattack by the conservatives *at the ideological level* must be held accountable for the reversals that have marked the recent past.

At Park East we shared all the misconceptions of the rest of the movement. We attributed alienation to the "straight curriculum" of the public schools, their authoritarian style of leadership, and the failure of the schools to inspire teachers to dedicated pedagogy. Our view was that the curriculum and governance had to (a) be relevant to students' lives by becoming more practical without succumbing to the anti-intellectualism of vocational education, (b) become less rigid to allow students a wider range of learning options and (c) involve students as well as parents in the processes of school governance. Of course, we made no political analysis of the reasons the old curriculum was inadequate or the administration had become arbitrary. We attributed its inadequacy merely to the fact that it was imposed from above, without regard to student needs. In short, we accepted the canons of student-centered education but, at the same time, made the claim that such an orientation had outcomes that would satisfy the concerns of parents, college admission criteria, and employers. We claimed that students could master the three Rs without recourse to teaching and curriculum styles that "turned them off." We accepted the implicit assumption that a "caring" learning environment was often the sufficient condition for motivating students to learning. At no time in our ruminations over the crisis in learning did it occur to us that the problem might be broader than the power of the schooling environment. We assumed that good teachers and excited students, given their autonomy by an activist but nondirective administration, and political support from parents and other community organizations, would reverse the tendency of schooling to grow more distant from education. Of course, school reformers and innovators in that period were dimly aware that among the reasons for the estrangement of black, Hispanic, and working-class white students from schools was their perception that the routes to opportunities to escape ghetto life were paved with nails. We knew that there was reason for kids to doubt that a degree from high school would pay off in concrete economic terms. Despite the boom engendered by the Vietnam War, the lives of those stuck in subworking class communities were little changed by Great Society programs. Yet, we were believers in the power of schools to provide these communities with a fair chance in the scramble for mobility for those historically excluded from the ball park, much less allowed to play the game.

Of course, we were wrong. All the alternative school movements accomplished was to give a few kids the chance to climb into the black or Hispanic middle class which, in the last analysis, was the objective of Great Society programs. We became unwitting agents (when successful) of the need for a new middle class of ghetto administrators, minority corporate public relations men and women, line supervisors in plants, stores and government agencies, and subprofessionals in education and social welfare sectors. Alternative education in the sixties and early seventies was a way to find a safety valve to place the most active, disruptive and talented kids away from the mainstream. It was also a way to return them to the mainstream as trained professionals who acted as mediators between their communities and the corridors of power. They were living proof to the community of the reality of mobility promises and simultaneously interpreters of community needs to the powerful. For the mass of the disenfranchised the alternative schools were confusing. Most of them never saw the inside of these weird places, and for many who did, the free or alternative school was a scam, a way to avoid the heavily guarded prison-like atmosphere of regular high schools. Moreover, after a few years it became painfully obvious that free schools were designed for the linguistically literate. The nondirective character of the school ambience abetted the self-motivated, those for whom traditional schools were actually a retardant. But for many who needed *a reason* to become educated in the ways of industrial or postindustrial society, there was nothing self-evident about the canons either of mathematical calculations or of bourgeois humanistic traditions.

The experiments came to a more or less abrupt ending in the public sector as some of its opponents mounted an effective attack on the ground that it was immoral, and even racist, when the child was black or Hispanic, to permit a ten year old to remain a nonreader. Only a reversion to the old curriculum could remedy the situation, according to advocates of "basic" education. Using the rhetoric of the civil rights movement's anti-elitism, educational conservatism took over in the mid-1970s leaving fervent ideologues of educational reform bewildered and ashamed. Soon even those who began the free school movement were uttering their *mea culpas*. Administrators and teachers who had furiously tried to "retool" in the hectic sixties breathed a sigh of relief and set out to invent a new ideology of learning which stressed "standards." Among these the writing of E. D. Hirsch was particularly refreshing because it attempted to incorporate the notion of standards into the concept of rhetoric akin to ancient meanings: rhetoric was not a means of persuasion alone; it was a way of knowing. Thus, expression had a cognitive content. In the manner of some modern students of language, the new drive for literacy found theoretical legitimacy in the unity of utterance and thought, a refusal of the ideas of such sociolinguists as William Labov who argued that forms of black speech could be transcoded into logical thought commensurable in every respect with canonical expression. The conservatives' insistence that standard English simply connoted the appropriate thought content against colloquialism that was fraught with illogicality convinced both professionals and laypeople that these hard times of stiffening competition for fewer jobs, the nadir of industrial work and its replacement by administrative and technical labor, and the dropping performance of students in schools demanded the end to a crippling permissiveness that had held sway for a decade.

Today free schools are no longer in evidence. They have been incorporated as vestigial structures into "alternative" programs or schools within conventional systems. Like the earlier movement, Progressive Education, the principles of these experiments exist as "traces" within a system that is moving rapidly towards a definition of educational excellence that antedates the older progressivism. The "new curriculum" devalues social learning as a content in education, replacing this notion with a much more direct concept: social reproduction. The schools are being mobilized to insure the reproduction of a society as a whole. Even though the slogan "critical thinking" has not disappeared from the discourse, it cannot be said that it has any major influence over the curriculum. In short, the "hidden curriculum" of American education, preparing students to take their place in the corporate order as disciplined, subordinate workers, has now become more overt. The counterattacks against the old new progressivism went much further than trying to correct some weaknesses in that palpably middle-class educational paradigm. The conservative onslaught argued explicitly for a restoration of old modes of administrative authority within schools, but not for its own sake. Instead the cry "illiteracy" became the rubric under which all forms of repression were subsumed. The old liberalism had swept the rebellion of the young against the arbitrary authority of school officials under the rug by labeling the rebels "hyperkinetic" (a reference to the growing use of psychological categories to eliminate opposition from the subject-objects of schooling, the young). The new conservatives found in "permissiveness" (an explicit attack against liberal notions of rehabilitation and against the critique of authority as a causal agent of the school crisis) a convenient target for justifying the return to the old order.

There are two main things to be said about the current state of education before discussing its future. First, it is perfectly true that progressives have placed entirely too much faith in its elementary principles, particularly the ideas of learning by doing and its view that authority relations that are not legitimated by democratic means are barriers to learning. To be sure, experience-based pedagogy is grounded in a theory of learning which argues that the separation of form and content and, specifically, the bifurcation of knowledge from its consequences is deleterious to learning. Goal-oriented learning that goes beyond intellectual achievement and enters the realm of status, honor, job advancement, and personal pride has already been adopted by the schools as one of the fragmented parts of progressivism consistent with their objectives. But the new conservative curriculum has posed a serious challenge to the epistemological assumptions of liberal educators. The new order argues that the authority of the *word* can be imposed without the crutch of instrumentalism if only the administration, teachers, and parents hold firm: "You shall learn because we say so." Moreover, if you don't, it is curtains for a decent life. America is the land of opportunity only if you do what we say.

Now, it must be admitted that the military model of learning works. Punishment is an effective tool of the reproduction of a hierarchical order, as well as one in which its subjects possess competencies. Of course, one would have to renounce critical thought as a goal of education or the effort to establish a democratic society in order to get kids to read and write under this regime. Or to be more exact, critical and democratic ideas would be produced as an outcome of the rebellion of kids against the authoritarian school, just as in the days before modern progressivism.

The second problem with the old liberal model is that it was based on the assumption of an expanding economy, one that may not be held as a basis for educational policy in the future. If jobs with mobility chances become scarce in the next decade, two consequences might follow. One that is already upon us is that students who believe they have acquired some literacy and cultural skills at home will become more obedient to school authorities and their methods, whether they like them or not. In this sense the conservative proposals under the new conditions may be far more effective than a liberal position might offer. In this culture competitive practices in all spheres and examinations are accorded preeminence as a criterion of competence. Learning how to pass the exam and getting good recommendations from school authorities take on pronounced importance.

Another consequence is the cleaning out of colleges and universities of those students who have been admitted under affirmative action programs including those called "open admissions." Even many liberals would agree with their antagonists that colleges are no place for the illiterate. So, tightening admissions criteria made necessary by fiscal crises (themselves the result of economic decline) will reduce the initiative of students in lower grades to seek higher education. Those who do not respond to the military/basic education model would be adjudged genetically (in the metaphoric sense of the word) incompetent, strengthening the moves towards a further vocationalization of education in the primary and secondary schools. Here the ideas of Plato's *Republic* seem already to have gained some currency among educators. Even more pronounced than the tracking system, the most recent policy has begun to exclude liberal arts from the lower rungs of the schooling hierarchy. A grotesque appropriator of the surface ideology of the old progressivism is the concentration of schools on technical subjects. The subordination of literature and history to "skills" acquisition, and the introduction of "hands on" computer training in the lower grades are all justified as a type of learning by doing as much as a different answer to the cry for relevance that pierced traditional curricula in the sixties and early seventies. What can be more relevant to the lives of students than a curriculum that stresses job preparation in an era that limits opportunities and is, at the same time, increasingly oriented to technique? The new conservatism, in short, preys on the anxiety of a generation that has finally got the news that America in the new era is *Hard Times*. At a time when colleges face declining enrollments, not because of the famous "demographic shift," but because those who might enter are persuaded by the argument that the liberal arts offer no definite payoff, even the institutions of higher learning are attempting to become "relevant" rather than remain academic. If the size of state colleges and universities does not shrink, say administrators, it will be a measure of the degree to which they can make their programs more practical (real job preparation oriented).

Thus, a major consequence of the drift (no, gallop) towards a reversal of the old liberal education, in both ideological and formal terms, will be to remove the elements of critical thinking that are inscribed in the traditional curricula. There is an irony here. The free or alternative school movement rose on the flag of relevance, as much as learning by doing. The argument of the new conservatives hinges on the appropriation of progressive ideology as much as its repudiation. All the conservatives had to do was *redefine* the meaning of a few terms and combine them in a new alternative education model that displaced progressivism as the vanguard of educational reform.

What of the decade that is already upon us? We believe that under the Clinton administration the American public is in for a heavy dose of the new technicalization of the curriculum corresponding to development within the labor market. The whole task set by contemporary educational policy is to keep up with rapidly shifting developments in technology. The only generalizing emphasis that has conquered so far is the now generally accepted campaign to improve reading and writing skills. There are many issues encapsulated in this back-to-basics movement. First, the theoretical assumptions of the new gurus of the movement are not commensurate with the ideology on which the movement rests. The movement triumphed on the basis of its claim that neither the traditional nor its alternative curricula were relevant to the new age. But the dominant mode of inquiry that had led to writing and composition programs at all levels, and focused on the three Rs is highly abstract. On the one hand, learning by doing is repudiated by reference to rhetorical studies, concepts such as standards, focus on parts of speech, vocabulary, and basic math. On the other hand, there are some "doings" underway in high schools, particularly the rapid spread of practically oriented vocational and technical education. Yet, if the former suffers from its other-worldliness, the latter's practical claims are defeated by the incredible degradation, segmentation, and reduction of skills in the job market. More importantly, entry-level jobs proliferate faster than any others in the new technology, and these require a minimum of training because *scientific* knowledge (not taught in the back-to-basics movement) is inscribed in a few machines and not in their operation. Those who design, maintain, and market these machines are a relatively small proportion of the labor force.

Second, the new learning ideology is encountering a major overhaul of educational resources in America. In the wake of a history of sharply higher defense costs, taxpayers' revolts, and economic instability, teaching has become nightmarish. Many classrooms are overcrowded, lack books and other materials, and are led by administrators and teachers who are weary after years of constant warfare and upheaval caused not so much by the kids as by the budget cutters.

Of course, the quest for literacy is paramount in any democratic society, not so much for vocational reasons (it's only during growth periods that genuine skills become in short supply), but for more important reasons.

Self-management of society at the political as well as social and economic levels requires a population possessed of detailed and complex knowledge of scientific and technological processes as well as the elements of policy. The issue in a society wishing to widen participation in its key decisions is whether these can be grasped by ordinary people, and reading and writing are essential elements of this process.

But the military model cannot insure democratic participation. On the contrary, it encourages subordination of a *conceptually* illiterate population whose skills extend to the technical plane. They are able to follow orders under the direction of managements that are responsive to bureaucracies and capital, but unable to examine critically public and private life, to determine how and what should be produced and by whom, and to make the public choices that become policy.

There is, of course, a serious problem with the literacy of the American people. Some aspects of this question reside in elementary skills. But, for the most part, this is a misplaced emphasis, a slogan that is oriented to promoting fear and anxiety so that a new wave of school policy may be accepted. Most Janeys and Johnnys can follow written orders, read newspapers, and make calculations in hundreds of thousands of jobs.[1]

Our problem is, who can think through what's going on in the world, the changes in our lives underway as a result of decisions made at the political level. More importantly, the changes in our ways of working and living, the relation of the United States to the rest of the world, especially those parts of it suffering chronic privation are changing. Our problems are preeminently public ones, for the gulf between the private and the public is no longer so wide that one may pursue his destiny without regard to institutional and political choices. Neither the old way, the alternative movement, nor the neo-conservatism back-to-basics movement proposes to deal with the problem of citizenship, the formation of a public that acts for itself, and the dangerous centralization of power in American life.

The illiteracy to which we refer can only be addressed in the context of social movements that wish to make serious social changes. The other model of rapid learning for whole populations is the *ideological* model. In a country lacking the conditions for rapid economic growth or the motivating force to accept a highly militarized educational process as grounds for learning, the only alternative is to argue for literacy on radical foundations. Democratic self-determination of all social institutions has been adequate as a spur to incredible advances in literacy conceived in both senses discussed here. The most notable example, Nicaragua under the Sandinista government, embarked on such a campaign with revolutionary participation as the fundamental argument.[2] This of course does not relieve educators of the responsibility to address specifically cognitive issues, the politics of learning itself. But given the objective of democracy, the abstract, "standards"-oriented proposals of conservative education cannot suffice. To be sure, language itself has a structure that must be mastered, or to be more exact, our structural capacity to transform grammar must be given an environment that transforms itself into the symbolic forms of speech and writing, and this task is somewhat distinct from practical and social applications. But as Wittgenstein has remarked, language is *"a* form of life," not *the* form of life. It is bound up with social relations, entwined with the ways of the world of which it is both an expression and through which the world lives. Therefore, the concept of relevance requires still another specification, one that insists that students must learn to examine their own lives, the ways in which they have been part of the system of social reproduction. Language learning is a way of distancing oneself from the self-evident, to discover the sense in which we have all been formed within the context of material practices of which schools as well as discourses are an essential aspect.

It may be that the autobiographical mode of inquiry is a way to help students discover their own relation to school and to language. They may see the ways in which the texts of everyday life such as family, peer relations, and mass culture are not merely activities or institutions "out there" but become fragments of that praxis by which we form ourselves. And, as Paul Willis has shown, self-formation does not occur merely mimetically, but also in the process of rebelling against the institutions that have the dominance over our existence.[3] The task of critical thinking, of course, does not end with the recognition that we are part of the system that has shaped us.

Critical education then proposes, not a student-centered practical step, but one that can only be directed, as it were, from without by persons (teachers) who share the goals of the students. Teachers are better able to guide students toward historical understanding and a critical scientific knowledge of the social and external, natural world, and to see how these may be changed by changing the ways people have conceptualized them over time. However, this does not exempt teachers from being self-critical about their own narratives. Nor does it exempt them from sharing power with students and giving students the opportunity to critically engage teacher authority and knowledge.

And, of course, an ideological education that wishes to critically examine its own presuppositions must show the ways in which ideology is defined not merely as a system of values and beliefs inculcated from above. Rather, the job is to help students see ideology as lived experience in literature, music, painting, and social interaction, without regard to distinctions between great canonical literature and the art of contemporary popular forms. For those who despair that students may no longer yield with awe and wonder to the lyrical Keats because the poison of our technological culture has occluded such a possibility have already entered a judgment that is at once problematic on two counts: first, as to Keats as *a priori* superior to anything produced today by popular lyrics in songs, and second, that technological domination subsumes all but a small avant-garde in recent art. The first responsibility of the educator is to validate the experience of the student, including her aesthetic experience, and then to be willing to learn from students. This view corresponds to Paulo Freire's notion of dialogic education, which is not the same as the old concept of student centeredness.

Critical education remembers that students, especially working-class and Third World kids, have been voiceless in this culture except in popular forms such as play and song. (Even commercial music allows the voice of the young to shine forth.) Voicelessness presupposes powerlessness, but it does not follow that the learning environment of schools may either abdicate to students or impose standards from without. If the objective of education is to empower students intellectually and, to some extent emotionally, their voice must receive validation. This entails *both* a critical stance toward their already acquired voice, obtained from the contradictory sources of mass culture and peer interaction, as well as an effort to enrich this voice with historical and critical dimension.

Thus, the antinomy between critical education and neo-conservatism does not engage at the level of the struggle for literacy. Critical education agrees that the problem exists; but it is less a question of *functional* illiteracy than historical and critical/conceptual illiteracy. The trend of current education policy seeks to persuade us that the basics movement can solve the economic crisis for students since it assumes that the problem of dead-end jobs, low income, and insecurity resides with the individual. The critical movement (still incipient but possessing some critical mass) reverses the causal relation. Functional illiteracy is produced by the constitution of the job market by economic and social inequality and political powerlessness. To combat this inequality students require knowledge (of which skills are derivative) and, most of all, hope in their collective powers to change the world so that democratic power replaces corporate control. Of course, some of these criticisms have been presupposed by various radical educators. But their criticisms have been characterized by some significant theoretical problems, and it is to this issue to which we will now turn to in the next chapter.

NOTES

1. See Jonathan Kozol, *Illiterate America* (New York: Doubleday, 1985).
2. Ministerio de Educacion. *Cinco Años de Educacion la Revolucion, 1979–1984* (Managua, Nicaragua: Government Printing, 1984).
3. P. Willis. *Learning to Labour* (England: Saxon House, 1977).

Chapter Four

Reproduction and Resistance in Radical Theories of Schooling

In the last decade, Karl Marx's concept of reproduction has been one of the major organizing ideas informing socialist theories of schooling. Marx states that "every social process of production is, at the same time, a process of reproduction. . . . Capitalist production, therefore . . . produces not only commodities, not only surplus-value, but it also produces and reproduces the capitalist relation, on the one side the capitalist, on the other the wage-labourer."[1] Radical educators have given this concept a central place in developing a critique of liberal views of schooling. Moreover, they have used it as the theoretical foundation for developing a critical science of education.[2] Thus far, the task has been only partially successful.

Contrary to the claims of liberal theorists and historians that public education offers possibilities for individual development, social mobility, and political and economic power to the disadvantaged and dispossessed, radical educators have generally argued that the main functions of schools are the reproduction of the dominant ideology, its forms of knowledge, and the distribution of skills needed to reproduce the social division of labor. In the radical perspective, schools as institutions could only be understood through an analysis of their relationship to the state and the economy. In this view, the deep structure or underlying significance of schooling could only be revealed through analyzing how schools functioned as agencies of social and cultural reproduction—that is, how they legitimated capitalist rationality and sustained dominant social practices.

Instead of blaming students for educational failure, radical educators blamed the dominant society. Instead of abstracting schools from the dynamics of inequality and class-race-gender modes of discrimination, schools were considered central agencies in the politics and processes of domination. In contrast to the liberal view of education as the great equalizer, radical educators saw the objectives of schooling quite differently. As Paul Willis states, "Education was not about equality, but inequality. . . . Education's main purpose of the social integration of a class society could be achieved only by preparing most kids for an unequal future, and by insuring their personal underdevelopment. Far from productive roles in the economy simply waiting to be 'fairly' filled by the products of education, the 'Reproduction' perspective reversed this to suggest that capitalist production and its roles required certain educational outcomes."[3]

In our view, radical educators presented a serious challenge to the discourse and logic of liberal views of schooling. But they did more than that. They also tried to fashion a new discourse and set of understandings around the reproduction thesis. Schools were stripped of their political innocence and connected to the social and cultural matrix of capitalist rationality. In effect, schools were portrayed as reproductive in three senses. First, schools provided different classes and social groups with the knowledge and skills they needed to occupy their respective places in a labor force stratified by class, race, and gender. Second, schools were seen as reproductive in the cultural sense, functioning in part to distribute and legitimate forms of knowledge, values, language, and modes of style that constitute the dominant culture and its interests. Third, schools were viewed as part of a state apparatus that produced and legitimated the economic and ideological imperatives that underlie the state's political power.

Radical reproduction theorists have used these forms of reproduction to fashion a number of specific concerns that have shaped the nature of their educational research and inquiry. These concerns have focused on analyses of the relationships between schooling and the workplace;[4] class-specific educational experiences and the job opportunities that emerge for different social groups;[5] the culture of the school and the class-defined cultures of the students who attend them;[6] the relationship among the economic, ideological, and repressive functions of the state and how they affect school policies and practices;[7] and the political economy of gender and textbooks.

Reproduction theory and its various explanations of the role and function of education have been invaluable in contributing to a broader understanding of the political nature of schooling and its relation to the dominant society. But it must be stressed that the theory has not achieved its promise to provide a comprehensive critical science of schooling. Reproduction theorists have largely overemphasized the idea of domination in their analysis and have inadequately gauged how teachers, students, and other human agents come together within specific historical and social contexts in order to both make and reproduce the conditions of their existence. More specifically, reproduction accounts of schooling have continually patterned themselves after structural-functionalist versions of Marxism which stress that history is made "behind the backs" of the members of society. The idea that people do make history, including its constraints, has been neglected. Indeed, human subjects generally "disappear" amidst a theory that leaves little room for moments of self-creation, mediation, and resistance. These accounts often leave us with a view of schooling and domination that appears to have been pressed out of an Orwellian fantasy; schools are often viewed as factories or prisons, and teachers and students alike act merely as pawns and role bearers constrained by the logic and social practices of the capitalist system.

By downplaying the importance of human agency and the notion of resistance, reproduction theories offer little hope for challenging and changing the repressive features of schooling. By ignoring the contradictions and struggles that exist in schools, these theories not only dissolve human "agency," but they also unknowingly provide a rationale for *not* examining teachers and students in concrete school settings. Thus, they miss the opportunity to determine whether there is a substantial difference between the existence of various structural and ideological modes of domination and their actual unfolding and effects.

Recent research on schooling in the United States, Europe, and Australia has both challenged and attempted to move beyond reproduction theories. This research emphasizes the importance of human agency and experience as the theoretical cornerstones for analyzing the complex relationship between schools and the dominant society. Organized around what we loosely label resistance theory, these analyses give central importance to the notions of conflict, struggle, and resistance.[8]

Combining ethnographic studies with European cultural studies, resistance theorists have attempted to demonstrate that the mechanisms of social and cultural reproduction are never complete and always meet with partially realized elements of opposition.[9] In effect, resistance theorists have developed a theoretical framework and method of inquiry that restores the critical notion of agency. They point not only to the role that students play in challenging the most oppressive aspects of schools but also to the ways in which students actively participate through oppositional behavior in a logic that very often consigns them to a position of class subordination and political defeat.

One of the most important assumptions of resistance theory is that working-class students are not merely the by-product of capital, compliantly submitting to the dictates of authoritarian teachers and schools that prepare them for a life of deadening labor. Rather, schools represent contested terrains marked not only by structural and ideological contradictions but also by collectively informed student resistance. In other words, schools are social sites characterized by overt and hidden curricula, tracking, dominant and subordinate cultures, and competing ideologies. Of course, conflict and resistance take place within asymmetrical relations of power which always favor dominant groups, but the essential point is that there are complex and creative fields of resistance through which class-, race- and gender-mediated practices often refuse, reject, and dismiss the central messages of the schools.

In resistance accounts, schools are relatively autonomous institutions that not only provide spaces for oppositional behavior and teaching but also represent a source of contradiction that sometimes make them dysfunctional to the material and ideological interests of the dominant society. Schools are not solely determined by the logic of the workplace or the dominant society; they are not merely economic institutions but are also political, cultural, and ideological sites that exist somewhat independently of the capitalist market economy. Of course, schools operate within limits set by society, but they function in part to influence and shape those limits, whether they be economic, ideological, or political. Moreover, instead of being homogeneous institutions operating under the direct control of dominant interests, schools are characterized by diverse forms of school knowledge, ideologies, organizational styles, and classroom social relations. Thus, schools often exist in a contradictory relation to the dominant society, alternately supporting and challenging its basic assumptions. For instance, schools sometimes support a notion of liberal education that is in sharp contradiction to the dominant society's demand for forms of education that are specialized, instrumental, and geared to the logic of the marketplace. In addition, schools still strongly define their role via their function as agencies for social mobility, even though they currently turn out graduates at a faster pace than the economy's capacity to employ them.

Whereas reproduction theorists focus almost exclusively on power and how the dominant culture ensures the consent and defeat of subordinate classes and groups, theories of resistance restore a degree of agency and innovation to the cultures of these groups. Culture, in this case, is constituted as much by the group itself as by the dominant society. Subordinate cultures, whether working class or otherwise, partake of moments of self-production as well as reproduction; they are contradictory in nature and bear the marks of both resistance and reproduction. Such cultures are forged within constraints shaped by capital and its institutions, such as schools, but the conditions within which such constraints function vary from school to school and from neighborhood to neighborhood. Moreover, there are never any guarantees that capitalist, patriarchal and racist values and ideologies will automatically succeed, regardless of how strongly they set the agenda. Put another way, "In the final analysis, human praxis is not determined by its preconditions; only the boundaries of possibility are given in advance."[10]

In this rather brief and abstract discussion, we have juxtaposed two models of educational analysis to suggest that theories of resistance represent a significant advance over the important but limited theoretical gains of reproduction models of schooling. But it is important to emphasize that, in spite of more complex modes of analysis, resistance theories are also marred by a number of theoretical flaws. In part, these flaws stem from a failure to recognize the degree to which resistance theories themselves are indebted to some of the more damaging features of reproduction theory. At the same time, however, resistance theories have too readily ignored the most valuable insights of reproduction theory and, in doing so, have failed to examine and appropriate those aspects of the reproduction model that are essential to developing a critical science of education. Furthermore, despite their concrete differences, resistance and reproduction approaches to education share the failure of recycling and reproducing the dualism between agency and structure, a failure that has plagued educational theory and practice for decades, while simultaneously representing its greatest challenge. Consequently, neither position provides the foundation for a theory of education that links structures and institutions to human agency and action in a dialectical manner.

The basis for overcoming this separation of human agency from structural determinants lies in the development of a theory of resistance that both questions its own assumptions and critically appropriates those aspects of schooling that are accurately presented and analyzed in the reproduction model. In other words, the task facing resistance theorists is twofold: first, they must structure their own assumptions to develop a more dialectical model of schooling and society; and second, they must reconstruct the major theories of reproduction in order to abstract from them their most radical and emancipatory insights.

The remainder of this chapter will first discuss three important theories that constitute various dimensions of the reproduction model of schooling: the economic-reproductive model, the cultural-reproductive model, and the hegemonic-state reproductive model. Since reproduction theorists have been the object of considerable criticism elsewhere, we shall focus primarily on the strengths of each of these models, and shall only summarize some of the general criticisms. Second, we shall look at what we generously call neo-Marxist theories of resistance that have recently emerged in the literature on education and schooling, examining their theoretical strengths and weaknesses, while at the same time analyzing how they are either positively or negatively informed by theories of reproduction. Finally, we shall attempt to develop a new theory of resistance and shall briefly analyze its implications for a critical practice of schooling.

SCHOOLING AND THEORIES OF REPRODUCTION

Economic-Reproductive Model

Within the last twenty years, the political-economy model of reproduction has exercised a strong influence on radical theories of schooling. Developed primarily around the work of Samuel Bowles and Herbert Gintis, it has had a major influence on theories about the hidden curriculum,[11] educational policy studies,[12] and a wide range of ethnographic research.[13] At the core of the political-economy approach are two fundamentally important questions. The most important of these focuses on the relationship between schooling and society and asks, "How does the educational system function within society?" The second question points to a related but more concrete concern regarding the issue of how subjectivities actually get constituted in schools, asking, "How do schools fundamentally influence the ideologies, personalities, and needs of students?" While theorists who work within this model give different answers, they generally agree on the relationship between power and domination, on the one hand, and the relationship between schooling and the economy on the other.

Power in these accounts is defined and examined primarily in terms of its function to mediate and legitimate the relations of dominance and subordinance in the economic sphere. In this perspective, power becomes the property of dominant groups and operates to reproduce class, gender, and racial inequalities that function in the interests of the accumulation and expansion of capital. This becomes clear in the way economic-reproductive theorists analyze the relations between the economy and schooling.

Central to this position is the notion that schools can only be understood by analyzing the structural effects of the workplace on them. In Bowles and Gintis's work, this notion becomes clear through their reliance on what they call the correspondence theory.[14] Broadly speaking, the correspondence theory posits that the hierarchically structured patterns of values, norms, and skills that characterize both the workforce and the dynamics of class interaction under capitalism are mirrored in the social dynamics of the daily classroom encounter. Through its classroom social relations, schooling functions to inculcate students with the attitudes and dispositions necessary to accept the social and economic imperatives of a capitalist economy.

In this view, the underlying experience and relations of schooling are animated by the power of capital to provide different skills, attitudes, and values to students of different classes, races, and genders. In effect, schools mirror not only the social division of labor but also the wider society's class structure. The theoretical construct that illuminates the structural and ideological connection between the schools and the workplace is the notion of the hidden curriculum. This term refers to those classroom social relations that embody specific messages which legitimize the particular views of work, authority, social rules, and values that sustain capitalist logic and rationality, particularly as manifested in the workplace. The power of these messages lies in their seemingly universal qualities—qualities that emerge as part of the structured silences that permeate all levels of school and classroom relations. The social relations that constitute the hidden curriculum provide ideological and material weight to questions regarding what counts as high- versus low-status knowledge (intellectual or manual), high- versus low-status forms of social organization (hierarchical or democratic), and, of course, what counts as high- versus low-status forms of personal interaction (interaction based on individual competitiveness or interaction based on collective sharing). The nature and meaning of the hidden curriculum is further extended through an understanding of how it contributes to the construction of student subjectivities—that is, those conscious and unconscious dimensions of experience that inform student behavior. Consideration of this issue leads into the work of the French social theorist, Louis Althusser.

Althusser also argues that schools represent an essential and important social site for reproducing capitalist relations of production.[15] In agreement with Bowles and Gintis, he argues that the school carries out two fundamental forms of reproduction: the reproduction of the skills and rules of labor power, and the reproduction of the relations of production.

The reproduction of the skills and rules of labor power is defined within the context of the formal curriculum and, in Althusser's terms, includes the kind of "know-how" students need in order to

> read, to write and to add—i.e., a number of techniques, and a number of other things as well, including elements of "scientific" or "literary culture," which are directly useful in the different jobs in production (one instruction for manual workers, another for technicians, a third for engineers, a final one for high management). . . . Children also learn the rules of good behaviour, i.e., the attitude that should be observed by every agent in the division of labor, according to the job he is "destined" for: rules of morality, civic and professional conscience, which actually means rules of respect for the socio-technical divisions of labour and ultimately the rules of the order established by class domination.[16]

Although both Althusser and Bowles and Gintis acknowledge the role that school knowledge plays in the reproductive process, it is not of much significance in their analyses. Domination and the reproduction of the workforce as constitutive elements of the schooling process take place primarily "behind the backs" of teachers and students through the hidden curriculum of schooling. But it is at this point that these theorists provide important and differing explanations. Unlike Bowles and Gintis, who situate the hidden curriculum in social relations that are somehow internalized by (read imposed on) students, Althusser attempts to explain this "hidden" process of socialization through a systematic theory of ideology.

Althusser's theory of ideology has a dual meaning, which becomes clear in his analysis of how ruling class domination is secured in schools. In its first meaning, the theory refers to a set of material practices through which teachers and students live out their daily experiences. Ideology has a material existence in the rituals, routines, and social practices that both structure and mediate the day-to-day workings of schools. This material aspect of ideology is clearly seen, for example, in the architecture of school buildings, with their separate rooms, offices, and recreational areas—each positing and reinforcing an aspect of the social division of labor. Space is arranged differently for the administrative staff, teachers, secretaries, and students within the school building. Furthermore, the ideological nature of the ecology of the school is somewhat obvious in the seating arrangements in university halls, or, for that matter, in the classrooms of many urban schools.

This material aspect of Althusser's notion of ideology corresponds somewhat to Bowles and Gintis's notion of the hidden curriculum in pointing to the political nature and use of space, time, and social processes as they function within specific institutional settings. Similarly, it also points to the class-specific source and control of power that bears down on ideological institutions such as schools—institutions deemed essential, according to Althusser, to the production of ideologies and experiences that support the dominant society.[17]

In the second meaning of Althusser's notion of ideology, the dynamics of the reproductive model unfold. In this sense, ideology is completely removed from any notion of intentionality, producing neither consciousness nor willing compliance. Instead, it is defined as those systems of meanings, representations, and values embedded in concrete practices that structure the unconsciousness of students. The effect of such practices and their mediations is to induce in teachers and students alike an "imaginary relationship . . . to their real conditions of existence."[18] Althusser explains:

> It is customary to suggest that ideology belongs to the region of "consciousness". . . . In truth, ideology has very little to do with "consciousness". . . . It is profoundly unconscious, even when it presents itself in a reflected form. Ideology is indeed a system of representations, but in the majority of cases these representations have nothing to do with "consciousness": they are usually images and occasionally concepts, but it is above all as structures that they impose on the vast majority of men, not via their "consciousness." They are perceived-accepted-suffered cultural objects and they act functionally on one in a process that escapes them. Men "live" their ideologies as the Cartesian "saw" the moon at two hundred paces away: not at all as a form of consciousness, but as an object of their "world"—as their world itself.[19]

The economic-reproductive model gains an added dimension in the work of Christian Baudelot and Roger Establet.[20] Baudelot and Establet also stress that the principal function of the school can only be understood in terms of the role it plays in the production of labor power, the accumulation of capital, and the reproduction of legitimating ideologies. Once again, schools are tied to the engine of domination and reproduction. But in this case, power does not collapse into an all-encompassing construct of ideological domination. Though still tied to the economic-reproductive model, Baudelot and Establet are not willing to dissolve the issue of social agency under the heavy hand of a one-sided notion of domination. Domination, they claim, does manifest itself through the imposition of bourgeois ideology in French schools, but the ideology is sometimes opposed and resisted by subordinate youths, particularly at the compulsory levels of schooling.

Several important but underdeveloped theoretical considerations begin to emerge in Baudelot and Establet's model of reproduction. First, schools are not viewed as sites that smoothly socialize working-class students into the dominant ideology. Instead, schools are seen as social sites informed by conflicting ideologies that are rooted, in part, in the antagonistic class relations and structured practices that shape the day-to-day workings of these institutions. But if schools are viewed as sites containing oppositional ideologies, the sources of these ideologies—which fuel student resistance— are to be found not only inside but outside the school as well. That is, the basis for both critique and resistance on the part of working-class students is partly produced through the knowledge and practices made available to them in schools, but the primary historical and material basis for such action is located in oppositional public spheres that exist outside of such institutions.

The question of the location of the basis of resistance leads to Baudelot and Establet's second major insight. They rightly argue that the source of working-class student consciousness cannot be limited to such spheres as the workplace and the school. Working-class student social formations— groups organized around specific cultural experiences, values, and class, gender, and racial relations—with their combination of hegemonic and oppositional ideologies, are primarily formed in the family, the neighborhood, and in the mass- and class-mediated youth cultures.[21] Social classes, in this account, are formed not through the primacy of their determined structural relation to the workplace, but through culture as well. The complex dynamic behind the construction of class formations is captured in the comment, "The class's capacity for self-representation is marked by common conditions of life, including, but not limited to, a common relation to the ownership and control of the means of production. Among other things, classes are . . . formed by culture, understood here as modes of discourse, a shared symbolic universe, rituals and customs that connote solidarity and distinguish a class from others."[22]

A third important but underdeveloped insight in Baudelot and Establet's analysis is that ideology is limited neither to the realm of the unconscious nor to a configuration of internalized personality traits. As mentioned elsewhere, Bowles and Gintis as well as Althusser have drawn accounts of schooling in which the logic of domination appears to be inscribed without the benefit of human mediation or struggle.[23] Baudelot and Establet modify these positions by giving ideology a more active nature. For them, ideology refers to that part of the realm of consciousness that produces *and* mediates the contradictory relations of capitalism and school life. Consequently, ideology becomes the locus of contradictory consciousness, informed by and containing both dominant and oppositional ideologies. This is evident in the contradictory logic exhibited in certain types of resistance. For example, some working-class students either resist or reject the notion of book learning and other forms of literacy in favor of subversive school behavior and a celebration of physicality and manual labor. In doing so, these students may undermine one of the fundamental ideologies of the school, but they do so at the cost of rejecting the possibility for developing modes of critical literacy that could be crucial to their own liberation.[24]

To summarize, the economic-reproductive model has made several important contributions to a radical theory of education. By focusing on the relationship between schools and the workplace, it has helped to illuminate the essential role that education plays in reproducing the social and technical division of labor. In addition, it has made visible the "structured silences" in liberal theory regarding how the imperatives of class and power bear down on and shape school experience, particularly through the hidden curriculum. Furthermore, this model of reproduction has provided important insights into the class and structural basis of inequality. By rejecting the "blaming the victim" ideology that informs much of the research on inequality, these accounts have blamed institutions such as the schools for inequality, and have traced the failure of such institutions to the very structure of capitalist society. Unfortunately, the economic-reproductive model has failed to capture the complexity of the relationship between schools and such other institutions as the workplace and the family. Within its grimly mechanistic and overly determined model of socialization, there appears little room for developing a theory of schooling that takes seriously the notions of culture, resistance, and mediation. Even where contradictions and mediations are mentioned, they generally disappear under the crushing weight of capitalist domination. As such, these accounts are marred not only by a reductionist instrumentalism regarding the meaning and role of schools, but also by a form of radical pessimism that offers little hope for social change and even less reason for developing alternative educational practices. In short, these accounts lack what we have labeled a language of possibility.

Cultural-Reproductive Model

Theories of cultural reproduction are also concerned with the question of how capitalist societies are able to reproduce themselves. Central to these theories is a sustained effort to develop a sociology of schooling that links culture, class, and domination. The mediating role of culture in reproducing class societies is given priority over the study of related issues, such as the source and consequences of economic inequality. The work of Pierre Bourdieu and his colleagues in France represents the most important perspective for studying the cultural-reproductive model.[25]

Bourdieu's theory of cultural reproduction begins with the notion that the logic of domination, whether manifested in schools or in other social sites, must be analyzed within a theoretical framework capable of dialectically linking human agents and dominant structures. Bourdieu rejects functionalist theories that either impute the effects of domination to a single, central apparatus or fail to see how the dominated participate in their own oppression. This rejection becomes clear in Bourdieu's theory of schooling in which he attempts to link the notions of structure, identity, and human agency through an analysis of the relationships among dominant culture, school knowledge, and individual biographies.[26] In his attempt to understand the role of culture in linking, first, schools to the logic of the dominant classes, and, second, the dynamics of capitalist reproduction to the subordinate classes, Bourdieu argues against the notion that schools simply mirror the dominant society. Instead, he claims that schools are relatively autonomous institutions that are influenced only indirectly by more powerful economic and political institutions. Rather than being linked directly to the power of an economic elite, schools are seen as part of a larger universe of symbolic institutions that do not overtly impose docility and oppression, but reproduce existing power relations more subtly through the production and distribution of a dominant culture that tacitly confirms what it means to be educated.

Bourdieu's theory of cultural reproduction begins with the assumption that class-divided societies and the ideological and material configurations on which they rest are partially mediated and reproduced through what he calls "symbolic violence." That is, class control is constituted through the subtle exercise of symbolic power waged by ruling classes in order "to impose a definition of the social world that is consistent with its interests."[27] Culture becomes the mediating link between ruling class interests and everyday life. It functions to portray the economic and political interests of the dominant classes, not as arbitrary and historically contingent, but as necessary and natural elements of the social order.

Education is seen as an important social and political force in the process of class reproduction. By appearing to be an impartial and neutral "transmitter" of the benefits of a valued culture, schools are able to promote inequality in the name of fairness and objectivity. Through this argument Bourdieu rejects both the idealist position, which views schools as independent of external forces, and orthodox radical critiques, in which schools merely mirror the needs of the economic system. According to

Bourdieu, it is precisely the relative autonomy of the educational system that "enables it to serve external demands under the guise of independence and neutrality, i.e., to conceal the social functions it performs and so to perform them more effectively."[28]

The notion of cultural capital is central to Bourdieu's analysis of how the mechanisms of cultural reproduction function within schools. He argues that the culture transmitted by the school is related to the various cultures that make up the wider society in that it confirms the culture of the ruling classes while simultaneously disconfirming the cultures of other groups. This becomes more understandable through an analysis of the notion of cultural capital—the different sets of linguistic and cultural competencies that individuals inherit by way of the class-located boundaries of their family. A child inherits from his or her family those sets of meanings, qualities of style, modes of thinking, and types of dispositions that are assigned a certain social value and status in accordance with what the dominant class(es) label as the most valued cultural capital. Schools play a particularly important role in legitimating and reproducing dominant cultural capital. They tend to legitimize certain forms of knowledge, ways of speaking, and ways of relating to the world that capitalize on the type of familiarity and skills that only certain students have received from their family backgrounds and class relations. Students whose families have only a tenuous connection to the dominant cultural capital are at a decided disadvantage. Bourdieu sums up this process:

> The culture of the elite is so near that of the school that children from the lower middle class (an *a fortiori* from the agricultural and industrial working class) can acquire only with great effort something which is *given* to the children of the cultivated classes—style, taste, wit—in short, those aptitudes which seem natural in members of the cultivated classes and naturally expected of them precisely because (in the ethnological sense) they are the *culture* of that class.[29]

By linking power and culture, Bourdieu provides a number of insights into how the hegemonic curriculum works in schools, pointing to the political interests underlying the selection and distribution of those bodies of knowledge that are given top priority.[30] These bodies of knowledge not only legitimate the interests and values of the dominant classes, but they also have the effect of marginalizing or disconfirming other kinds of knowledge, particularly knowledge important to women, the working class, and minority groups. For example, working-class students often find themselves subjected to a school curriculum in which the distinction between high-status and low-status knowledge is organized around the difference between theoretical and practical subjects. Courses that deal with practical subjects, whether they be industrial arts or culinary arts, are seen as marginal and inferior. In this case, working-class knowledge and culture are often placed in competition with what the school legitimates as dominant culture and knowledge. In the end, working-class knowledge and culture are seen not as different and equal, but as different and inferior. It is important to note that high-status knowledge often corresponds to bodies of knowledge that provide a stepping stone to professional careers via higher education. Such knowledge embodies the cultural capital of the middle and upper classes and presupposes a certain familiarity with the linguistic and social practices it supports. Needless to say, such knowledge is not only more accessible to the upper classes, but also functions to confirm and legitimate their privileged positions in schools. Thus, the importance of the hegemonic curriculum lies in both what it includes—with its emphasis on Western history, science, and so forth—and what it excludes—women's history, black studies, labor history, in-depth courses in the arts, and other forms of knowledge important to the working class and other subordinate groups.[31]

Thus, schools legitimize the dominant cultural capital through the hierarchically arranged bodies of school knowledge in the hegemonic curriculum, and by rewarding students who use the linguistic style of the ruling class. Certain linguistic styles, along with the body postures and the social relations they reinforce (lowered voice, disinterested tone, nontactile interaction), act as identifiable forms of cultural capital that either reveal or betray a student's social background. In effect, certain linguistic practices and modes of discourse become privileged by being treated as natural to the gifted, when in fact they are the speech habits of dominant classes and thus serve to perpetuate cultural privileges.

Class and power connect with the production of dominant cultural capital not only in the structure and evaluation of the school curriculum but also in the dispositions of the oppressed themselves, who sometimes actively participate in their own subjugation. This point is central to Bourdieu's theory of cultural reproduction and can be examined more closely through a discussion of his notions of *habitat* (positions) and *habitus* (dispositions).[32]

In Bourdieu's later writings, he examines the relationship between action and structure through forms of historical action that bring together two histories. The first is the habitat, or *objectified history,* "the history which has accumulated over the passage of time in things, machines, buildings, monuments, books, theories, customs, law, etc."[33] The second refers to the *embodied history* of the habitus, and points to a set of internalized competencies and structured needs, an internalized style of knowing and relating to the world that is grounded in the body itself. Habitus, then, becomes a "matrix of perceptions, appreciations and actions,"[34] "a system of durably acquired schemes of perception, thought and action, engendered by objective conditions but tending to persist even after an alteration of those conditions."[35] The habitus is a product of both socialization and embodied history, and differs for various dominant and subordinate groups within society. As principles inscribed deeply within the needs and dispositions of the body, the habitus becomes a powerful force in organizing an individual's experience and is the central category in situating human agency within practical activity.

It is in the dialectical relationship between institutions as objectified history and the habitus or dispositions of different classes that Bourdieu attempts to fashion a theory of domination and learning. Bourdieu explains the process of domination by arguing that it is often forged through a correlation between a certain disposition (habitus) and the expectations and interests embedded in the position of specific institutions (habitat). Thus, it is in this correspondence between the tacitly inscribed values and ideologies that make up the individual's disposition and the norms and ideologies embedded in the positions characterizing institutions such as schools that the dynamics of domination become manifest. Furthermore, for Bourdieu the notions of habitus and habitat reveal how domination is forged in a logic that draws together those corresponding ideologies and practices that constitute both agents and structures. "The dispositions inculcated by a childhood experience of the social world which, in certain historical conditions, can predispose young workers to accept and even wish for entry into a world of manual labor which they identify with the adult world, are reinforced by work experience itself and by all the consequent changes in their dispositions."[36]

The importance of the notion of habitus to a theory of schooling becomes evident in the expanded theory of learning that it suggests. Bourdieu argues that individuals from different social groups and classes undergo processes of socialization that are not only intellectual but also emotional, sensory, and physical. Learning, in this case, is actively situated in the practical activity of the body, senses, and emotions. It is organized around class-specific cultural practices that inscribe their messages beyond consciousness, in the materiality of the body and the values and dispositions it signifies. Bourdieu explains:

> The principles em-bodied in [the habitus] . . . are placed beyond the grasp of consciousness, and hence cannot be touched by voluntary deliberate transformation, cannot even be made explicit; nothing seems more ineffable, more incommunicable, more inimitable, and, therefore, more precious, than the values given body, *made* body by the transubstantiation achieved by the hidden persuasion of an implicit pedagogy, capable of instilling a whole cosmology, an ethic, a metaphysic, a political philosophy, through injunctions as insignificant as "stand up straight" as "don't hold your knife in your left hand."[37]

Bourdieu's work is significant in that it provides a theoretical model for understanding aspects of schooling and social control that have been virtually ignored in conservative and liberal accounts. Its politicization of school knowledge, culture, and linguistic practices formulates a new discourse for examining ideologies embedded in the formal school curriculum. Similarly, Bourdieu adds a new dimension to analyses of the hidden curriculum by focusing on the importance of the body as an object of learning and social control.[38] In effect, what emerges in this account are the theoretical rudiments of a cultural-reproductive model that attempts to take seriously the notions of history, sociology, and psychology.

Yet, Bourdieu's work is not without some serious theoretical flaws. The most glaring flaws concern the mechanistic notions of power and domination and the overly determined view of human agency that characterizes much of this work. For example, Bourdieu's formulation of the notion of habitus is based on a theory of social control and depth psychology that appears to be fashioned almost exclusively in the logic of domination. The following comment by Bourdieu is representative of this position.

> The uses of the body, of languages, and of time are all privileged objects of social control: innumerable elements of explicit education—not to mention practical, mimetic transmission—relate to uses of the body ("sit up straight," "don't touch") or uses of language ("say this" or "don't say that"). Through bodily and linguistic discipline . . . the choices constituting a certain relation to the world are internalized in the form of durable patternings not accessible to consciousness nor even, in part, amenable to will. Politeness contains a politics, a practical immediate recognition of social classifications and of hierarchies between the sexes, the generations, the classes, etc.[39]

Unfortunately, where the conceptual possibility for resistance does appear in Bourdieu's work—that is, in the mismatch between one's habitus and the position one occupies—the foundation for such action rests not on a notion of reflexivity or critical self-consciousness, but on the incompatibility between two structures—the historical structure of the disposition and the historical structure embodied in the institution. Thus, resistance becomes the outcome of a conflict between two formalistic structures, one situated in the realm of the unconscious and the other situated in the social practices that make up institutions such as schools. The result is that the power of reflexive thought and historical agency are relegated to a minor theoretical detail in Bourdieu's theory of change.

Another theoretical flaw in Bourdieu's work is that culture represents a somewhat one-way process of domination. As a result, his theory suggests falsely that working-class cultural forms and knowledge are homogeneous and merely a pale reflection of dominant cultural capital. Working-class cultural production and its relation to cultural reproduction through the complex dynamics of resistance, incorporation, and accommodation are not acknowledged by Bourdieu. The collapse of culture and class into the processes of cultural reproduction raises a number of significant problems. First, such a portrayal eliminates conflict both within and between different classes, resulting in the loss of such notions as struggle, diversity, and human agency in a somewhat reductionist view of human nature and history. Second, by reducing classes to homogeneous groups whose only differences are based on whether they exercise or respond to power, Bourdieu provides no theoretical opportunity to unravel how cultural domination and resistance are mediated through the complex interface of race, gender, and class. What is missing from Bourdieu's work is the notion that culture is both a structuring and transforming process. David Davies captures this dynamic in his comment: "Culture refers paradoxically to conservative adaptation and lived subordination of classes and to opposition, resistance, and creative struggle for change."[40]

Bourdieu's analyses of schooling also suffer from a one-sided treatment of ideology.[41] While it is useful to argue, as Bourdieu does, that dominant ideologies are transmitted by schools and actively incorporated by students, it is equally important to remember that ideologies are also *imposed* on students, who occasionally view them as contrary to their own interests and either resist them openly or conform to them under pressure from school authorities. In other words, dominant ideologies are not just transmitted in schools, nor are they practiced in a void. On the contrary, they are often met with resistance by teachers, students, and parents. Furthermore, it is reasonable to argue that in order to be successful, schools have to repress the production of counter-ideologies. Roger Dale illuminates this process in his discussion of how hegemony functions in schools, writing that "hegemony is not so much about winning approval for the status quo. . . . Rather what seems to be involved is the prevention of rejection, opposition or alternatives to the status quo through denying the use of the school for such purposes."[42] Similarly, it must be noted that schools are not simply static institutions that reproduce the dominant ideology; they are active agents in its construction as well. This is aptly portrayed in an ethnographic study of ruling class schools conducted by Robert Connell and his colleagues. They write:

> The school generates practices by which the class is renewed, integrated and re-constituted in the face of changes in its own composition and in the general social circumstances in which it tries to survive and prosper. (This is an embracing practice, ranging from the school fete, Saturday sport and week-night dinners with parents, to the organization of a marriage market—e.g., inter-school dances—and informal networks in business and the professions, to the regulation of class memberships, updating of ideology, and subordi-

nation of particular interests to those of class as a whole). The ruling-class school is no mere agent of the class; it is an important and active part of it. In short, it is organic to its class. Bourdieu wrote a famous essay about the "school as conserver"; we would suggest an equal stress should be laid on the school as constructor.[43]

By failing to develop a theory of ideology that speaks to the way in which human beings dialectically create, resist, and accommodate themselves to dominant ideologies, Bourdieu excludes the active nature of both domination and resistance. In spite of his claims, it is important to argue that schools do not simply usurp the cultural capital of working-class families and neighborhoods. Complex relations develop between the schools and working-class families, and they need to be analyzed in terms of the conflicts and struggles that inform them. This point is highlighted in an ethnographic study by R. Timothy Sieber which chronicles the history of a power struggle over an elementary school in New York City.[44]

This study reinforces one aspect of Bourdieu's analysis in revealing that middle-class students, with their respective cultural competencies and experiences, were accorded specific academic privileges and freedoms denied to working-class and Puerto Rican students in the same school. But the more interesting aspect of Sieber's study indicates that the "privileged standing" and educational benefits provided to middle-class students were the outcome of a long struggle between the middle-class segment of the community and its predominantly working-class residents. The predominance of middle-class culture in this school was the outcome of a political struggle, and contrary to Bourdieu's position, was actively and systematically developed "both inside and outside of the school" by middle-class parents.[45]

Finally, there is a serious flaw in Bourdieu's work regarding his unwillingness to link the notion of domination with the materiality of economic forces. There is no insight in Bourdieu's analyses regarding how the economic system, with its asymmetrical relations of power, produces concrete constraints on working-class students. Michel Foucault's notion that power works on the body, the family, sexuality, and the nature of learning itself serves to remind us that the relations of power weigh down on more than just the mind.[46] In other words, the constraints of power are not exhausted within the concept of symbolic violence. Domination as an objective, concrete instance cannot be ignored in any discussion of schooling. For instance, the privileged classes have a relationship to time that enables them to make long-term plans regarding their futures. In contrast, the children of the dispossessed, especially those who are in higher education, often are burdened by economic constraints that lock them into the present and limit their goals to short-term plans. Time is a privation, not a possession, for most working-class students.[47] It is the economic dimension that often plays a crucial role in the decision over whether a working-class student can go to school full or part time, or in some cases can afford to go at all, just as the economic issue is often the determining factor in deciding whether or not a student will have to work part time while attending school. Bourdieu appears to have forgotten that domination has to be grounded in something other than mere ideology, that it also has a material foundation. This is no small matter, because it points to a major gap in Bourdieu's reasoning regarding working-class failure. The internalization of dominant ideology is not the only force that motivates working-class students or secures their failure. Their behaviors, failures, and choices are also grounded in material conditions.

As a result of Bourdieu's one-sided emphasis on ruling class domination and its attendant cultural practices, it becomes clear that both the concept of capital and the notion of class are treated as static categories. In our view, class involves a notion of social relations that are in opposition to each other. It refers to the shifting relations of domination and resistance and to capital and its institutions as they constantly regroup and attempt to reconstruct the logic of domination and incorporation. These oppositions are missing from Bourdieu's analyses.[48] What we are left with is a theory of reproduction that displays little faith in subordinate classes and groups and little hope in their ability or willingness to reconstruct the conditions under which they live, work, and learn. Consequently, most reproduction theories informed by Bourdieu's notion of domination ultimately fail to provide the comprehensive theoretical elements needed for a radical pedagogy.

Hegemonic-State Reproductive Model

Marxist theorists have argued that understanding the role of the state is central to any analysis of how domination operates.[49] Thus, a major concern now among a number of educational theorists focuses on the complex role of state intervention in the educational system.[50] These theorists believe that educational change cannot be understood by looking only at capital's domination of the labor process or the way capitalist domination is reproduced through culture. Neither of these explanations, they claim, has given adequate attention to the underlying structural determinants of inequality that characterize the advanced industrial countries of the West. They argue that such accounts display little understanding of how political factors lead to state interventionist policies that serve to structure and shape the reproductive functions of education.

In spite of the agreement among reproductive theorists about the importance of the state, there are significant differences among them as to what the state actually is, how it works, and what the precise relationship is between the state and capital, on the one hand, and the state and education, on the other. Michael Apple captures the complexity of this issue in his review of some of the major questions with which theorists of the state are currently grappling. He writes:

> Does the state only serve the interests of capital or is it more complex than that? Is the state instead an arena of class conflict and a site where hegemony must be worked for, not a foregone conclusion where it is simply imposed? Are schools—as important sites of the state—simply "ideological state apparatuses" (to quote Althusser), ones whose primary role is to reproduce the ideological and "manpower" requirements of the social relations of production? Or, do they also embody contradictory tendencies and provide sites where ideological struggles within and among classes, races, and sexes can and do occur?[51]

It is not our intent to unravel how different theorists of the state deal with these issues. Instead, we will focus on two major themes. First, we will explore some of the dynamics that characterize the relationship between the state and capitalism. Second, we will explore some of the underlying dynamics at work in the relationship between the state and schooling.

The state and capitalism. One of the major assumptions in Marxist accounts regarding the relationship between the state and capitalism has been developed around the work of the late Italian theorist, Antonio Gramsci.[52] For Gramsci, any discussion about the state had to begin with the reality of class relations and the exercise of hegemony by the dominant classes. Gramsci's dialectical formulation of hegemony as an ever-changing combination of force and consent provides the basis for analyzing the nature of the state in capitalist society.

Hegemony, in Gramsci's terms, appears to have two meanings. First, it refers to a process of domination whereby a ruling class exercises control through its intellectual and moral leadership over allied classes.[53] In other words, an alliance is formed among ruling classes as a result of the power and "ability of one class to articulate the interest of other social groups to its own."[54] Hegemony in this instance signifies, first, a pedagogic and politically transformative process whereby the dominant class articulates the common elements embedded in the world views of allied groups. Second, hegemony refers to the dual use of force and ideology to reproduce societal relations between dominant classes and subordinate groups. Gramsci strongly emphasizes the role of ideology as an active force used by dominant classes to shape and incorporate the common sense views, needs, and interests of subordinate groups. This is an important issue. Hegemony in this account represents more than the exercise of coercion: it is a process of continuous creation and includes the constant structuring of consciousness as well as a battle for the control of consciousness. The production of knowledge is linked to the political sphere and becomes a central element in the state's construction of power. The primary issue for Gramsci centers around demonstrating how the state can be defined, in part, by referring to its active involvement as a repressive and cultural (educative) apparatus.

This brings us directly to Gramsci's definition of the state. Rejecting orthodox Marxist formulations of the state as merely the repressive tool of the dominant classes, Gramsci divides the state into two specific realms: political society and civil society. Political society refers to the state apparatuses of administrative, law, and other coercive institutions whose primary, though not exclusive, function is based on the logic of force and repression. Civil society refers to those private and public institutions that rely on meanings, symbols, and ideas to universalize ruling class ideologies, while simultaneously shaping and limiting oppositional discourse and practice.

Two issues need to be stressed in conjunction with Gramsci's view of the state. All state apparatuses have coercive and consensual functions; it is the dominance of one function over the other that gives the apparatuses of either political or civil society their defining characteristic. Furthermore, as a mode of ideological control, hegemony—whether it takes place in the schools, the mass media, or the trade unions—must be fought for constantly in order to be maintained. It is not something "that simply consists of the projection of the ideas of the dominant classes into the heads of the subordinate classes."[55] The footing on which hegemony moves and functions has to shift ground in order to accommodate the changing nature of historical circumstances and the complex demands and critical actions of human beings. This view of the function of the state redefines class rule and the complex use of power. Power as used here is both a positive and a negative force. It functions negatively in the repressive and ideological apparatuses of the government and civil society to reproduce the relations of domination. It functions positively as a feature of active opposition and struggle, the terrain on which men and women question, act, and refuse to be incorporated into the logic of capital and its institutions.

In short, Gramsci provides a definition of the state that links power and culture to the traditional Marxist emphasis on the repressive aspects of the state. Gramsci is rather succinct on this issue: "The state is the entire complex of practical and theoretical activities with which the ruling class not only justifies and maintains its dominance, but manages to win the active consent of those over whom it rules."[56]

Gramsci's writings are crucial to an understanding of the meaning and workings of the state and have influenced a wide range of Marxist writers who argue that "all state formations under capitalism articulate class power."[57] The crucial starting point for many of these theorists is a sustained attack on the liberal assumption that the state is a neutral, administrative structure that operates in the interests of the general will. This attack generally takes the form of an historical critique that rejects the liberal notion of the state as a naturally evolving structure of human progress which stands above class and sectional interests. Marxist critics have argued in different ways that the state is a specific set of social relations linked historically to the conditions of capitalist production. In effect, the state is an organization, an embodiment of a changing pattern of class relations organized around the dynamics of class struggle, domination, and contestation. Furthermore, as a set of relations organized around class divisions, the state expresses ideological and economic interests through repressive as well as legitimating institutions. "The state is not a structure, it is an organization; or better, it is a complex of social forms organized so that it inflects all relations and ideas about relations in such a way that capitalist production, and all it entails, becomes thought of as lived and natural."[58]

This leads to a related and important issue concerning the defining features of the state's operation. Theorists such as Nicos Poulantzas have rightly argued that the state and its various agencies, including public schools, cannot be seen merely as tools manipulated at will by the ruling classes.[59] On the contrary, as the concrete representation of class relations, the state is constituted through continuing conflicts and contradictions, which, it can be argued, take two primary forms. First, there are conflicts among different factions of the ruling class, who often represent varied and competing approaches to social control and capital accumulation. But it is important to note that the relative autonomy of the state, secured partly through the existence of competing dominant classes, often tends to obscure what various factions of the ruling class have in common. That is, the state's short-term policies are firmly committed to maintaining the underlying economic and ideological structures of capitalist society. Thus, behind the discourse of diverging political, sectional, and social interests, there is the underlying grammar of class domination and structured inequality. Dominant classes may battle over the size of the military budget, monetary cutbacks in social services, and the nature of the tax structure, but they do not challenge basic capitalist production relations.

The definitive feature of the relative autonomy of the state is to be found, then, not in its chorus of oppositional discourses, but in its structured silences regarding the underlying basis of capitalist society. Moreover, the state is defined less by the interest of any one dominant group than by the specific set of social relations it mediates and sustains. Claus Offe and Volker Ronge summarize this position well: "What the state protects and sanctions is a set of rules and social relations which are presupposed by the class rule of the capitalist class. The state does not defend the interests of one class but the common interest of all members of a capitalist society."[60]

The second defining feature of the state centers around the relationship between the dominant and dominated classes. The state is not only an object of struggle among members of the ruling class; it is also a defining force in the production of conflict and struggle between the ruling class and other subordinate groups. The underlying logic of state formation is situated in the state's dual role of performing the often contradictory tasks of establishing the conditions for the accumulation of capital, on the one hand, and the ideological task of moral regulation on the other. In other words, the state has the task of meeting the basic needs of capital by providing, for instance, the necessary flow of workers, knowledge, skills, and values for the reproduction of labor power.[61] But at the same time, the state has the task of winning the consent of the dominated classes, which it attempts by legitimating the social relations and values that structure the capital accumulation process either through remaining silent about the class interests that benefit from such relations, or through marginalizing or disqualifying any serious critique or alternative to them. Furthermore, the state attempts to win the consent of the working class for its policies by making an appeal to three types of specific outcomes—economic (social mobility), ideological (democratic rights), and psychological (happiness). Philip Corrigan and his colleagues point to this issue in their argument:

> We stress that the state is constructed and fought over. Central to this is a two-fold set of historical practices: (i) the constant "rewriting" of history to naturalize what has been, in fact, an extremely changeable set of state relations, to claim that there is, and has always been, one "optimal institutional structure" which is what "any" civilization needs; and (ii) to marginalize (disrupt, deny, destroy, dilute, "help") all alternative forms of state, particularly any which announces any form of organization that established difference at the level of the national social formation (or crime of all crimes!, that established any form of international solidarity along class lines).[62]

The contradictions that arise out of the differences between the reality and the promise of capitalist social relations are evident in a number of instances, some of which directly involve schooling. For example, schools often promote an ideology of social mobility that is at odds with high levels of unemployment and the overabundance of highly qualified workers. Furthermore, the ideology of the work ethic is often contradicted by the increasing number of routinized and alienating jobs. In addition, capitalism's appeal to the satisfaction of higher needs often rests on an image of leisure, beauty, and happiness, the fulfillment of which lies beyond the capabilities of the existing society.

What emerges from this analysis of the relationship between the state and the economy are a number of crucial issues that have a significant bearing on educational policy and practice. First, it is rightly claimed that the state is neither the instrument of any one dominant class faction nor simply a pale reflection of the needs of the economic system. Second, the state is accurately portrayed as a site marked by ongoing conflicts among and between various class, gender, and racial groups. Third, the state is not merely an expression of class struggle; it is primarily an organization that actively defends capitalist society through repressive as well as ideological means. Finally, in its capacity as an ideological and repressive apparatus, the state limits and channels the responses that schools can make to the ideology, culture, and practices that characterize the dominant society. The following section contains a more detailed examination of these issues.

The state and schooling. In order to adequately investigate the relationship between the state and schooling, two questions need to be posed and analyzed. How does the state exercise control over schools in terms of its economic, ideological, and repressive functions? How does the school function not only to further the interests of the state and the dominant classes but also to contradict and resist the logic of capital?

As part of the state apparatus, schools and universities play a major role in furthering the economic interests of the dominant classes. Several theorists have argued that schools are actively involved in establishing the conditions for capital accumulation, and they point specifically to a number of instances in which the state intervenes to influence this process.[63] For example, through state-established certification requirements, educational systems are heavily weighted toward a highly technocratic rationality that relies on a logic drawn primarily from the natural sciences. The effects can be seen in the distinction schools at all levels make between high-status knowledge—usually the "hard sciences"—and low-status knowledge—subjects in the humanities. This bias also puts pressures on schools to utilize methods of inquiry and evaluation that stress efficiency, prediction, and the logic of the mathematical formula. The extent of state intervention is obvious in the favorable political orientation exercised through small- and large-scale government funding for educational research programs. Apple, for instance, illuminates this point:

> The state will take on the large initial cost of basic research and development. It then "transfers" the fruits of it back to the "private sector" once it becomes profitable. The state's role in capital accumulation is very evident in its subsidization of the production of technical/administrative knowledge. . . . Like the economy, examples of this pattern of intervention are becoming more visible. They include the emphasis on competency-based education, systems management, career education, futurism (often a code word for manpower planning), continued major funding for mathematics and science curriculum development (when compared to the arts), national testing programs. . . . All of these and more signal the sometimes subtle and sometimes quite overt role of state intervention into schooling to attempt to maximize

efficient production of both the agents and the knowledge required by an unequal economy.[64]

The rationality that supports state intervention into schools also influences the development of curricula and classroom social relations, the success of which is often measured against how well they "equip" different groups of students with the knowledge and skills they will need to perform productively in the workplace. Moreover, beneath the production of this type of curriculum and socialization there is the brute reality that schools function partly to keep students out of the labor force. As Dale points out, "schools keep children off the streets, and insure that for a large part of most days in the year they cannot engage in activities which might disrupt a social context amenable to capital accumulation but are exposed to attempts to socialize them into ways compatible with the maintenance of that context."[65]

State intervention is also manifested in the way policy is formulated outside of the control of teachers and parents. The economic interest underlying such policy is present not only in the rationality of control, planning, and other bureaucratic emphases on rule following but also in the way in which the state funds programs to handle what Apple calls "negative outcomes" in the accumulation process.

> By defining large groups of children as deviant (slow learners, remedial problems, discipline problems, etc.), and giving funding and legislative support for special teachers and for "diagnosis" and for "treatment" the state will fund extensive remedial projects. While these projects seem neutral, helpful, and may seem aimed at increasing mobility, they will actually defuse the debate over the role of schooling in the reproduction of the knowledge and people "required" by society. It will do this in part by defining the ultimate causes of such deviance as within the child or his or her culture and not due to, say, poverty, the conflicts and disparities generated by the historically evolving cultural and economic hierarchies of the society, etc. This will be hidden from us as well by our assumption, that schools are primarily organized as distribution agencies, instead of, at least in part, important agencies in the accumulation process.[66]

One of the major questions pursued by educational theorists studying the state focuses on the relationship between power and knowledge—specifically, how the state "exercises and imposes its power through the production of 'truth' and 'knowledge' about education."[67] Poulantzas, for example, argues that the production of dominant ideologies in the schools is to be found not only in the high-status knowledge and social relations sanctioned by the state bureaucracy but, more importantly, in the reproduction of the mental-manual division. The state appropriates, trains, and legitimates "intellectuals" who serve as experts in the production and conception of school knowledge, and who ultimately function to separate knowledge from both manual work and popular consumption. Behind this facade of credentialized expertise and professionalism lies a major feature of dominant ideology—the separation of knowledge from power. Poulantzas states, "The knowledge-power relationship finds expression in particular techniques of the exercise of power-exact devices inscribed in the texture of the state whereby the popular masses are permanently kept at a distance from the centres of decision making. These comprise a series of rituals and styles of speech, as well as structural modes of formulating and tackling problems that monopolize knowledge in such a way that the popular masses are effectively excluded."[68]

This separation becomes more pronounced in the special status that state certification programs and schools give to curriculum "experts"; the underlying logic of this status suggests that teachers should implement rather than conceptualize and develop curriculum approaches. The knowledge-power relation also finds expression in the active production and distribution of knowledge itself. For instance, one of the main roles of the schools is to valorize mental labor and disqualify manual labor. This division finds its highest representation in tracking, classroom social relations, and other aspects of school legitimation that function to exclude and devalue the history, culture, and experience of women, people of color, and working-class students. Furthermore, this division between mental and manual labor underlies the school's socializing process which prepares minority and working-class students for their respective places in the workforce.

Schools, of course, do more than mediate the logic of domination, and this can be seen in the contradictions that emerge around the ideology of democratic rights often reproduced in the school curriculum. Schools play an active role in legitimating the view that politics and power are primarily defined around the issues of individual rights and through the dynamics of the electoral process. Central to this liberal ideology of democratic rights are assumptions that define the political sphere and the role of the state in that sphere. The importance of this ideology as a contradictory part of the hegemonic curriculum cannot be overstated. On the one hand, it functions to separate the issues of politics and democracy from the economic sphere and to displace the notion of conflict from its class-specific social context to the terrain of individual rights and struggle. On the other hand, there is a certain counter-logic in democratic liberal ideology that provides the basis for resistance and conflict. That is, liberal democratic ideology contains concerns for human rights that are often at odds with capitalist rationality, its ethos of commodity fetish, and its drive for profits.

Finally, it must be remembered that the most direct intervention exercised by the state is constituted by law. Though impossible to discuss here in detail, this intervention often takes forms that link schools to the logic of repression rather than ideological domination. One instance of this linkage is that the foundation of school policy is sometimes established in the courts, such as the push toward racial integration of public schooling. Another instance is that school attendance is established through the rule of law and provides the "legal" cement that brings students into the schools. Relatedly, it is the courts, the police, and other state agencies that attempt to enforce involuntary school attendance. Of course, involuntary school attendance does not guarantee student obedience, and in some respects becomes a major issue promoting student resistance, a fact often forgotten by resistance theorists.

In conclusion, it must be emphasized that theories of the state perform a theoretical service by adding to our understanding of how the processes of social and cultural reproduction function in the political sphere. They rightly draw our attention to the importance of the relative autonomy of the state and its apparatuses (such as schools), the contradictory character of the state, and the economic, ideological, and repressive pressures the state exerts on schooling. But it must be acknowledged that, as part of a wider theory of reproduction, hegemonic-state accounts exhibit some major theoretical failings. First, theories of the state focus primarily on macro and structural issues, resulting in a mode of analysis that points to contradictions and struggle, but says little about how human agency works through such conflicts at the level of everyday life and concrete school relations. A second failing is that some theories of the state display an inadequate understanding of culture as a relatively autonomous realm with its own inherent counter-logic. For instance, Poulantzas's heavy-handed notion of the schools as merely an ideological state apparatus provides no theoretical space for investigating the emergence and dynamics of student countercultures as they develop in the interplay of concrete, antagonistic school relations.[69] Culture is, however, both the subject and object of resistance; the driving force of culture is contained not only in how it functions to dominate subordinate groups, but also in the way in which oppressed groups draw from their own cultural capital and set of experiences to develop an oppositional logic. Despite theoretical lip service to the contrary, this dialectical view of culture is often subsumed within a view of power that leans too heavily on the logic of domination in defining culture simply as an *object* of resistance rather than its *source*. In order to obtain a more concrete view of the dynamics of resistance and struggle as they inform subordinate school cultures operating under the ideological and material constraints partly constructed by the state, it is necessary to turn to theories of resistance.

SCHOOLING AND THEORIES OF RESISTANCE

The concept of resistance is relatively new in educational theory. The reasons behind this theoretical neglect can be traced partly to the failings of both conservative and radical approaches to schooling. Conservative educators analyzed oppositional behavior primarily through psychological categories that served to define such behavior not only as deviant, but more importantly, as disruptive and inferior—a failing on the part of the individuals and social groups that exhibited it. Radical educators, on the other hand, have generally ignored the internal workings of the school and have tended to treat schools as "black boxes." Beneath a discourse primarily concerned with the notions of domination, class conflict, and hegemony, there has been a structured silence regarding how teachers, students, and others live out their daily lives in schools. Consequently, there has been an overemphasis on how structural determinants promote economic and cultural inequality, and an underemphasis on how human agency accommodates, mediates, and resists the logic of capital and its dominating social practices.

Within the last fifteen years, a number of educational studies have emerged that attempt to move beyond the important but somewhat limited theoretical gains of reproduction theory. Taking the concepts of identity conflict and resistance as starting points for their analyses, these accounts have sought to redefine the importance of mediation, power, and culture in understanding the complex relations between schools and the dominant society. Consequently, the work of a number of theorists has been instrumental in providing a rich body of detailed literature that integrates feminist and neo-Marxist social theory with ethnographic studies in order to illuminate the dynamics of accommodation and resistance as they work through countercultural groups both inside and outside schools.[70]

Resistance, in these accounts, represents a significant critique of school as an institution and points to social activities and practices whose meanings are ultimately political and cultural. In contrast to a vast amount of ethnographic literature on schooling in both the United States and England, neo-Marxist resistance theories have not sacrificed theoretical depth for methodological refinement.[71] That is, neo-Marxist studies have not followed the method of merely providing overly exhaustive descriptive analyses of the internal workings of the school. Instead, they have attempted to analyze how determinant socioeconomic structures embedded in the dominant society work through the mediations of class and culture to shape the antagonistic experiences of students' everyday lives. Rejecting the functionalism inherent in both conservative and radical versions of educational theory, neo-Marxist accounts have analyzed curriculum as a complex discourse that not only serves the interests of domination but also contains aspects that provide emancipatory possibilities.

The attempt to link social structures and human agency in order to explore the way they interact in a dialectical manner represents a significant advance in educational theory. Of course, neo-Marxist resistance theories are also beset with problems, and we will mention some of the more outstanding ones here. Their singular achievement is the primary importance they allot to critical theory and human agency as the basic categories to be used in analyzing the daily experiences that constitute the internal workings of the school.

Central to theories of resistance is an emphasis on the tensions and conflicts that mediate relationships among home, school, and workplace. For example, Willis demonstrates in his study of the "lads"—a group of working-class males who constitute the "counterculture" in an English secondary school—that much of their opposition to the labels, meanings, and values of the official and hidden curricula is informed by an ideology of resistance, the roots of which are in the shop-floor cultures occupied by their family members and other members of their class.[72] The most powerful example of this mode of resistance is exhibited by the lads in their rejection of the primacy of mental over manual labor. Not only do the lads reject the alleged superiority of mental labor, but they also reject its underlying ideology that respect and obedience will be exchanged for knowledge and success. The lads oppose this ideology because the counter-logic embodied in the families, workplaces, and street life that make up *their* culture points to a different and more convincing reality. Thus, one major contribution that has emerged from resistance studies is the insight that the mechanisms of reproduction are never complete and are always faced with partially realized elements of opposition.

Furthermore, this work points to a dialectical model of domination, one that offers valuable alternatives to many of the radical models of reproduction analyzed previously. Instead of seeing domination as simply the by-product of external forces—for example, capital or the state—resistance theorists have developed a notion of reproduction in which working-class subordination is viewed not only as a result of the structural and ideological constraints embedded in capitalist social relationships, but also as part of the process of self-formation within the working class itself.

One key issue posed by this notion of domination is the question, "How does the logic that promotes varied forms of resistance become implicated in the logic of reproduction?" For example, theories of resistance have attempted to demonstrate how students who actively reject school culture often display a deeper logic and view of the world that confirms rather than challenges existing capitalist social relations. Two illustrations demonstrate this point. Willis's lads rejected the primacy of mental labor and its ethos of individual appropriation, but in doing so they closed off any possibility of pursuing an emancipatory relationship between knowledge and dissent. By rejecting intellectual labor, the lads discounted the power of critical thinking as a tool of social transformation.[73]

The same logic is displayed by the students in Michelle Fine's study of dropouts from alternative high schools in New York City's South Bronx.[74] Fine had assumed that the students who dropped out of these schools were victims of "learned helplessness," but she discovered instead that they were the most critical and politically astute students in the alternative schools: "Much to our collective surprise (and dismay) the drop outs were those students who were most likely to identify injustice in their social lives and at school, and most ready to correct injustice by criticizing or challenging a teacher. The drop outs were least depressed, and had attained academic levels equivalent to students who remained in school."[75] There is a certain irony here: while such students were capable of challenging the dominant ideology of the school, they failed to recognize the limits of their own resistance. By leaving school, these students placed themselves in a structural position that cuts them off from political and social avenues conducive to the task of radical reconstruction.

Another important and distinctive feature of resistance theories is their emphasis on the importance of culture and, more specifically, cultural production. In the concept of cultural production we find the basis for a theory of human agency, one that is constructed through the active, ongoing, collective medium of oppressed groups' experiences. In a more recent work, Willis elaborates on this issue, arguing that the notion of cultural production

> insists on the active, transformative natures of cultures and on the collective ability of social agents, not only to think like theorists, but to act like activists. Life experiences, individual and group projects, secret illicit and informal knowledge, private fears and fantasies, the threatening anarchic power arising from irreverent association . . . are not merely interesting additions. . . . These things are central: determined but also determining. They must occupy, fully fledged in their own right, a vital theoretical and political transformative stage in our analyses. This is, in part, the project of showing the capacities of the working class to generate albeit ambiguous, complex, and often ironic, collective and cultural forms of knowledge not reducible back to the bourgeois forms and the importance of this as one of the bases for political change.[76]

As Willis suggests, theories of resistance point to new ways of constructing a radical pedagogy by developing analyses of the ways in which class and culture combine to offer the outlines for a "cultural politics." At the core of such a politics is a semiotic reading of the style, rituals, language, and systems of meaning that inform the cultural terrains of subordinate groups. Through this process, it becomes possible to analyze what counterhegemonic elements such cultural fields contain, and how they tend to become incorporated into the dominant culture and subsequently stripped of their political possibilities. Implicit in such an analysis is the need to develop strategies in schools in which oppositional cultures might be rescued from the processes of incorporation in order to provide the basis for a viable political force. An essential element of such a task, which has been generally neglected by radical educators, is the development of a radical pedagogy that links a politics of the concrete not just with the processes of reproduction but also with the dynamics of social transformation. The possibility for such a task already exists and is present in the attempt by resistance theorists to view the cultures of subordinate groups as more than simply the by-product of hegemony and defeat.[77]

Another important feature of resistance theory is a deeper understanding of the notion of relative autonomy. This notion is developed through a number of analyses that point to those nonreproductive moments that constitute and support the critical notion of human agency. As we have mentioned, resistance theory assigns an active role to human agency and experience as key mediating links between structural determinants and lived effects. Consequently, there is the recognition that different spheres or cultural sites—schools, families, mass media—are governed by complex ideological properties that often generate contradictions both within and among them. At the same time, the notion of ideological domination as all-encompassing and unitary in its form and content is rejected, and it is rightly argued that dominant ideologies themselves are often contradictory, as are different factions of the ruling classes, the institutions that serve them, and the subordinate groups under their control.

In considering the weaknesses in theories of resistance, we will make several criticisms that represent starting points for the further development of a critical theory of schooling. First, although studies of resistance point to those social sites and "spaces" in which the dominant culture is encountered and challenged by subordinate groups, they do not adequately conceptualize the historical development of the conditions that promote and reinforce contradictory modes of resistance and struggle. What is missing in this perspective are analyses of those historically and culturally mediated factors that produce a *range* of oppositional behaviors, some of which constitute resistance and some of which do not. Put simply, not all oppositional behavior has "radical significance," nor is all oppositional behavior a clear-cut response to domination. The issue here is that there have been too few attempts by educational theorists to understand how subordinate groups embody and express a combination of reactionary and progressive behaviors—behaviors that embody ideologies both underlying the structure of social domination and containing the logic necessary to overcome it.

Oppositional behavior may not be simply a reaction to powerlessness, but might be an expression of power that is fueled by and reproduces the most powerful grammar of domination. Thus, on one level, resistance may be the simple appropriation and display of power, and may manifest itself through the interests and discourse of the worst aspects of capitalist rationality. For example, students may violate school rules, but the logic that informs such behavior may be rooted in forms of ideological hegemony such as racism and sexism. Moreover, the source of such hegemony often originates outside of the school. Under such circumstances, schools become social sites where oppositional behavior is simply played out, emerging less as a critique of schooling than as an expression of dominant ideology.

This becomes clearer in Angela McRobbie's account of sixth-form female students in England who, by aggressively asserting their own sexuality, appear to be rejecting the official ideology of the school with its sexually repressive emphasis on neatness, passivity, compliance, and "femininity."[78] Their opposition takes the form of carving boyfriends' names on school desks, wearing makeup and tight-fitting clothes, flaunting their sexual preferences for older, more mature boys, and spending endless amounts of time talking about boys and boyfriends. It could be argued that this type of oppositional behavior, rather than suggesting resistance, primarily displays an oppressive mode of sexism. Its organizing principle appears to be linked to social practices informed by the objective of developing a sexual, and ultimately successful, marriage. Thus, it appears to underscore a logic that has little to do with resistance to school norms and a great deal to do with the sexism that characterizes working-class life and mass culture in general. This is not to say that such behavior can simply be written off as reactionary. Obviously, the fact that these young women are acting collectively and attempting to define for themselves what they want out of life contains an emancipatory moment. But in the final analysis, this type of opposition is informed by a dominating, rather than liberating, logic.

This leads to a related issue. Resistance theories have gone too far in viewing schools as institutions characterized exclusively by forms of ideological domination. Lost from this view is an insight provided by theorists who deal with the hegemonic-state reproductive model: the notion that schools are also repressive institutions that use various coercive state agencies, including the police and the courts, to enforce involuntary school attendance. The point here is that resistance theories must recognize that in some cases students may be totally indifferent to the dominant ideology of the school with its respective rewards and demands. Their behavior in school may be fueled by ideological imperatives that signify issues and concerns that have very little to do with school directly. School simply becomes the place where the oppositional nature of these concerns is expressed.

In short, oppositional behaviors are produced amid contradictory discourses and values. The logic that informs a given act of resistance may, on the one hand, be linked to interests that are class-, gender- or race-specific. On the other hand, it may express the repressive moments inscribed in such behavior by the dominant culture rather than a message of protest against their existence. To understand the nature of such resistance, we must place it in a wider context to see how it is mediated and articulated in the culture of such oppositional groups. Because of a failure to understand the dialectical nature of resistance, most theories of education have treated the concept somewhat superficially. For instance, when domination is stressed in such studies, the portrayals of schools, working-class students, and classroom pedagogy often appear too homogeneous and static to be taken seriously. When resistance is discussed, its contradictory nature is usually not analyzed seriously, nor is the contradictory consciousness of the students and teachers treated dialectically.[79]

A second weakness in theories of resistance is that they rarely take into account issues of gender and race. As a number of feminists have pointed out, resistance studies, when analyzing domination, struggle, and schooling, generally ignore women and gender issues and focus instead on males and class issues.[80] This has meant that women are either disregarded altogether or are included only in terms that echo the sentiments of the male countercultural groups being portrayed. This raises a number of important problems that future analyses must resolve. One problem is that such studies have failed to account for the notion of patriarchy as a mode of domination that both cuts across various social sites and mediates between men and women within and between different social class formations. The point here, of course, is that domination is not singularly informed or exhausted by the logic of class oppression, nor does it affect men and women in similar ways. Women, though in different degrees, experience dual forms of domination in both the home and the workplace. How the dynamics of these forms are interconnected, reproduced, and mediated in schools represents an important area of continuing research. Another problem is that these studies contain no theoretical room for exploring forms of resistance that are race- and gender-specific, particularly as these mediate the sexual and social divisions of labor in various social sites such as schools. The failure to include women and racial minorities in such studies has resulted in a rather uncritical theoretical tendency to romanticize modes of resistance even when they contain reactionary racial and gender views. The irony here is that a large amount of neo-Marxist work on resistance, although allegedly committed to emancipatory concerns, ends up contributing to the reproduction of sexist and racist attitudes and practices.

A third weakness characterizing theories of resistance, as Jim Walker points out, is that they have focused primarily on overt acts of rebellious student behavior.[81] By so limiting their analyses, resistance theorists have ignored less obvious forms of resistance among students and have often misconstrued the political value of overt resistance. For example, some students minimize their participation in routine school practices while simultaneously displaying outward conformity to the school's ideology, opting for modes of resistance that are quietly subversive in the most immediate sense, but that have the potential to be politically progressive in the long run. These students may use humor to disrupt a class, use collective pressure to draw teachers away from class lessons, or purposely ignore the teacher's directions while attempting to develop collective spaces that allow them to escape the ethos of individualism permeating school life. Each type of behavior can indicate a form of resistance if it emerges out of a latent or overt ideological condemnation of the underlying repressive ideologies that characterize schools in general. That is, if we view these acts as practices involving a conscious or semiconscious political response to school-constructed relations of domination, then these students are resisting school ideology in a manner that gives them the power to reject the system on a level that will not make them powerless to protest it in the future. They have not renounced access to knowledge and skills that may allow them to move beyond the class-specific positions of dead-end, alienating labor that most of the showy rebels will eventually occupy.[82]

What resistance theorists have failed to acknowledge is that some students are able to see through the lies and promises of the dominant school ideology but decide not to translate this insight into extreme forms of rebelliousness. In some cases the reason for this decision may be an understanding that overt rebelliousness may result in powerlessness now and in the future. Needless to say, they may also go through school on their own terms and still face limited opportunities in the future. But what is of major importance here is that any other alternative seems ideologically naive and limits whatever transcendent hopes for the future these students may have.[83]

It is the tension between the present reality of their lives and their willingness to dream of a better world that makes such students potential political leaders. Of course, in some cases students may not be aware of the political grounds of their position toward school, except for a general awareness of its dominating nature and the need to somehow escape from it without relegating themselves to a future they do not want. Even this vague understanding and its attendant behavior portend a politically progressive logic, a logic that needs to be incorporated into a theory of resistance.

A fourth weakness of theories of resistance is that they have not given enough attention to the issue of how domination reaches into the structure of personality itself. There is little concern with the often contradictory relation between understanding and action. Part of the solution to this problem may lie in uncovering the genesis and operation of those socially constructed needs that tie people to larger structures of domination. Radical educators have shown a lamentable tendency to ignore the question of needs and desires in favor of issues that center around ideology and consciousness. A critical psychology is needed that points to the way in which "un-freedom" reproduces itself in the psyche of human beings. We need to understand how dominating ideologies prevent many-sided needs from developing in the oppressed, or, in other words, how hegemonic ideologies function to exclude oppressed groups from creating needs that extend beyond the instrumental logic of the market. We are concerned here with such radical needs as those that represent the vital drive toward new relationships between men and women, the generations, different races, and humanity and nature. More specifically, we need to understand how to substitute radical needs organized around the desire for meaningful work, solidarity, an aesthetic sensibility, eros, and emancipatory freedoms for the egoistic, aggressive, calculable greed of capitalist interests. Alienating need structures—those dimensions of our psyche and personality that tie us to social practices and relationships that perpetuate systems of exploitation and the servitude of humanity—represent one of the most crucial areas from which to address a radical pedagogy.

The question of the historical genesis and transformation of needs constitutes, in our minds, the most important basis for a theory of radical educational praxis. Until educators can point to possibilities for the development of "radical needs that both challenge the existing system of interest and production and point to an emancipated society,"[84] it will be exceptionally difficult to understand how schools function to incorporate people, or what that might mean to the establishment of a basis for critical thinking and responsible action. Put another way, without a theory of radical needs and critical psychology, educators have no way of understanding the grip and force of alienating social structures as they manifest themselves in the lived but often nondiscursive aspects of everyday life.[85]

TOWARD A THEORY OF RESISTANCE

Resistance is a valuable theoretical and ideological construct that provides an important focus for analyzing the relationship between school and the wider society. More importantly, it provides a new means for understanding the complex ways in which subordinate groups experience educational failure, pointing to new ways of thinking about and restructuring modes of critical pedagogy. As we have noted, the current use of the concept of resistance by radical educators suggests a lack of intellectual rigor and an overdose of theoretical sloppiness. It is imperative that educators be more precise about what resistance actually is and what it is not, and be more specific about how the concept can be used to develop a critical pedagogy. It is also clear that a rationale for employing the concept needs to be considered more fully. We will now discuss these issues and briefly outline some basic theoretical concerns for developing a more intellectually rigorous and politically useful foundation for pursuing such a task.

In the most general sense, resistance must be grounded in a theoretical rationale that provides a new framework for examining schools as social sites that structure the experiences of subordinate groups. The concept of resistance, in other words, represents more than a new heuristic catchword in the language of radical pedagogy; it depicts a mode of discourse that rejects traditional explanations of school failure and oppositional behavior and shifts the analysis of oppositional behavior from the theoretical terrains of functionalism and mainstream educational psychology to those of political science and sociology. Resistance in this case redefines the causes and meaning of oppositional behavior by arguing that it has little to do with deviance and learned helplessness, but a great deal to do with moral and political indignation.

Aside from shifting the theoretical ground for analyzing oppositional behavior, the concept of resistance points to a number of assumptions and concerns about schooling that are generally neglected in both traditional views of schooling and radical theories of reproduction. First, it celebrates a dialectical notion of human agency that rightly portrays domination as a process that is neither static nor complete. Concomitantly, the oppressed are not seen as being simply passive in the face of domination. The notion of resistance points to the need to understand more thoroughly the complex ways in which people mediate and respond to the connection between their own experiences and structures of domination and constraint. Central categories that emerge in a theory of resistance are intentionality, consciousness, the meaning of common sense, and the nature and value of nondiscursive behavior. Second, resistance adds new depth to the notion that power is exercised on and by people within different contexts that structure interacting relations of dominance and autonomy. Thus, power is never unidimensional; it is exercised not only as a mode of domination, but also as an act of resistance. Last, inherent in a radical notion of resistance is an expressed hope for radical transformation, an element of possibility that seems to be missing in radical theories of education which appear trapped in the theoretical cemetery of Orwellian pessimism.

In addition to developing a rationale for the notion of resistance, there is a need to formulate criteria against which the term can be defined as a central category of analysis in theories of schooling. In the most general sense, we think resistance must be situated in a perspective that takes the notion of emancipation as its guiding interest. That is, the nature and meaning of an act of resistance must be defined by the degree to which it contains possibilities to develop what Herbert Marcuse termed "a commitment to an emancipation of sensibility, imagination and reason in all spheres of subjectivity and objectivity."[86] Thus, the central element of analyzing any act of resistance must be a concern with uncovering the degree to which it highlights, implicitly or explicitly, the need to struggle against domination and submission. In other words, the concept of resistance must have a revealing function that contains a critique of domination and provides theoretical opportunities for self-reflection and struggle in the interest of social and self-emancipation. To the degree that oppositional behavior suppresses social contradictions while simultaneously merging with, rather than challenging, the logic of ideological domination, it does not fall under the category of resistance, but under its opposite—accommodation and conformism. The value of the concept of resistance lies in its critical function and in its potential to utilize both the radical possibilities embedded in its own logic and the interests contained in the object of its expression. In other words, the concept of resistance represents an element of difference, a counter-logic, that must be analyzed to reveal its underlying interest in freedom and its rejection of those forms of domination inherent in the social relations against which it reacts. Of course, this is a rather general set of standards on which to ground the notion of resistance, but it does provide a notion of interest and a theoretical scaffold on which to make a distinction between forms of oppositional behavior that can be used for either the amelioration of human life or the destruction and denigration of basic human values.

Some acts of resistance reveal quite visibly their radical potential, while others are rather ambiguous; still others may reveal nothing more than an affinity for the logic of domination and destruction. It is the ambiguous area that we want to analyze briefly, since the other two areas are self-explanatory. Recently, we heard a "radical" educator argue that teachers who rush home early after school are, in fact, committing acts of resistance. She also claimed that teachers who do not adequately prepare for their classroom lessons are participating in a form of resistance as well. Of course, it is equally debatable that the teachers in question are simply lazy or care very little about teaching, and that what in fact is being displayed is not resistance but unprofessional and unethical behavior. In these cases, there is no logical, convincing response to either argument. The behaviors displayed do not speak for themselves. To call them resistance is to turn the concept into a term that has no analytical precision. In cases like these, one must either link the behavior under analysis with an interpretation provided by the subjects themselves, or dig deeply into the historical and relational conditions from which the behavior develops. Only then will the interest embedded in such behavior be open to interrogation.

It follows from our argument that the interests underlying a specific form of behavior may become clear once the nature of that behavior is interpreted by the person who exhibits it. But we do not mean to imply that such interests will automatically be revealed. Individuals may not be able to explain the reasons for their behavior, or the interpretation may be distorted. In this case, the interest underlying such behavior may be illuminated against the backdrop of social practices and values from which the behavior emerges. Such a referent may be found in the historical conditions that prompted the behavior, the collective values of a peer group, or the practices embedded in other social sites such as the family, the workplace, or the church. We want to stress that the concept of resistance must not be allowed to become a category indiscriminately hung over every expression of "oppositional behavior." On the contrary, it must become an analytical construct and mode of inquiry that is self-critical and sensitive to its own interests—radical consciousness-raising and collective critical action.

Let us now return to the question of how we define resistance and view oppositional behavior, and to the implications for making such distinctions. On one level, it is important to be theoretically precise about which forms of oppositional behavior constitute resistance and which do not. On another level, it is equally important to argue that all forms of oppositional behavior represent a focal point for critical analysis and should be analyzed to see if they represent a form of resistance by uncovering their emancipatory interests. This is a matter of theoretical preciseness and definition. On the other hand, as a matter of radical strategy, *all* forms of oppositional behavior, whether or not actual resistance, must be examined for their possible use as a basis for critical analysis. Thus, oppositional behavior becomes the object of theoretical clarification and the subject of pedagogical considerations.

On a more philosophical level, we want to stress that the theoretical construct of resistance rejects the positivist notion that the meaning of behavior is synonymous with a literal reading based on immediate action. Instead, resistance must be viewed from a theoretical starting point that links the display of behavior to the interest it embodies, going beyond the immediacy of behavior to the interest that underlies its often hidden logic, a logic that also must be interpreted through the historical and cultural mediations that shape it. Finally, we want to emphasize that the ultimate value of the notion of resistance must be measured not only by the degree to which it promotes critical thinking and reflective action but, more importantly, by the degree to which it contains the possibility of galvanizing collective political struggle among parents, teachers, and students around the issues of power and social determination.

We will now briefly discuss the value of a dialectical notion of resistance for a critical theory of schooling. The pedagogical value of resistance lies, in part, in the connections it makes between structure and human agency, on the one hand, and culture and the process of self-formation on the other. Resistance theory rejects the idea that schools are simply instructional sites by not only politicizing the notion of culture, but also by analyzing school cultures within the shifting terrain of struggle and contestation. In effect, this represents a new theoretical framework for understanding the process of schooling which places educational knowledge, values, and social relations within the context of antagonistic relations and examines them within the interplay of dominant and subordinate school cultures. When a theory of resistance is incorporated into radical pedagogy, elements of oppositional behavior in schools become the focal point for analyzing different, and often antagonistic, social relations and experiences among students from dominant and subordinate cultures. Within this mode of critical analysis, it becomes possible to illuminate how students draw on the limited resources at their disposal in order to reaffirm the positive dimensions of their own cultures and histories.

Resistance theory highlights the complexity of student responses to the logic of schooling. Thus, it highlights the need for radical educators to unravel how oppositional behavior often emerges within forms of contradictory consciousness that are never free from the reproductive rationality embedded in capitalist social relations. A radical pedagogy, then, must recognize that student resistance in all of its forms represents manifestations of struggle and solidarity that, in their incompleteness, both challenge and confirm capitalist hegemony. What is most important is the willingness of radical educators to search for the emancipatory interests that underlie such resistance and to make them visible to students and others so that they can become the object of debate and political analysis.

A theory of resistance is central to the development of a radical pedagogy for other reasons as well. It helps bring into focus those social practices in schools whose ultimate aim is the control of both the learning process and the capacity for critical thought and action. For example, it points to the ideology underlying the hegemonic curriculum, to its hierarchically organized bodies of knowledge, and particularly to the way in which this curriculum marginalizes or disqualifies working-class knowledge as well as knowledge about women and minorities. Furthermore, resistance theory reveals the ideology underlying such a curriculum, with its emphasis on individual rather than collective appropriation of knowledge, and how this emphasis drives a wedge between students from different social classes. This is particularly evident in the different approaches to knowledge supported in many working-class and middle-class families. Knowledge in the working-class culture is often constructed on the principles of solidarity and sharing, whereas within middle-class culture, knowledge is forged in individual competition and is seen as a badge of separateness.

In short, resistance theory calls attention to the need for radical educators to unravel the ideological interests embedded in the various message systems of the school, particularly those embedded in its curriculum, systems of instruction, and modes of evaluation. What is most important is that resistance theory reinforces the need for radical educators to decipher how the forms of cultural production displayed by subordinate groups can be analyzed to reveal both their limitations and their possibilities for enabling critical thinking, analytical discourse, and learning through collective practice.

Finally, resistance theory suggests that radical educators must develop a critical rather than a pragmatic relationship with students. This means that any viable form of radical pedagogy must analyze how the relations of domination in schools originate, how they are sustained, and how students and teachers, in particular, relate to them. This means looking beyond schools. It suggests taking seriously the counter-logic that pulls students away from schools into the streets, the bars, and the shop-floor culture. For many working-class students, these realms are "real time" as opposed to the "dead time" they often experience in schools. The social spheres that make up this counter-logic may represent the few remaining terrains that provide the oppressed with the possibility of human agency and autonomy. Yet, these terrains appear to represent less a form of resistance than an expression of solidarity and self-affirmation.

The pull of this counter-logic must be critically engaged and built into the framework of a radical pedagogy. Yet, this is not to suggest that it must be absorbed into a theory of schooling. On the contrary, it must be supported by radical educators and others from both inside and outside of schools. But as an object of pedagogical analysis, this counter-logic must be seen as an important theoretical terrain in which one finds fleeting images of freedom that point to fundamentally new structures in the public organization of experience.

Inherent in the oppositional public spheres that constitute a counter-logic are the conditions around which the oppressed organize important needs and relations. Thus, it represents an important terrain in the ideological battle for the appropriation of meaning and experience. For this reason, it provides educators with an opportunity to link the political with the personal in order to understand how power is mediated, resisted, and reproduced in daily life. Furthermore, it situates the relationship between schools and the larger society within a theoretical framework informed by a fundamentally political question, "How do we develop a radical pedagogy that makes schools meaningful so as to make them critical, and how do we make them critical so as to make them emancipatory?"

But the basis for a radical pedagogy demands more than the development of a theory of resistance; it also needs to develop a new discourse, one that appropriates the most critical dimensions of Marxist theory while simultaneously moving beyond it. In other words, if the language of possibility is to become a constitutive part of radical educational theory, it will have to ground itself in a theoretical discourse that draws expansively from a number of radical traditions, which address the interrelationships among race, gender, and class as they are specifically constituted between the material politics of containment and various discourses and projects of possibility. This is the issue we will deal with in the next chapter.

NOTES

1. Marx, *Capital*, I (Moscow: Progress Publishers, 1969), pp. 531, 532.
2. For a critical analysis of the significance of Marx's notion of reproduction in social theory, see Henri Lefebvre, *The Survival of Capitalism*, trans. Frank Bryant (New York: St. Martin's Press, 1973). For a critical review of the literature on

schooling that takes the notion of reproduction as its starting point, see Michael Apple, *Ideology and Curriculum* (London: Routledge and Kegan Paul, 1979); Henry A. Giroux, *Ideology, Culture and the Process of Schooling* (Philadelphia: Temple University Press, 1981); Geoff Whitty and Michael Young, ed., *Society, State, and Schooling* (Sussex, England: Falmer Press, 1977); Len Barton, Roland Meighan, and Stephen Walker, eds., *Schooling, Ideology and Curriculum* (Sussex, England: Falmer Press, 1980); Samuel Bowles and Herbert Gintis, *Schooling in Capitalist America* (New York: Basic Books, 1977).

3. Willis, "Cultural Production and Theories of Reproduction," in *Race, Class and Education,* eds. Len Barton and Stephen Walker (London: Croom-Helm, 1983), p. 110.

4. Bowles and Gintis, op. cit.

5. Jean Anyon, "Social Class and the Hidden Curriculum of Work," *Journal of Education* 162 (1980), pp. 67–92.

6. Pierre Bourdieu and Jean Claude Passeron, *Reproduction in Education, Society, and Culture* (Beverly Hills, Calif.: Sage, 1977).

7. Nicos Poulantzas, *Classes in Contemporary Society* (London: Verso Books, 1978).

8. Representative examples include Michael Apple, *Education and Power* (London: Routledge and Kegan Paul, 1982); Richard Bates, "New Developments in the New Sociology of Education," *British Journal of Sociology of Education* 1 (1980), pp. 67–79; Robert W. Connell, Dean J. Ashenden, Sandra Kessler, and Gary W. Dowsett, *Making the Difference* (Sydney: Allen and Unwin, 1982); Geoff Whitty, *Ideology, Politics, and Curriculum* (London: Open University Press, 1981); Henry A. Giroux, *Theory and Resistance in Education* (South Hadley, Mass.: Bergin and Garvey, 1983); Stanley Aronowitz and Henry Giroux, *Postmodern Education* (Minneapolis: University of Minnesota Press, 1990).

9. Paul Willis, *Learning to Labor* (New York: Columbia University Press, 1981); Women's Study Group, Centre for Contemporary Cultural Studies, ed., *Women Take Issue* (London: Hutchinson, 1978); David Robins and Philip Cohen, *Knuckle Sandwich: Growing Up in a Working Class City* (London: Pelican Books, 1978); Paul Corrigan, *Schooling and the Smash Street Kids* (London: Macmillan, 1979); Angela McRobbie and Trisha McCabe, *Feminism for Girls* (London: Routledge and Kegan Paul, 1981); Thomas Popkewitz, B. Robert Tabachnick, and Gary Wehlage, *The Myth of Educational Reform* (Madison, Wis.: University of Wisconsin Press, 1982); Robert B. Everhart, "Classroom Management, Student Opposition, and the Labor Process" in *Ideology and Practice in Schooling,* eds. Michael Apple and Lois Weiss (Philadelphia: Temple University Press, 1983); Paul Olson, "Inequality Remade: The Theory of Correspondence and the Context of French Immersion in Northern Ontario," *Journal of Education* 165 (1983), pp. 75–78.

10. Stanley Aronowitz, "Marx, Braverman, and the Logic of Capital," *The Insurgent Sociologist* 8 (1977), pp. 126–146.

11. Michael Apple, "The Hidden Curriculum and the Nature of Conflict," *Interchange* 2 (1971), pp. 27–40; Henry A. Giroux and Anthony N. Penna, "Social Education in the Classroom: The Dynamics of the Hidden Curriculum," *Theory and Research in Social Education* 7 (1979), pp. 21–42; Henry A. Giroux and David Purpel, eds., *The Hidden Curriculum and Moral Education* (Berkeley, Calif.: McCutchan, 1983).

12. Martin Carnoy and Henry Levin, *The Limits of Educational Reform* (New York: McKay, 1976); W. Timothy Weaver, *The Contest for Educational Resources* (Lexington, Mass.: Lexington Books, 1982).

13. Kathleen Wilcox and Pia Moriarity, "Schooling and Work: Social Constraints on Educational Opportunity," in *Education: Straitjacket or Opportunity,* eds. James Benet and Arlene Kaplan Daniels (New York: Transaction Books, 1980); Roslyn Arlin Mickelson, "The Secondary School's Role in Social Stratification: A Comparison of Beverly Hills High School and Morningside High School," *Journal of Education* 162 (1980), pp. 83–112; Jean Anyon, "Social Class and School Knowledge," *Curriculum Inquiry* 11 (1981), pp. 3–42.

14. Bowles and Gintis, op. cit., p. 131.

15. Althusser, *For Marx* (New York: Vintage Books, 1969), *Reading Capital* (London: New Left Books, 1970), and "Ideology and the Ideological State Apparatuses," in his *Lenin and Philosophy, and Other Essays,* trans. Ben Brewster (New York: Monthly Review Press, 1971).

16. Althusser, "Ideological State Apparatuses," p. 132.

17. Ibid., pp. 148–158.

18. Ibid., p. 162.

19. Althusser, *For Marx,* p. 233.

20. Baudelot and Establet, *L'Ecole Capitaliste en France* (Paris: Maspero, 1971).

21. Hegemonic as it is used here refers to elements of unconsciousness, common sense, and consciousness that are compatible with ideologies and social practices that perpetuate existing practices of domination and oppression. This is discussed in greater detail in Giroux, *Theory and Resistance.*

22. Stanley Aronowitz, "Cracks in the Bloc: American Labor's Historic Compromise and the Present Crisis," *Social Text* 5 (1982), pp. 22–52.

23. See Henry A. Giroux, "Hegemony, Resistance, and the Paradox of Educational Reform," *Interchange* 12 (1981), pp. 3–26.

24. James Donald, "How Illiteracy Became a Problem and Literacy Stopped Being One," *Journal of Education* 165 (1983), pp. 35–52.

25. Bourdieu and Passeron, *Reproduction;* Bourdieu, *Outline of Theory and Practice* (Cambridge, England: Cambridge University Press, 1977). It must be noted that the pioneering work in this area was done by Paulo Freire, *Pedagogy of the Oppressed* (New York: Seabury Press, 1970).

26. Bourdieu and Passeron, *Reproduction;* Bourdieu, "Symbolic Power," *Critique of Anthropology* 4 (1979), pp. 77–85.

27. Bourdieu, "Symbolic Power," p. 30.

28. Bourdieu and Passeron, *Reproduction,* p. 178.

29. Bourdieu, "The School as a Conservative Force: Scholastic and Cultural Inequalities," in *Contemporary Research in the Sociology of Education,* ed. John Eggleston (London: Methuen, 1974), p. 39.

30. The hegemonic curriculum refers to the way in which "schools are organized around a particular organization of learning and content. . . . The crucial features of this curriculum are hierarchically organized bodies of academic knowledge appropriated in individual competition" (Connell et al., *Making the Difference,* p. 120). The curriculum is hegemonic in that it functions to exclude large numbers of students who are from subordinate classes. Connell et al. were the first

to use the term, while Bourdieu and his associates have demonstrated how the hegemonic curriculum works in France's system of higher education.

31. For an illuminating analysis of this issue, see Jean Anyon, "Ideology and United States History Textbooks," *Harvard Educational Review* 49 (1979), pp. 361–386; and Joshua Brown, "Into the Minds of Babes: A Journey Through Recent Children's History Books," *Radical History Review* 25 (1981), pp. 127–145.

32. Bourdieu, *Outline of Theory and Practice*; Bourdieu, "Men and Machines," in *Advances in Social Theory and Methodology,* eds. Karin Knorr-Cetina and Aaron V. Cicourel (London: Routledge and Kegan Paul, 1981).

33. Bourdieu, "Men and Machines," p. 305.

34. Bourdieu, *Outline of Theory and Practice,* p. 83.

35. Pierre Bourdieu and Jean-Claude Passeron, *The Inheritors: French Students and Their Relations to Culture* (Chicago: University of Chicago Press, 1979).

36. Bourdieu, "Men and Machines," p. 314.

37. Bourdieu, *Outline of Theory and Practice,* p. 94.

38. It must be stressed that the most important work on the politics of the body is to be found in Maurice Merleau-Ponty, *Phenomenology of Perception* (London: Routledge and Kegan Paul, 1962), esp. pp. 67–199.

39. Bourdieu, "The Economics of Linguistic Exchanges," *Social Science Information* 16 (1977), pp. 645–668.

40. Davies, *Popular Culture, Class, and Schooling* (London: Open University Press, 1981), p. 60.

41. This is particularly true in Bourdieu and Passeron's *Reproduction*.

42. Dale, "Education and the Capitalist State: Contributions and Contradictions," in *Cultural and Economic Reproduction in Education,* ed. Michael Apple (London: Routledge and Kegan Paul, 1982), p. 157.

43. Robert W. Connell, Dean J. Ashenden, Sandra Kessler, and Gary W. Dowsett, "Class and Gender Dynamics in a Ruling Class School," *Interchange* 12 (1981), pp. 102–117.

44. Sieber, "The Politics of Middle-Class Success in an Inner-City School," *Journal of Education* 164 (1981), pp. 30–47.

45. Ibid., p. 45.

46. Foucault, *Power and Knowledge: Selected Interviews and Other Writings,* ed. Colin Gordon (New York: Pantheon, 1980).

47. Noelle Bisseret, *Education, Class Language, and Ideology* (London: Routledge and Kegan Paul, 1979).

48. See esp. Bourdieu, "Cultural Reproduction and Social Reproduction," in *Power and Ideology in Education,* eds. Jerome Karabel and Albert H. Halsey (New York: Oxford University Press, 1979); and Bourdieu and Passeron, *Reproduction*.

49. Some representative examples include Ralph Miliband, *The State in Capitalist Society* (New York: Basic Books, 1969); James O'Connor, *The Fiscal Crisis of the State* (New York: St. Martin's Press, 1973); Nicos Poulantzas, *Political Power and Social Classes* (London: New Left Books, 1973), and *Classes in Contemporary Society;* Goran Therborn, *What Does the Ruling Class Do When It Rules* (London: New Left Books, 1978); Philip Corrigan, ed., *Capitalism, State Formation, and Marxist Theory* (London: Quartet Books, 1980).

50. This is a small but growing and important body of literature. Among the

more recent works are Roger Dale, Geoff Easland, and Madeleine Macdonald, eds., *Education and the State,* I and II (Sussex, England: Falmer Press, 1980); Mariam E. David, *The State, the Family, and Education* (London: Routledge and Kegan Paul, 1980); Madan Sarup, *Education, State and Crisis* (London: Routledge and Kegan Paul, 1982); Apple, *Education and Power.*

51. Apple, "Reproduction and Contradiction in Education," in *Cultural and Economic Reproduction in Education,* p. 14.

52. Gramsci, *Selections from Prison Notebooks,* ed. and trans. Quintin Hoare and Geoffrey Smith (New York: International Publishers, 1971).

53. Ibid., pp. 57–58.

54. Chantal Mouffe, "Hegemony and Ideology in Gramsci," in *Gramsci and Marxist Theory,* ed. Chantal Mouffe (London: Routledge and Kegan Paul, 1979), pp. 182–183. It is important to stress that hegemony is not a static concept; on the contrary, hegemony is an active process realized as an uneven and tenuous situation and outcome through which oppositional forces are either accommodated, constrained, or defeated. The relationship between hegemony and political education is treated extensively in Walter Adamson, *Hegemony and Revolution: A Study of Antonio Gramsci's Political and Cultural Theory* (Berkeley: University of California Press, 1980); see also Philip Wexler and Tony Whitson, "Hegemony and Education," *Psychology and Social Theory* 3 (1982), pp. 31–42.

55. Kenneth Neild and John Seed, "The Theoretical Poverty or the Poverty of Theory," *Economy and Society* 8 (1979), pp. 383–416.

56. Gramsci, op. cit., p. 244.

57. Philip Corrigan, Harvie Ramsey, and Derek Sayer, "The State as a Relation of Production," in *Capitalism, State Formation and Marxist Theory,* ed. Philip Corrigan (London: Quartet Books, 1980), p. 21.

58. Ibid., p. 10.

59. Poulantzas, *Classes in Contemporary Society.* For an important discussion of Marxist theories of the state and the issue of relative autonomy, see Ralph Miliband, "State Power and Class Interests," *New Left Review* 138 (1983), pp. 57–68.

60. Offe and Ronge, "Thesis on the Theory of the State," *New German Critique* 6 (1975), pp. 137–147.

61. Althusser, "Ideological State Apparatuses," pp. 127–186.

62. Corrigan, Ramsey, and Sayer, op. cit., p. 17.

63. See esp. Martin Carnoy, "Education, Economy and the State"; Roger Dale, "Education and the Capitalist State," in *Cultural and Economic Reproduction in Education.*

64. Apple, *Education and Power,* pp. 54–55.

65. Dale, op. cit., pp. 146–147.

66. Apple, *Education and Power,* p. 95.

67. James Donald, "Green Paper: Noise of a Crisis," *Screen Education* 30 (1979), pp. 13–49.

68. Poulantzas, quoted in Donald, "Green Paper," p. 21.

69. Poulantzas, *Classes in Contemporary Society,* pp. 259–270.

70. See, for example, Willis, *Learning to Labor;* McRobbie and McCabe, *Feminism for Girls;* Robins and Cohen, *Knuckle Sandwich;* Dick Hebdige, *Subculture: The Meaning of Style* (London: Methuen, 1980).

71. Representative examples of the ethnographic literature in the United States include Howard Becker, *Boys in White* (Chicago: University of Chicago Press, 1961); Arthur Stinchombe, *Rebellion in a High School* (New York: Quadrangle Books, 1964); Harry Wolcott, *The Man in the Principal's Office: An Ethnography* (New York: Holt, Rinehart and Winston, 1973); George Spindler, ed., *Ethnography of Schooling* (New York: Holt, Rinehart and Winston, 1982). Works from England include David Hargreaves, *Social Relations in a Secondary School* (London: Routledge and Kegan Paul, 1967); Colin Lacey, *Hightown Grammar* (Manchester: Manchester University Press, 1970); Peter Woods, *The Divided School* (London: Routledge and Kegan Paul, 1979); Stephen Ball, *Beachside Comprehensive: A Case Study of Secondary Schooling* (London: Cambridge University Press, 1981); and Ralph Larkin, *Suburban Youth in Cultural Crisis* (New York: Oxford University Press, 1979).

72. Willis, *Learning to Labor,* pp. 99–116.

73. Ibid., pp. 89–116.

74. Fine, "Examining Inequity: View from Urban Schools," University of Pennsylvania, Unpublished manuscript, 1982.

75. Ibid., p. 6.

76. Willis, "Cultural Production and Theories of Reproduction," p. 114.

77. It is important to stress that the opposition displayed by a subordinate group must be seen not only as a form of resistance but also as an expression of a group's struggle to constitute its social identity.

78. Angela McRobbie, "Working Class Girls and the Culture of Femininity," in *Women Take Issue.*

79. A representative example of the work we are criticizing can be found in Nancy King, "Children's Play as a Form of Resistance in the Classroom," *Journal of Education* 164 (1982), pp. 320–329; Valerie Suransky, "Tale of Rebellion and Resistance: The Landscape of Early Institutional Life," *Journal of Education* (forthcoming). There is a certain irony in that these articles are organized around the concept of resistance without ever providing a rigorous theoretical definition of what the term means.

80. See, for example, Angela McRobbie, "Settling Accounts with Subcultures," *Screen Education* 34 (1980), pp. 37–49.

81. Walker, "Rebels with Our Applause: A Critique of Resistance Theories," *Journal of Education* (forthcoming).

82. Willis, *Learning to Labor,* pp. 130–137.

83. See Willis, *Learning to Labor,* chs. 8 and 9; Connell et al., *Making the Difference,* chapter 5.

84. Jean Cohen, review of *Theory and Need in Marx,* by Agnes Heller, *Telos* 33 (1977), pp. 170–184.

85. For an excellent analysis of the relationship between Marxist theory and psychoanalysis, see the differing interpretations by Richard Lichtman, *The Production of Desire* (New York: Free Press, 1982); and Russell Jacoby, *Social Amnesia* (Boston: Beacon Press, 1973). For a more informative and recent analysis of the critical potential that poststructuralist psychology can make to a critical pedagogy, see the following: Julian Henriques, Wendy Hollway, Cathy Vrmin, Couze Venn, and Valerie Walkerdinc, *Changing the Subject* (New York: Methuen, 1984); Roger Simon, "Work Experience as the Production of Subjectivity," in *Critical Pedagogy*

and Cultural Power, ed. David Livingstone (South Hadley, Mass.: Bergin and Garvey, 1987.

86. Marcuse, *The Aesthetic Dimension* (Boston: Beacon Press, 1977).

Material in this chapter was adopted from *Theory and Resistance in Education* (South Hadley, Mass.: Bergin and Garvey, 1983).

Chapter Five

Radical Pedagogy and the Legacy of Marxist Discourse

As we pointed out in another chapter, Marxist theory has exercised a major influence on the development of radical theories of schooling. In many respects, this influence has been part of a wider revival of Marxist thought that has been going on in the United States, Europe, and other sections of the world.[1] On the surface, this Marxist revival has generated not only various "new" readings of Marx's work; it has also essentially developed into the production of a plethora of discourses, many of which have been used to redefine the way radicals view a host of academic disciplines, not to mention Marxist theory itself. What becomes evident even to the casual observer is that the notion of a unifying and homogeneous Marxist discourse belongs to history. Success breeds its own problems. One needs to consult a consumer's guide to keep abreast of the latest Marxist offerings that tumble out from the publishing houses and university symposiums. As one surveys the offerings, the theoretical landscape appears cluttered with structural Marxism, hermeneutical Marxism, phenomenological Marxism, feminist Marxism, semiotic Marxism, post-Marxism, along with standbys such as Marxist-Leninism, Trotskyism, and so forth.

An unsettling and unsettled paradox has accompanied the revival of Marxist theory and its influence on areas such as educational theory and practice. The paradox lies in the fact that as the literature and influence of Marxism have grown, so has the magnitude of the crisis that besets it. In our view, the nature of the crisis is defined by two different but related issues.

First, there is the attempt by intellectuals of various Marxist persuasions to confront the changing social, political, and economic conditions of the twentieth century by either revising Marxist thought or by "returning to Marx" in order to unravel a new insight or undiscovered truth for understanding the existing social reality. Capitalizing on a history of "critical" revisionist Marxist theory that draws from such luminaries as Rosa Luxemburg, George Lukacs, Karl Korsch, Antonio Gramsci, the Frankfurt School, and others, this approach is characterized largely by an attempt to develop a perspective on struggle and emancipation that stays within a Marxist paradigm and discourse. In other words, Marxism remains the basis for a new critical or radical theory. Underlying the crisis that confronts this approach are a plethora of discourses that remain abstracted from the terrain of power and struggle. Acknowledging the limits of Marxist thought has not only prompted plain, neo-, and post-Marxists to produce many variations on traditional orthodox concerns; it has also shifted the nature of the struggle from the terrain of everyday life and the streets to the lecture halls and classrooms of the university. The struggle for power appears to have been reduced to merely the struggle over meaning. This is not meant to attack the importance of theory production as much as to argue against the severing of theory as a political endeavor from the task of creating an organic connection with excluded majorities, that is, workers, women, racial minorities, and various social movements.

Second, there is the failure to recognize that the basis for generating a new critical and radical theory appropriate to the problems and lived experiences of the twentieth century demands a new discourse, one that is informed by the legacy of a critical Marxism but that, in the final analysis, has to break with its most fundamental assumptions and, as such, break with Marxism as the master discourse of any emancipatory project.

What we are suggesting is that, while the crisis in Marxism is not new, it is now confronted by a series of social, political, and economic events that not only indict its orthodox or classical strains, which have always been dominated by a rigid economism, but also reveal the limitations of more recent Marxist developments that have produced a critical assessment of the original theory. The failure of the working class to assume the role of the historical agent of revolution, the failure of existing socialisms in Eastern Europe and other parts of the world to provide and demonstrate an emancipatory vision, and the appearance of new social movements that have redefined the meaning of domination and emancipation appear to have dealt Marxism in all of its forms a devastating blow. Not only do the fundamental Marxist categories of class, history, and economy fail to address or change the new social antagonisms that exist in society, but they also fail to interrogate critically Marxism's own complicity with the rationality of domination. The task of radical theory, especially in the case of radical educational theory, is to see Marxism not as a doctrine valid for all times under all historical conditions, but as a critical "way of seeing." In this case, the primacy of universal categories is replaced by a discourse linked to the spirit of critical inquiry. This suggests creating a new discourse, one that is informed by the Marxist project of social, and, hence, self-emancipation but not limited by its most fundamental categories. It is the legacy of this need to move beyond Marx, rather than rescue him from his critics and followers, that haunts the American left, and the radical educational American left in particular.

In this chapter, we first want to examine some of the major categories of classical and critical Marxism and review critically some of the issues that have emerged around their usefulness for radical social theory. Second, we want to analyze their strengths and limitations with regard to the way they have influenced the course of radical educational theory. We conclude by turning to the broader project of providing a theoretical discourse for developing an alternative radical theory of education.

At the core of our critique of the Marxist tradition is the claim that Marxism has failed to show how its most fundamental categories remain valid as the basis for a theory of social transformation and emancipation. As a number of social theorists have pointed out, Marxism has been held captive by the formulation of theoretical and philosophical presuppositions developed almost entirely within a discourse that stresses the primacy of the economic sphere in shaping society, on the one hand, and the primacy of class as the exclusive referent for understanding history and the dynamics of domination and struggle, on the other. One consequence has been the devaluing of politics, ideology, and culture in both theoretical and practical terms. Another problem has centered on the inability of Marxist theory to free itself from forms of class and historical reductionism. What needs to be stressed here is that any approach to developing a critical theory of emancipation demands that the Marxist theory of class and history be revised and that the theoretical terrains of culture and ideology be given primary importance as a constitutive force in the shaping of consciousness and historical agency. Such critique demands not only a reformulation of the central categories of critical theory and praxis. It also demands as a starting point some understanding of how the central categories of Marxism have failed both in their orthodox usage and in their most radical formulations in the last seventy to eighty years.

CLASS AND ECONOMISM IN CLASSICAL AND CRITICAL MARXIST TRADITIONS

The significance of the primacy of class and most generally the economic sphere, particularly production relations, in Marxist theory cannot be overestimated. For Marx, class was the fundamental theoretical category explaining history and the nature of human struggle. His famous formulation that "the history of all hitherto existing society is the history of class struggle" became the theoretical cornerstone for various shades of Marxists in understanding and explaining the underlying logic of capitalist exploitation as it evolved within the sphere of production. Moreover, against those views of history in which great ideas or great men became the central explanatory categories, it provided an alternative analysis. History, in this account, was made through the struggle of different classes and social groups, defined primarily through their relations to the means of production. Moreover, it was the working class which, because of the nature of its misery and oppression as well as centrality to the process of material production, became the designated subject of history. In this form of analysis, almost irrespective of the theoretical differences that have arisen about how to define class, class consciousness, the nature of radical agency, and so on, there is an underlying belief in the notion that labor is the most important social process creating the material world and the cultural forms that are the expressions of its various social groups. We believe that Catharine MacKinnon is correct in her assessment that Marxist theory is wedded to the notion that productive work is the central "activity by which people become what they are. Class is its structure, production its consequence, capital its congealed form, and control its issue."[2]

Implicit in historical materialism's views about class and the primacy of the economic are a number of assumptions that have defined the Marxist problematic in its most orthodox and radical strains. In its orthodox versions, particularly as supported by the Second International, the working class was constituted as an *a priori* subject, characterized by its objective place in the relations of production, and defined by a homogeneous discourse. As an *a priori* subject, the working class made history without the benefit of being influenced by it. That is, as an objective *a priori* class, it was defined through its structural location in the economy and its objective revolutionary mission to overthrow capitalist exploitation. The working class, in other words, constituted history through its historical mission to liberate humanity through liberating itself and to usher in socialism. But this was not done under the banner of a dialectical conception of history, one in which the working class was both constituted and shaped by history. On the contrary, it was done under the banner of determinism, guided by the thesis of the inevitability of socialism.[3] Furthermore, within the confines of a Marxism informed by a theory of historical necessity, the economy was viewed as a homogeneous sphere guided by a single logic and its own laws of development. That is, conceived as a homogeneous milieu, the economy "was a level of society, but a level governed by a single logic which started from the category of commodity to produce out of itself all the other categories. In the end, the whole historical process was considered to be governed by the unique contradiction between forces and relations of production."[4] Similarly, the working class itself was seen as a homogeneous cultural formation, categorized through such all-embracing labels as "industrial proletariat" or "proletarian class."

In its more radical versions, Marxist theory has modified or rejected those assumptions about class and the primacy of the economic at the core of the orthodox Marxian tradition. For instance, Lukacs argued that the working class could be neither understood, nor its political behavior predicted, by pointing to its location in the relations of production. By providing a theory that pointed to the specificity of culture and everyday life in the shaping of consciousness, Lukacs claimed that domination had to be seen as a moment of lived experience, a form of ideological hegemony, rather than simply as a form of economic imposition.[5] In other words, class consciousness could not be explained as merely a reflection of the logic of capital. Instead, working-class existence had to be seen as being produced not only in the economic sphere, but also on the terrains of culture and ideology. Political struggle, in this case, was not subordinated to the laws of historical necessity, but to the ability of a working class to mediate critically and transform the nature of its own existence.

In our view, Lukacs's major contribution was to revive considerations of ideology and culture within Marxist theory, while at the same time rendering problematic the notion of the working class as a revolutionary subject. But in the end, Lukacs failed because of his belief in the classical Marxian view that the capitalist class, the degree of working-class organization, and socialist leadership were sufficient to produce revolutionary praxis, even as the ideological and material conditions of capitalism worked against such a development.

Like Lukacs, the Frankfurt School, especially Adorno, Horkheimer, and Marcuse, believed that the failings in classical Marxism did not signal the need to abandon Marxism as much as the theoretical imperative to revise it. And yet the theoretical scalpel wielded by the Frankfurt theorists cut deep into the body of Marxist doctrine. On the one hand, in the face of the rise of fascism, Stalinism, and the New Deal in the United States, they rejected the notion that the working class was fated to become the revolutionary negation of capitalism. On the other hand, they extended this critique and further argued that the basic categories of Marxism had failed as a sufficient basis for an emancipatory social theory.[6]

Underlying the claim that the fundamental categories of Marxism had failed, the Frankfurt School theorists not only rejected the notion that the working class occupied a privileged position as an *a priori* historical agent, but they also redefined the notion of domination and laid the theoretical groundwork for linking Marxism to the dominating logic of capitalist rationality. Regarding the working class, the Frankfurt School differed with Lukacs's formulation that the introduction of a theory of mediation and ideology was all that was necessary to help workers develop a self-conscious awareness of their oppression and the political strategy needed to overcome it. While Adorno, Horkheimer, and Marcuse did not devalue the importance of developing a theory of ideology, they believed that the forces of domination have rendered problematic the very possibility for critical thinking. Underlying this view was the Weberian notion that technocratic rationality, not the relations of production, represented the primary source of domination. For the Frankfurt School, classical Marxism's view of both history and its doctrine of historical inevitability was rendered inoperative as a result of the rise of the capitalist state, the politicization of science, and the end of the free-market economy. The state was not merely the instrument of the ruling class; it had become a new source of administrative domination arising out of the twentieth-century conjuncture between capital and technocratic rationality. Domination had to be understood as part of a theory of administration, not merely as part of a critique of capitalist production relations. Moreover, as the ideology of domination, technocratic rationality had to be analyzed as part of the totality of societal relations and not viewed exclusively within the realm of economic relations. Domination, as the Frankfurt School analyzed it, was equated with a notion of total administration that extended into the far reaches of the individual psyche as well as into all corners of everyday life and lived experience. While Marcuse and Horkheimer either searched for a revolutionary subject (students) in order to spark the working class or argued that worker self-management rather than the Marxist or capitalist infatuation with "progress" was the real path to socialist democracy, Adorno believed that only through a revival of theory that promoted human emancipation could the preconditions for oppositional practice be established.[7]

The importance of Adorno's position centers around his insistence on the centrality of theory as a separate but fundamental dimension of emancipatory practice, his rejection of Marxist identity theory, with its uncritical acceptance of science and its repressive view of nature as an object of domination, and his stress on the notion of difference as a condition of arriving at truth and negativity as the condition of freedom. In short, Adorno laid bare the links between capitalist rationality and Marxism by exposing how both ideologies shared the basic notions of identity theory. That is, common to both positions is a search for overcoming the contradictions between classes, the refusal to recognize the difference between nature and human society, and the refusal to accept negativity as the driving force of critical thought and human agency. In other words, for Adorno, Marxism negates the importance of difference and contradiction by arguing that if classes in the Marxist sense of the term disappear, the historical basis of contradiction also disintegrates. Similarly, Adorno's critique of identity theory is also a critique of positivist science. Like Marxism, positivist science posits the absolute difference between humans and nature, but paves the way for the objectification of both humans and nature. That is, under the twin imperatives of the logic of progress and control, contradictions disappear, and both humans and nature become revered as objects without qualities, objects to be worked on rather than to be understood in terms of their distinctiveness and place within an emancipatory view of life. Put another way, just as nature is reduced to its abstract, measurable features, so the labor process, consumption, politics, and public life are subordinated to the logic of administrative and specialization. Under this theoretical rubric, the management of things and persons becomes homologous. Needless to say, our external environment and our psychic structure are concrete material objects that can neither be reduced to their quantitative aspects for the purposes of control nor exploited instrumentally without dire consequences for the human race.

Similarly, as a result of their efforts to develop a theory of culture, the Frankfurt School also dealt a serious blow to classical Marxism's view of economism. In effect, this is developed around the position that Marxism had failed to grasp the materiality and relative autonomy of culture because of its notion that the mode of production was the motive force of society. As one of us has noted elsewhere:

> Here, the sharp separation of base and superstructure, in which production is not only accorded primacy with respect to historical development of the human species, but also the basis for all social, cultural, and ideological forms of discourse, is rejected. Instead, for the Frankfurt Marxists, within a complex totality, cultural phenomena cannot be accorded the status of merely a "reflex" of the relations of production. At certain historical periods, particularly in the era of late capitalism, ideas, mores and mass culture become material forces because they have gripped masses of people and serve, on the whole, to maintain the social cohesion of the existing order, despite frequent economic crises and wars that tend to produce the "objective conditions" for revolutionary change.[8]

In our view, the Frankfurt School's theoretical and empirical demonstrations of the role that culture played as part of the dominant society's attempt at the total administration of both human beings and things represents one of its most important, though flawed, insights. On the positive side, the Frankfurt theorists argued that the political grammar of cultural production was to be found not only in the artistic sphere, but throughout the realm of everyday life. For Adorno, Marcuse, and Horkheimer, modern culture was permeated with the imperatives of technocratic rationality, and its logic was played out in the culture industry, which shaped personal and political relationships according to the dictates of instrumental thought.[9] In this formulation, all thought was reduced to the demands of the existing society, occupied by the utility of ideas within the prevailing order rather than their transcendent qualities. On the negative side, the Frankfurt School theorists often assumed that the relationship between the dominating ideologies of the culture industry and the actual consciousness of the masses was one of cause and effect, or simple determinism. Consequently, complex mediating factors—social, psychological, and ideological—were treated in a reductionist fashion. Furthermore, a deep pessimism emerges from this perspective, one that is evident in its failure to highlight the contradictions, forms of resistance, and struggle that are part of oppositional cultures. Finally, there is a failure to examine the oppositional and emancipatory elements that exist in forms of popular culture such as music, art, and literature. The Frankfurt School's celebration of high culture may have helped to illuminate the oppositional nature of art sometimes present in its form and content, but this is done at the theoretical expense of removing the possibilities for locating similar oppositional elements in the spheres of popular and mass culture.

As important as the Frankfurt School was in reconstituting the fundamental categories of Marxism, in the end it remained wedded to the original theory. Despite its many revisions of Marxism, critical theory contained a highly orthodox strain. Underlying its notion of domination and its deep-rooted political pessimism there existed a flawed view of working-class agency and an unwarranted retreat from the terrain of critical praxis. In the first instance, the working class was unfairly viewed as the reified object of history, caught between the forces of an all-embracing mode of domination and its own unwillingness to actively resist it. In the second instance, there is no space for conscious praxis, especially in the later work of Adorno.[10] This represents a position based on a view of theory that lacks any viable conception of social contestation, while simultaneously supporting the orthodox notion that what history offered the future was either a crisis in capitalism and the victory of the working class, or increasing forms of domination, a one-dimensionality capable of eliminating revolutionary agency, integrating forms of oppositional culture, and ultimately containing any possibilities for social change.

RECONSTRUCTING MARXIST DISCOURSE:
BEYOND CLASS AND ECONOMISM

Faced with the dilemma of appropriating the most important insights provided by a critical Marxist tradition while simultaneously reaching beyond its discourse, a number of radical theorists have attempted to provide the theoretical foundation for rejecting the Marxian notion of class and class formation and the primacy of the economic in shaping society. At the core of their argument is the attempt to place the debate about class and economism in the wider context of radical theory and practice. That is, they boldly attempt to evaluate these issues not only as problems of theory and discourse but also as problems regarding the issues of power and strategy. This is an important theoretical task for radical social theory in general since such a project not only proposes to refute the central Marxian notions of class and history, but it also attempts to generate a discourse or counter-logic that points to new possibilities for social struggle and transformation.

According to Laclau and Mouffe, for example, Marxism in its various forms has failed to escape from the economistic logic that is its driving force.[11] They develop this position around the view that the grammar of economism can be seen in the classical Marxist reading of those institutions that occupy the terrains of culture and everyday life, that is, institutions or "superstructures" involved in the production of ideologies, social values, and social practices. In addition, the logic of economism can also be seen in the reductionist belief that the history, subjectivity, and consciousness of a group is determined by the nature of its class location. Finally, Marxist economism reveals itself in its view of history and the scientism that underlies it.

Classical Marxism has rarely taken seriously the categories of culture, ideology, and the lived experiences of everyday life. Trapped within the belief that the mode of production is the structuring force of human societies, classical Marxism has relied on a notion of power that sees domination as an outgrowth of capitalist economies governed by the dynamics of commodity production and history as a process primarily informed by contradictions rooted in the forces and relations of production. Conversely, contestation and struggle have been associated with the exercise of working-class power within the sphere of production. Production relations, in the classical Marxian view, have defined the nature and limits of both domination and contestation. This position fails for a number of reasons. The economic sphere is not governed by a single logic. Rather than being a homogeneous sphere, the economic realm is characterized by a number of discourses, which are ideological, political, and cultural in nature. Instead of existing prior to and independent of ideological and political conditions, the economic sphere is a site marked by various political and ideological determinations which point to an "hegemonic articulation of a complex of social relations."[12] As Noble,[13] Braverman,[14] and others[15] have shown, the labor process itself is a locus of domination and struggle. Rather than existing separately and being determined by the economic sphere, the political realm is a constituting aspect of the labor process existing both within and outside of the production sphere.

In this case, the discursive practices that characterize the institutions of everyday life become both a constituted and constituting aspect of social reality. In other words, to understand how subjectivities get established, ideologies formed, and struggles defeated, and how individual and collective histories unfold, it is necessary to view classes and the cultural formations of which they are a part as *not* being uniquely located and determined in the relations of production. Put another way, human beings are formed out of complex interactions, a multiplicity of determinations, which may be specified in advance in their structural limits but not their temporal course. The theoretical implications of this position are far reaching with respect to a number of issues. Class formation is now viewed as an *effect* of various relations, which are economic, ideological, and political in nature. Workers occupy a position in the labor process but are not formed exclusively within its context. Instead, class formation is linked to the larger social totality with its many-faceted relations and practices. That is, social agents are formed through their activities in neighborhoods, religious institutions, various political organizations, and other cultural associations. Not only are we arguing that a specific relation to the means of production is not an adequate condition for class formation, but we are also pointing out that the relationship between class and ideology is highly problematic. That is, since human agents are created within political and ideological spheres that cannot be viewed as a mere reflection of the economic sphere, social consciousness cannot be reduced to a particular class interest or ideology.[16]

Our refusal to limit the meaning of culture and ideology to the primacy of class boundaries provides a theoretical basis for rejecting the logic of the two-class model of capitalist society that has been the hallmark of both classical and revisionist Marxist theory. Underlying our rejection of this model is a more dialectical notion of ideology, contestation, and historical change. On one level, we claim that there is no universal class interest that defines the substance and nature of class struggle. Since workers are formed as a result of many different ideological and social interactions, there is no privileged economic interest that either shapes their consciousness or mediates their political activity. This becomes more clear when it is understood that class position represents only *one* terrain where contradictions are rooted and struggles emerge.

Contradictions and forms of oppression are also rooted in sexual, ethnic, and racial social practices and hierarchies, which cause antagonisms within the working class itself and make problematic the Marxist notion of historical inevitability. That is, Marxism's obsession with the two-class model of capitalist society has been falsely predicated on the notions that class formation and political struggle can be reduced to the ineluctable laws and structure of history. Far from being the outcome of contradictions produced exclusively or primarily in the labor process, the march of history represents the intervention of political subjects formed in many different sites who engage in struggles around which there may be many different outcomes. This is not to deny the importance of immediate producers as a possible source of struggle, as much as it is to point to the way in which culture and ideology become primary determinants in the shaping of human behavior. Moreover, it suggests that radical theory needs a new view of both hegemony and social time.

A principal assumption underlying our argument is that the notion of hegemony is a much broader category than class as a unit of analysis suggests. Neither the exercise of power in the interest of domination, nor the attempt of a social group to attain political ascendancy can be defined solely through the category of class rule and formation. For instance, the rise of new social movements around issues such as race, ecology, feminism, and sexual freedom refers to forms of hegemony and struggle that cannot be subsumed within the logic of class struggle. Such movements generally circumvent traditional Marxist analysis by posing questions about both domination and liberation that not only exist outside of most Marxist discourse, but are also often at odds with basic Marxist assumptions regarding how human subjects get constituted through their relations with nature and each other. This is evident regarding the traditional Marxian notion of social time.

By combining somewhat unevenly the theoretical insights of Bloch, Benjamin, Foucault, and others we can gain insight into how the Marxian notion of social time is flawed in a double sense.[17] First, its notion of historical necessity has given rise to an approach that underplays the radical discontinuities that exist in history. Underlying the Marxist theory of history is the assumption that an internal evolutionary logic characterizes the development of the forces of production along with class relations and class struggles.[18] We are arguing that it is in the internal tensions, the ruptures and the margins of history that one "squeezes" out the events, the details, the apparent insignificance or trivial features of institutional life in order to find something that may discover the *episteme,* a category connoting the way a historical period "sees" social life. Great historical events may conceal more than they reveal. Moreover, as Foucault has demonstrated, the issue of historical understanding is predicated on the deconstructing of events, texts, and images that make up the past. History has no essence, its meaning is to be found not only in what is included in mainstream explanations but also in what is excluded. What this type of historical explanation suggests is that the present gives rise to the past, a notion derived from a reading of the radical discontinuities of history: for example, discontinuities such as the Nazi-Soviet pact of the 1930s, the integration of the working class as part of capitalist society, and the rise of the welfare state in Western societies. To understand these events is to turn away from the logic of historical necessity as it informs Marxist theory and to focus instead on what Benjamin called the traces and fleeting images of history for clues to how history is constituted and what the future portends.[19]

Second, the notion of social time in Marxist discourse is flawed because of its refusal to acknowledge how the multilayering of the past, present and the future is present in the sedimented histories and discourses that constitute various individuals and social groups. There is no pure notion of uniform time characterizing either the historical subject or material culture. For instance, as Bloch's notion of the nonsynchronous indicates, not all people exist in the same "now." Moreover, it is further suggested that Marxism reveals its positivist ideology in its willingness to ignore the mul-

tilayered and dialectical nature of reality, to ignore all differences and contradictions except those granted to class formation and struggle. This is an
important theoretical insight. It is within a critique of economic and class
reductionism that Marxism remains a captive of scientism. It is to these
issues that we will now turn.

SCIENTISM, NATURE, AND THE RISE OF
NEW SOCIAL MOVEMENTS

The status of Marxism as a science as well as its view of science has
been an object of intense debate both within and outside of the Marxist
tradition.[20] But in spite of the problematic nature of Marxism as a science,
it is clear that the tradition of "scientific Marxism" has dominated socialist
and communist movements in the West as well as most governments that
act in the name of some brand of Marxism. Moreover, it is fair to argue
that, with few exceptions, the tradition that informs Marxist theory is in-
fatuated with science. Douglas Kellner comments on the nature of this
infatuation and some of its theoretical and political implications:

> This tradition of Marxism has fetishised science as if it were the sole source
> of knowledge and guide to action. 'Scientific Marxism' has also accommo-
> dated Marxism to positivist models of knowledge that sharply distinguished
> between value and fact, or subject and object, so as to portray value judg-
> ments from objective facts or laws. This bourgeois model of "scientificity"
> has informed left models of history which relegate human aspirations and
> powers to a subsidiary role in the march of History. From the time of the
> original German Social Democrats and Bolsheviks through the present, left
> political leaders have appealed for authority to "laws of history" or to "his-
> torical/objective necessity." This appeal helps legitimate their power by vir-
> tue of their scientific knowledge which ensures their own political correct-
> ness.[21]

Thus, the real tension in Marxism historically has centered around its
uncritical appropriation of positivist science rather than its attempt to create the theoretical foundation for a science that is both critical and emancipatory. Scientism rather than science has plagued Marxist theory from
its inception. This becomes clear in the way Marxists of various persuasions have been strongly influenced by central elements drawn from mainstream scientific and epistemological models. For instance, in orthodox
Marxist theories of culture and art, the notions of multiple causality and
indeterminacy are replaced by cause and effect models informed by theories of scientific explanation based on the instrumental logic of lawfulness,
falsifiability, quantification, and formulaic simplicity.[22] The instrumentalism and technical rationality that underlies Marxist theory also finds

expression in those theories of the state in which the latter is accorded no relative autonomy and as such is reduced to a purely instrumental role. The problem is no less severe in so-called revisionist Marxist discourse. In much of Althusser's work, for example, science is separated from ideology and granted some transhistorical objective validity.[23] He discards anything that smacks of humanism, moral critique, or Hegelianism as aspects of pre-Marxist ideology. The technological rationality at work in this view of science is particularly evident in Marxist theories of political economy. The general analysis of the relationship between scientism and Marxist political economy theory is captured in the following comment:

> Despite concrete differences, the new Marxist political economy shares many of the assumptions of its bourgeois counterparts. Among the most important is the classical conception of scientificity. While Marxists try to preserve the critical edge of political economy by insisting on the primacy of production relations for finding the dynamics of capitalist development, it proceeds, having inserted this sphere into economic theory, to an alternative within the science of economics rather than constituting itself as counterhegemonic to economic science as such. For the hegemony of bourgeois economic paradigms are reproduced not only by their practical orientation to policy, but also by their adherence to method as defined by eighteenth century natural science. Among the major premises of this is the requirement that all relations shall be subject to quantification—since the book of nature, including human nature is held to be written in the language of mathematics. Thus, the ability to penetrate the nature of the economic process is contingent upon framing questions that may be answered by mathematic calculation.[24]

One of the most disturbing aspects of Marxist scientism is revealed in its treatment of nature and the link this has to the subjugation of women and blacks in American society. The starting point for such an analysis is Marx's view of the relationship between labor and nature. For Marx, one of the presuppositions of human emancipation rested on the steady and progressive mastery of nature. Nature was seen as a laboratory and tool house to be subsumed under labor and converted into raw material for the production of use values. In other words, nature is seen as an object to be dominated and worked on in the interest of human mastery. It is the instrumentalization of nature, not its celebration, that links Marxism, once again, to the logic of scientific rationality. Nature, like objective knowledge, is something that exists "for us," its value mediated through the use of a science and technology that take manipulation and objectification as their defining qualities.

The rationality that informs this view of nature is grounded in a form of self-interest almost incapable of understanding either the limits of its own rationalism or the limits to which nature can be manipulated. Science in this case becomes an extension of the logic of domination. That is, it takes the mastery of nature as its central task with little or no understanding that embodied in such a view is a rationale that implies no normative stance against science and technique as forms of reification and domination that constitute specific ideological and political relations. Conversely, a critical science would be based on a rationality that recognizes the limits of nature's tolerance to scientific and technological manipulation. Such a rationality would take seriously the claims of an ecological movement that argues for developing a respect for nature's boundaries in order to sustain the life-giving support systems that make up the biosphere; it would take seriously the claims of a romantic tradition that views nature in noninstrumental terms and celebrates its aesthetic value. Finally, it would take seriously the claims of more recent social theorists who argue that the domination of humans and nature by capital is a related phenomenon of which Marxism remains captive.[25] It is this last point that provides a rationale for both indicting Marxism while simultaneously arguing for a radical discourse that supports the rise of a number of new social movements.

Since the late 1960s, four key social movements have emerged in the United States and have provided the theoretical basis for a new critical view of the current period of capitalist development. In their attempt to develop the elements of a counterhegemonic logic and oppositional culture, feminist, ecological, racial, and gay/lesbian movements have raised fundamental criticisms regarding the existing nature of social and political domination and the ways in which it is supported by both liberal and Marxist discourses. All of these movements are addressing an entirely new range of problems and in doing so are challenging cultural models and hierarchical structures that have refused to make the domination of nature problematic. What is unique about these perspectives is that they not only have challenged the underlying rationale of modern capitalist technology and science, which emphasizes the logic of expanding production as the measure of human progress, but they have also begun to articulate how this rationale has led to new forms of social domination.

It is imperative to take up the challenge of the new social movements and in doing so attempt to demonstrate how the link between the domination of nature and humanity works itself out on the terrain of everyday life. For instance, it can be argued that the impulses that lead to sexism and racism are connected to the violence waged against nature. That is, the logic that underlies patriarchal normative structures, that identifies blacks with forbidden sexuality, and that links women with dark, uncontrollable emotional and sexual feelings is deeply rooted in forms of hegemonic instrumental rationality and asceticism which the Marxist tradition shares. At the core of this rationality is the logic of domination, a logic aimed at reducing liberation to the mastery of nature, on the one hand, and overcoming the realm of necessity, on the other. A scientific method that reduces the external world to its merely quantitative dimensions has both influenced and prevented Marxism from developing an adequate critique of everyday life; another consequence has been that Marxism often finds itself pitted against the demands of feminists and ecology activists. For example, Marxism's view of liberation reduces desire and the obliteration of human suffering to freedom *from* nature through the development of technique and in the social realm as the concept of individual right. The message here is that Marxism lacks a discourse that seems capable of challenging more than the economic hegemony of capitalist relations. It does not recognize the need for a new historic bloc that can challenge the political and social basis of domination—that is, a number of autonomous movements that both demonstrate and argue for principles of self-management in opposition to male supremacy, modes of science and technology that perpetuate hierarchies, racial repression, and the domination of nature. We believe that Marxism has failed to recognize the real differences that exist between the positions and demands of blacks, Hispanics, and whites, women and men, and has refused to alter the parameters of its class-based discourse to make room for these insights. Trapped within its two-class model of domination, Marxist discourse fails to understand the ways in which the various forms of domination pit different factions of the working class against each other. Moreover, it fails to understand that a new praxis necessitates the emergence of oppositional cultures and spheres organized around the demands of autonomous social movements that take the elimination of all forms of domination, and not simply class domination, as their starting point. Underlying such an approach is the need to take seriously the desires, goals, and social practices that characterize those social groups organizing around new forms of democratic participation. Such movements not only point to new forms of social contestation, but they also reveal orthodox Marxism's deep-seated antagonism for any movement that challenges the Marxist claim to universal validity on the basis of the categories of class and economics. Jacoby's comment on the failure of Marxism in this regard is revealing:

> Against the dirty words—romanticism, subjectivism, aestheticism, utopianism—the clean ones are invoked—science, objectivity, rigor, structure. Here the final, almost psychological, contours of orthodox Marxism come into view. Adorno's characterization of positivism as "the puritanism of knowledge" holds true for orthodox Marxism. The goal is rigorous self-control and self-discipline. The asceticism of orthodox Marxism despises unregulated insight as if it were the threat it actually is. The sexual code is internalized as conceptual commandments: Suggestions of utopia and romanticism are tabooed as too suggestive. Scientific Marxism dreams not a life without anxiety but of master plans and interoffice memos. . . . Asceticism is the conceptual center of gravity of orthodox Marxism. . . . Along with Benjamin Franklin, orthodox Marxism is infused with the spirit of puritanism. The mental apparatus with permanent-press concepts tames the chaos

of desire. Orthodox Marxism confirms what Mary Douglas called the "purity rule": An increase "to disembody or etherealize the forms of expression" corresponds to a tightening net of social domination."[26]

One issue that needs to be raised here is that while the autonomous nature and demands of the new social movements represent an expression of democratic pluralism, it is important to recognize that such movements need also to organize at various times as part of a broader left movement. This becomes imperative, for instance, within the field of electoral politics, or, in some cases, as part of a radical attempt to promote forms of collective action against obvious and pressing forms of domination. Of course, how these groups might be reconciled around common issues is rather problematic at the present historical juncture.[27]

TOWARD A RECONSTRUCTED THEORY OF SCHOOLING

The work in this chapter points to three major theoretical tasks that have to be addressed in the reconstruction of a radical theory of schooling. First, it is necessary to articulate a new critical view that recognizes the political and strategic relevance of distinguishing between education and schooling. Second, it is imperative to develop a discourse and set of concepts around which this distinction becomes theoretically operational for developing more viable forms of political pedagogy. Third, theoretical work that focuses on social and cultural reproduction has to be developed in conjunction with analyses of *social and cultural production,* particularly in relation to historical studies of oppositional public spheres and the emergence of critical social movements.

More specifically, if radical pedagogy is to become conscious of its own limitations and strengths within the existing society, it must be viewed as having an important but limited role in the struggle for creating a more just society. This suggests that radical teachers not only reevaluate the material and ideological conditions under which they work, but also raise new questions about the educative role they may undertake outside of schools. At stake here is the need to extend the possibilities for developing educational work by redefining the distinction between radical forms of schooling and radical forms of education. Moreover, there is an urgent need to create a new discourse regarding the debate over the nature of education and what it means as a process of social and, hence, self-formation. Underlying the call for a new discourse about educational theory and practice is a dual concern. On the one hand, radical educators have to reconsider the content and purpose of school reform. On the other hand, they have to construct organic links with community people around the injustices that work in and through the schools. Furthermore, radical educators have to actively involve themselves with social movements and groups involved in developing oppositional public spheres outside of schools around broader educational issues. The dual role for radical pedagogues implicit in this analysis can be clarified by providing a distinction between schooling and education. Schooling as we use the term takes place within institutions that are directly or indirectly linked to the state through public funding or state certification requirements. Institutions that operate within the sphere of schooling embody the legitimating ideologies of the dominant society. Such institutions generally define their relationship to the dominant society in functional and instrumental terms, though, of course, room is also provided for forms of critical pedagogy. (But it is important to remember that, while such "room" is often provided within varied and changing circumstances, it exists within constraining ideological and material conditions.) Education is much more broadly defined and, used in this context, takes place outside of established institutions and spheres. In a radical sense, education represents a collectively produced set of experiences organized around issues and concerns that allow for a critical understanding of everyday oppression as well as the dynamics involved in constructing alternative political cultures. As the embodiment of an ideal, it refers to forms of learning and action based on a commitment to the elimination of class, racial, and gender oppression. As a mode of intellectual development and growth, its focus is political in the broadest sense in that it functions to create organic intellectuals and to develop a notion of active citizenry based on the self-dedication of a group to forms of education that promote models of learning and social interaction that have a fundamental connection to the idea of human emancipation.

For radical teachers, it is imperative that strategies be developed that take as their starting point an understanding of how knowledge and patterns of social relations steeped in domination come into being in schools, how they are maintained, how students, teachers, and others relate to them, and how they can be exposed, modified, and overcome, if possible. We suggest that such a strategy can be organized around a pedagogy that argues for a notion of critical literacy and cultural power, while simultaneously presenting a strong defense for schooling as a public service.

In the first instance, critical literacy would make clear the connection between knowledge and power. It would present knowledge as a social construction linked to norms and values, and it would demonstrate modes of critique that illuminate how, in some cases, knowledge serves very specific economic, political, and social interests. Moreover, critical literacy would function as a theoretical tool to help students and others develop a critical relationship to their own knowledge. In this case, it would function to help students and others understand what this society has made of them (in a dialectical sense) and what it is they no longer want to be, as well as what it is they need to appropriate critically in order to become knowledgeable about the world in which they live. Thus, critical literacy is linked to notions of self- and social empowerment as well as to the processes of democratization. In the most general sense, critical literacy means helping students, teachers, and others learn how to read the world and their lives critically and relatedly; it means developing a deeper understanding of how knowledge gets produced, sustained, and legitimated; and most importantly, it points to forms of social action and collective struggle.

As a form of critique, critical literacy would raise questions about modes of discourse and organization in schools that reduce learning and social practices to narrow technical dimensions. In other words, it would make problematic the instrumentalization and technicization of American education. Such a critique would analyze the technocratic ideology that dominates teacher education, the empiricist and technical thinking that governs state certification policies, and the "methodological madness" that generally characterizes curriculum theorizing, classroom social relations, and technicist modes of evaluation and selection. Of course, the reduction of thought to its strictly technical dimensions is only one aspect of how schools promote forms of political and conceptual illiteracy. At another level, schools disempower students, parents, and community people by disconfirming their histories, experiences, and, in effect, their role as historical agents. It is worth stressing that the concept of critical literacy moves beyond the call for counterhegemonic knowledge and social relations by acknowledging the need for educators to incorporate in their pedagogies the experiences and social practices that give a collective voice to specific individuals and groups. Critical literacy interrogates the cultural capital of the oppressed in order to learn from it; it functions to confirm rather than disconfirm the presence and voices of the oppressed in institutions that are generally alienating and hostile to them. But the call to take the cultural capital of oppressed and oppositional groups seriously should not be mistaken for the traditional liberal argument for educational relevance. The latter makes an appeal to a pedagogy responsive to the individual interests of the student in order to motivate him or her. Critical literacy responds to the cultural capital of a specific group or class and looks at the way in which it can be confirmed, and also at the ways in which the dominant society disconfirms students by either ignoring or denigrating the knowledge and experiences that characterize their everyday lives. The unit of analysis here is social, and the key concern is not with individual interests but with individual and collective empowerment.

It must be remembered that many students grow up within the boundaries of a class culture, popular culture, and a school culture. It is on the terrains of class and popular culture that students primarily develop an active voice. On the other hand, for many students school culture has little to do with either their histories or their interests; instead, it becomes the culture of "dead time," something to be endured and from which to escape. Of course, school culture is really a battleground around which meanings are defined, knowledge is legitimated, and futures are sometimes created and destroyed. It is a place of ideological and cultural struggle favored primarily to benefit the wealthy, males, and whites. But it is precisely because there is room for struggle and contestation in schools around cultural and ideological issues that pedagogies can be developed in the interest of critical thinking and civic courage.

Struggles within the schools have to be understood and linked to alliances and social formations that can affect policy decisions over the control and content of schooling. In effect, this means that radical teachers will have to establish organic connections with those parents and progressive groups who inhabit the neighborhoods, towns, and cities in which schools are located. Such alliances point to the need for radical teachers to join with feminists, ecology groups, neighborhood organizations, and parents in order to question and strongly influence school policy. Critical literacy in this case points to forms of knowledge and social practice that take seriously the notion of school democracy. Moreover, it points to the need to develop a real defense of schools as institutions that perform a public service, a service defined by the imperative to create a literate, democratic, and active citizenry—in this case, citizens who would be self-governing and actively involved in the shaping of public welfare.

The concept of radical education suggests some specific roles for radical pedagogues. It points to the necessity of struggle in sites other than those influenced and controlled by the state. It points to developing and working in oppositional public spheres aimed at achieving forms of collective power. Radical educational reform cannot rely on existing institutions to promote emancipatory change. The power of such institutions to set and limit the agenda for debate, the disrespect they exhibit for the oppressed, and their willingness to take economic and political action against oppositional voices make them unreliable as primary institutions for social change. Oppositional public spheres, on the other hand, provide the possibility for using collective aspirations and criticisms in the development of alternative cultures.

One reason for the development of an oppositional public sphere would be to help people develop what we call a healthy narcissism; that is, to provide the conditions through which people who have been excluded from making political decisions are able to recover their self, to find the basis on which to validate their own pleasures as well as their own work.

For radical educators, this means working with community groups to develop pockets of cultural resistance based on new forms of social relations and practices. It also means working with adults around those issues directly related to their lives, and acting as educative citizens struggling to establish a social and economic democracy. As radical educators, we can help to destroy the myth that education and schooling are the same thing, we can debunk the idea that expertise and academic credentials are the distinguishing marks of the intellectual; and, equally important, such educational work could also promote critical analyses of schooling itself and its relations to other institutions included in the state public sphere. Furthermore, radical educators could provide, discuss, and learn from historical and contemporary examples in which various social groups have come together to create alternative public spheres. Clearly, the elements of a democratic pedagogy can be exhibited through an examination of historically specific examples of alternative public spheres: the various organizations, clubs, cultural activities, and media productions created at the turn of the century by the nationality federations associated with the socialist party.

One of the most important reasons for creating alternative public spheres is to provide the conditions for the development of what we previously referred to as transformative intellectuals—that is, intellectuals who are part of a specific class and/or movement and who serve to give it an awareness of its own function not only in the economic but also in the social and political fields. The notion of transformative intellectual is important for educators because it broadens our understanding of the role of intellectuals by highlighting their social function as mediators between the state and everyday life. In this definition, the concept of intellectual is politicized. It rejects the current meaning of the term which restricts it to scholars, writers, and so on. Moreover, it suggests that oppositional groups have to form their own leadership, a leadership rooted in and committed to the history, experience, and set of goals they share with the people such intellectuals represent. It is worth repeating that this concept is important because it lays the theoretical ground for radical educators to examine their own organic connections to specific groups. At the same time, it points to establishing social relations with social groups in concrete institutional contexts such as neighborhoods and trade unions. Furthermore, its logic argues for democratic organizations in which intellectuals and the masses coalesce around building their ascendancy as groups fighting the material and ideological forces of domination, while simultaneously and self-consciously educating every member of the community to develop the general skills, knowledge, and capacities to govern.

Of course, at the present time only shadows of a left public sphere exist in the United States. These are organized mainly around journals, magazines, and academic publications. Some counter-institutions also exist in the form of alternative schools, but generally the left has given little political attention to creating cultural sites where people who share a common language, set of problems, and cultural experience can come to argue, learn, and act collectively to transform their lives. The obstacles against the development of alternative public spheres are enormous. The media, the power of the corporations, the culture industry, and the state all function to keep oppositional groups on the defensive. Under these circumstances, it becomes difficult but absolutely essential to establish new agendas that can examine the preconditions for establishing a left public sphere. As one of us has noted elsewhere:

> [The left's] independent role is primarily to create a left "public sphere," that is, to find the basis for enlarging the left political culture in ways that address existing conditions, but also to find ways of going beyond them. This task has several practical specifications: (1) a major effort to study the formation of intellectuals in the American context, both those who were destined to serve the prevailing order and those who attempted to define themselves as the opposition; (2) recognition that mass communications is the mainstream public sphere in which political and social ideas are disseminated and some-times debated—mostly among the organic intellectuals of capital; (3) investigation into the relations between economic, political, and ideological spheres in the United States as a specifically "late" capitalist society; and (4) a concrete and unsentimental analysis of the evolution and devolution of the American working class—particularly its ideological formation and changing composition—and the trade unions. This would deepen our understanding of the centrality of race, sex, and ecological politics in both the discourses of domination and the political culture of the left.[28]

In conclusion, it seems imperative that radical educators recognize the limits of orthodox and neo-Marxian discourses. This is not a call to abandon Marxism as much as it is to critically appropriate what is relevant to the present historical and contemporary juncture and to develop it as part of a new radical social theory that points to existing possibilities and more expanded opportunities for radical educational work. Of course, what we have provided in this chapter is a broad theoretical sweep that draws from the work of a number of critical theorists. The point has been to make a small contribution to rethinking those ideologies that have traditionally informed radical educational theory and practice and to provide some theoretical contributions for creating the basis for a new and more viable radical educational discourse. We will continue this theoretical effort in the next chapter by narrowing the focus of our analysis to the radical tradition of curricula criticism and the form of discourse needed to engage in radical forms of curriculum production.

NOTES

1. See A. Giddens, *Profiles and Critiques in Social Theory* (Berkeley: University of California Press, 1982); P. Piccone, *Italian Marxism* (Berkeley: University of California Press, 1983); B. Jessop, *The Capitalist State* (Oxford, England: Martin Robertson and Co., 1982); E. Lunn, *Marxism and Modernity* (Berkeley: University of California Press, 1982); R. Ryan, *Marxism and Deconstruction* (Baltimore: Johns Hopkins University Press, 1982).

2. Catharine A. MacKinnon, "Feminism, Marxism, Method, and the State: An

Agenda for Theory," in N. O. Keohane, M. Z. Rosaldo, and B. C. Gelpi, eds., *Feminist Theory: A Critique of Ideology* (Chicago: University of Chicago Press, 1982).

3. Examples of theorists who have recently engaged in this type of analysis include: J. Cohen, *Class and Civil Society: The Limits of Marxian Critical Theory* (Amherst: University of Massachusetts Press, 1982); A. Gorz, *Farewell to the Working Class* (Boston: South End Press, 1982); A. Touraine, *The Voice and the Eye* (New York: Oxford University Press, 1981); C. Castoriadis, *La Societe Bureaucratique* (Paris: Editions 10/18, 1973–76, Vols. 1–4); A. Gouldner, *The Two Marxisms* (New York: Seabury Press, 1980); R. Jacoby, *Dialectic of Defeat: Contours of Western Marxism* (New York: Cambridge University Press, 1981); J. Habermas, *Communication and the Evolution of Society* (Boston: Beacon Press, 1979); J. Baudrillard,*The Mirror of Production* (St. Louis: Telos Press, 1975).

4. Interview with E. Laclau and C. Mouffe, "Recasting Marxism: Hegemony and New Social Movements," *Socialist Review,* 12:6 (1982), p. 93.

5. G. Lukacs, *History and Class Consciousness,* trans. R. Livingstone (Cambridge, Mass.: MIT Press, 1971), pp. 46–81.

6. M. Horkheimer, *Eclipse of Reason* (New York: Oxford University Press, 1947); T. Adorno, *Negative Dialectics* (New York: Seabury Press, 1973); H. Marcuse, *One Dimensional Man* (Boston: Beacon Press, 1964).

7. An excellent compilation and commentary on the Frankfurt School can be found in A. Arato and E. Gebhardt, eds., *The Essential Frankfurt School Reader* (New York: Urizon Books, 1978); also see D. Held, *Introduction to Critical Theory* (Berkeley: University of California Press, 1980).

8. S. Aronowitz, *Crisis in Historical Materialism* (South Hadley, Mass.: Bergin and Garvey, 1981), p. 231.

9. See especially, T. Adorno and M. Horkheimer, *Dialectic of Enlightenment,* trans . J. Cumming (New York: Seabury Press, 1972) (originally published in 1947).

10. Adorno, op. cit.

11. Laclau and Mouffe, op. cit.

12. Ibid., p. 93.

13. D. Noble, *America by Design* (New York: Alfred A. Knopf, 1977).

14. H. Braverman, *Labor and Monopoly Capital* (New York: Basic Books, 1979).

15. M. Buraway, *Manufacturing Consent* (Chicago: University of Chicago Press, 1979); R. Edwards, *Contested Terrain* (New York: Basic Books, 1979).

16. See also A. Przeworski, "Proletariat into Class: The Process of Class Formation from Karl Kautsky's 'Class Struggle' to Recent Controversies," *Politics and Society* (1977), pp. 343–401; G. Therborn, "Which Class Wins," *New Left Review* 138 (March–April 1983), pp. 37–55.

17. E. Bloch, "Nonsynchronism and Dialectics," *New German Critique* 11 (Spring 1977), pp. 22–38; E. Bloch, *On Karl Marx* (New York: Herder and Herder, 1977); W. Benjamin, *Illuminations,* ed. Hannah Arendt, trans. Harry Zohn (New York: Schocken Books, 1969); M. Foucault, *Discipline and Punish: The Birth of the Prison* (New York: Pantheon, 1977); M. Foucault, *Power and Knowledge: Selected Interviews and Other Writings,* ed. Colin Gordon (New York: Pantheon Press, 1981).

18. Theoretical support for this position can be found in E. O. Wright, "Gid-

dens' Critique of Marxism," *New Left Review* 138 (March–April 1983), pp. 11–35.

19. Benjamin, *Illuminations,* op. cit., pp. 252–267.

20. See P. Feyerabend, *Against Method* (London: Verso Books, 1975); C. O. Schrag, *Radical Reflections and the Origin of the Human Sciences* (West Lafayette, Ind.: Purdue University Press, 1980); L. Levidow and B. Young, eds., *Science, Technology and the Labor Process,* vol. 1 (Atlantic Highlands, N.J.: Humanities Press, 1981); H. Gadamer, *Reason in the Age of Sciences,* trans. F. Laurence (Cambridge , Mass.: MIT Press, 1981).

21. D. Kellner, "Science and Method in Marx's *Capital,* " *Radical Science Journal,* no. 13 (1983), p. 39.

22. For two major discussions on this issue, see A. S. Vasquez, *Art and Society: Essays in Marxist Aesthetics* (New York: Monthly Review Press, 1973); S. Morawski, *Inquiries into the Fundamentals of Aesthetics* (Cambridge, Mass.: MIT Press, 1974), especially chapter 7; for a classic example of the reduction of art to a class analysis, see A. Lunarcharsky, *On Literature and Art* (Moscow: Progress Publishers 1973), pp. 9–21.

23. L. Althusser and E. Balibar, *Reading Capital* (London: New Left Books, 1970).

24. Aronowitz, *Crisis in Historical Materialism,* p. 142.

25. A. Gorz, *Ecology as Politics,* trans. Patsy Vegderman and Jonathan Cloud (Boston: South End Press, 1980); W. Leiss, *The Limits to Satisfaction* (Toronto: University of Toronto Press, 1978).

26. Jacoby, *The Dialectic of Defeat,* p. 35.

27. See. E. Feher and A. Heller, "From Red to Green," *Telos* 59 (Spring 1984), pp. 35–44.

28. S. Aronowitz, "Socialism and Beyond," *Socialist Review* 13:3 (May–June 1983), pp. 16–17.

Chapter Six

Curriculum Theory, Power, and Cultural Politics

The relationship between school culture and power has suffered tradition-ally from the unwillingness of conservative and critical educators to give serious consideration to how schools as political sites *both* repress and produce subjectivities. The key term here is "both," a term that suggests that schools not only constitute subjectivities through language, knowl-edge, and social practices, but also function in a related fashion to dis-credit, disorganize, and dismantle specific ways of experiencing and mak-ing sense of the world. Conservative educators, for example, have focused on the production and maintenance of what is legitimated as a universal set of symbolic values and knowledge forms.[1] This defense of, call it high culture, classical culture, or simply a common culture, has also found sup-port among many progressive educators who have criticized schools less for reproducing it in the curriculum than for failing to democratize domi-nant school culture to make it accessible to all students.

On the other hand, the leading tradition within radical educational the-ory has argued that curricula and school culture share a particular rela-tionship with ruling class forms of social life and function to primarily repress those active forms of cultural capital that express and affirm the histories, languages, and social practices of subordinate groups. In this view, culture becomes a political category linked to the power of a ruling class to define its own values and practices as universal and beyond reproach.[2]

We hold that both of these pedagogical positions share a view of power and curriculum theory that disables rather than enables critical learning and social transformation. Power is something that either works through the curriculum in a way that goes unquestioned, specifically as it defines what counts as legitimate forms of school knowledge, or is seen as a neg-ative instance of social control that represses the possibilities for struggle and resistance. In either case, power loses its dialectical quality as a positive and negative force that works both on and through people. Consequently, the notion of historical agency in both positions (and their many variants) either disappears under the rubric of producing a universal culture or collapses under the logic of capital and its necessity to reproduce the dominant culture. Furthermore, radical discourses about curriculum theory and schooling generally do not see oppositional cultures as a form of production around which different levels of contestation are organized over contrasting orders of representation, lived experiences, and values. Similarly, orthodox radical critics limit the notion of cultural practices to specific cultural forms as they work in the schools, in the popular media, or in the family. They make but little effort to extend the dynamics of the cultural field (with its emphasis on the production, organization, and control of signifying practices) to other spheres such as the workplace and a number of other public spheres where human beings produce meanings within relations of exchange and power.

Our brief critical commentary on conservative and radical views of curriculum and culture points to the need to rethink the very nature of curriculum theory and its fundamental relationship to emancipatory practice. We will suggest a radically different set of categories and discourses on which to develop a model of curriculum theory and practice. But before examining the language of critique as it has developed in various radical theories of schooling, we want to provide some theoretical categories that might help rethink curriculum discourse and practice as it is currently constituted. These categories are both defined and organized around the following theoretical concerns: (1) an expanded notion of the political, (2) an attempt to link the languages of critique and possibility, (3) a discourse that views teachers as public intellectuals, (4) and a reformulation of the relationship between theory and practice. As major organizing principles that will inform our view of curriculum theory and study, we want to articulate a general definition of each of these categories and then develop their implications in the final sections of this chapter.

First, we want to rescue the notion of the political from its conservative and liberal advocates by arguing that its meaning should include the entire way we organize social life along with the power relations that inform its underlying social practices. In this case, curriculum theory becomes both a form of representation and a set of social practices that are inextricably related to specific cultural and social forms as well as particular ideologies. As a starting point for assessing any discourse labeled as curriculum theory, the deeper political grammar that structures its view of power, sexuality, history, identity, and the future would be openly engaged and subject to critical analysis as a form of political discourse. In short, schooling is a matter of social practice and is both permeated with normative considerations and relations of power. In essence, it is a political process that simply cannot be seen as either neutral or objective.

Second, we believe that any notion of curriculum theory has to be organized and developed around what we have in previous chapters called the languages of possibility and critique. With respect to the discourse of possibility, we are proposing that the study of curriculum be informed by a language that acknowledges curriculum as the introduction, preparation, and legitimation for particular forms of social life. Underlying such a political project would be a fundamental commitment to the notions of hope and emancipation. Curriculum theory as a form of cultural politics would be linked to the goals of self- and social empowerment. Moreover, as an expression of specific forms of knowledge, values, and skills, it would take as its object the task of educating students to become active and critical citizens, capable of intellectual skills and willing to exercise the forms of civic courage needed to struggle for a self-determined, thoughtful, and meaningful life.

Informed by the language of possibility and hope, curriculum theory must acknowledge the partisan nature of human learning and provide a theoretical foundation for linking knowledge to power and commitment to the development of forms of community life that take seriously the principles of fraternity, liberty, and equality. Thus, curriculum theory would be steeped in the ethical and political imperative of educating students to provide the moral and intellectual leadership necessary to struggle for a qualitatively better life for all. It is worth pointing out that curriculum discourse would relate knowledge and power in a threefold sense. First, it would interrogate all knowledge claims for the interests that structure both the questions they raise as well as the questions they exclude. Second, knowledge claims about all aspects of schooling and society would be analyzed as part of wider cultural processes intimately connected with the production and legitimation of class, racial, and gender social formations as they are reproduced within asymmetrical relations of power. Third, knowledge would be viewed as part of a collective learning process intimately connected to the dynamics of struggle and contestation both within and outside of schools.

Far from being treated as "objective" and as something simply to be mastered, knowledge claims that emerge within the curriculum would be analyzed as part of a wider struggle over different orders of representation, conflicting forms of cultural experience, and diverse visions of the future. Underlying this view of curriculum theory lies the important task of helping students rethink both the democratic possibilities within schools and the wider society of which they are a part. It is at this nexus between school reform and societal reconstruction that the languages of critique and possibility both meet and inform each other.

Third, if the theoretical significance of the languages of critique and possibility is not to be reduced to empty abstraction, we must point to another fundamental category for rethinking the meaning of curriculum theory. Simply put, curriculum theory must define the role of teacher-educators as intellectuals engaged in various forms of political struggle. The importance of this category has to be judged, in part, against the assumption that curriculum theory and the programs in which it is produced in many universities not only have been stripped of a democratic vision, but they have also correspondingly functioned to educate students less as intellectuals and reflective practitioners than as obedient civil servants and skillful technicians. Viewing teachers as intellectuals provides the opportunity to counter this process and to link emancipatory possibilities to critical forms of leadership by rethinking and restructuring the role of curriculum workers.

But it is important to reemphasize the argument we made in chapter two that the concept of "intellectual" does more than suggest the political processes that structure the ideological and material conditions that make up what is known as curriculum work, specifically, and schooling in the more general sense. It also provides a starting point for educators to examine their own histories, that is, their connections to the past and to particular social formations, cultures, and sedimented experiences, which, in part, define who they are and how they assimilate everyday experience. Central to such a task is having teachers recognize the partiality and historically formed politics of their own location. Furthermore, viewing teachers as intellectuals highlights for students the importance for them to examine the dialectical character of power as both an ideological and material force. In other words, students need to understand how power works dialectically as a positive and negative process within the many contradictions that make up school life. More specifically, this suggests the need for a mode of curriculum theorizing that makes concrete studies around how power functions to structure language, how it is used as a force to administer and shape the politics of the body,* and how it is implicated in the organization of time and space. Underlying these concerns is the need to understand the conscious and tacit role that curriculum workers as intellectuals play in mediating such processes. We will return to this issue later in this chapter.

Fourth, if curriculum theory is to be linked to what we call a *cultural politics,* it will be necessary to redefine the relationship between theory and practice as it has unfolded traditionally within the curriculum field itself.[3] In order to develop methods of inquiry that overcome rather than reinforce the division of labor between theory and practice, particularly as it defines the university—public school relationship, curriculum research will

* We mean to suggest that the body is not merely a vehicle through which "mind" or "consciousness" functions, but a field of contestation and a site by which subjectivity is constructed socially and politically.

have to become more closely tied to active forms of community life. This suggests that theory be understood as the production of forms of discourse that arise from specific social sites and that each context involves a particular locus of practice intimately related to a specific discourse. Thus, while university people theorize out of one particular site, public school teachers and administrators theorize from a different but equally important context. The point is that we recognize that these sites give rise to various forms of theoretical production and cannot be seen as, respectively, representative for the development of theory, on the one hand, and the implementation of practice, on the other. Each of these different institutional spheres provides diverse and critical insights into the problems of curriculum production and schooling. And it is around common projects developed primarily in the public schools and other public spheres that research programs should be organized in cooperation with university people, neighborhood groups, oppositional social movements, labor unions, and other cultural workers.

It is at this point that we want to shift the theoretical terrain from a general discussion of what the discourse of a critical theory of curriculum and cultural politics might look like to a more specific analysis of how the language of critique has emerged within the last fifteen years around a radical educational discourse. It is to this issue that we will now turn.

RADICAL PEDAGOGY AND THE LANGUAGE OF CRITIQUE

Within the last fifteen years, a number of alternative pedagogical traditions have attempted to take as a fundamental beginning in their analysis of schools the relationship between knowledge and power. Underlying all of these approaches has been the concerted effort to link schooling with the notions of domination and liberation. As we detailed in chapter five, schools were seen as having a one-sided relationship with the social dynamics of power. In some cases, schools were viewed as being neither all-encompassing footholds of domination nor untainted repositories of freedom. But more often than not, schools were viewed as having a particular relationship with the existing society, one in which they generally served to reproduce dominant interests and values. In effect, schools were seen as agencies of social and cultural reproduction, exercising power through the underlying interests embodied in the overt and hidden curricula, while at the same time offering limited possibilities for critical teaching and student empowerment.

We want to argue that the various perspectives that developed within and out of these alternative views of education, sometimes labeled the "new" sociology of education, have provided an important theoretical foundation for grappling with the fundamental questions of what schools actually do as political and cultural spheres and how they might be used in the quest for human freedom and dignity. We will begin by summarizing some of the arguments we presented in chapters four and five. In the most general sense, the "new" sociology of education provided a discourse for reexamining the relationship among knowledge, culture, and power, on the one hand, and schooling and the issue of social control, on the other. That is, the alternative perspectives that emerged out of this tradition played a significant role in undermining mainstream assumptions about the political and social neutrality of the school curriculum. In addition, they made clear that all knowledge claims are forms of intelligibility rooted in specific normative and political interests, the importance of which we mentioned earlier. Furthermore, they made a strong case for the significance of honoring forms of life and language that characterized the cultures of subordinated groups, whether they be the excluded majorities of women, ethnics, or members of the working classes.

We want to comment on some of the major contributions that each of these various alternative positions have made to understanding how power, culture, and knowledge function as part of the fabric of school life and curricula discourse. We also want to argue that these approaches to schooling ultimately fall short in providing the theoretical elements necessary for a comprehensive and critical theory of curriculum and cultural politics. More specifically, in failing to delineate a dialectical notion of power, culture, and an adequate answer to the question of what counts as really useful knowledge, these positions have not been successful enough in moving from a language of critique to a language of possibility and transformation.

In the early 1970s Michael Young and his associates launched a major critique of traditional educational theory and practice by arguing that it offered no real basis for understanding the relationship between knowledge and power.[4] It criticized, for example, traditional theory's claim that school knowledge and culture were relatively objective; it decried mainstream educational theory's silence about how schools might be influenced by interest groups that reproduced and benefited from deeply rooted ideological and structural inequalities in the dominant society; and it launched a sophisticated critique of mainstream theory's use of an epistemology that largely reduced pedagogy to the celebration of methodological refinement rather than critical thought. Rather than viewing knowledge as objective, as merely something to transmit to students, proponents of the new sociology of education argued that the school curriculum represented an ordering of school knowledge, one that was constructed through a selection process of emphasis and exclusion. Knowledge, in this case, like the culture it legitimated was deeply implicated in specific power relations.

The call for a critical sociology of education was important because it called into question the production, organization, transmission, stratification, allocation, and evaluation of *knowledge* within schools. And in doing so, it made school knowledge problematic and thereby gave us a measure against which to analyze many of the common sense assumptions and meanings that underscored oppressive, yet often tacit, forms of classroom control. This problematic can be characterized by a series of questions that became the basis for a new model for educational theory and research. These included:

What counts as school knowledge?

How is school knowledge organized?

What are the underlying codes that structure such knowledge?

How is what counts as school knowledge transmitted?

How is access to such knowledge determined?

What kind of cultural system does school knowledge legitimate?

Whose interests are served by the production and legitimation of school knowledge?[5]

As important as the early approaches of the "new" sociology of education were in analyzing the relationship between knowledge and control, they ultimately fell short of developing an adequate theory of culture, schooling, and power. In effect, social control in this view was linked to power relations defined primarily through the various ways in which teachers and other educators defined and legitimated school knowledge. Furthermore, the relationship between power and repression was reduced to the connection between knowledge as a form of cultural production and its uncritical implementation by teachers. At the same time, the pedagogical strategy for change that emerged from this position centered around demystifying the common sense and taken-for-granted assumptions that structured teacher practice and school organization.[6]

The problems that emerged from this position centered around a number of issues that were taken up by later supporters of the "new" sociology of education. These included: an uncritical emphasis on the social construction of school culture and knowledge forms, one that eventually developed into a relativist posture suggesting that all forms of knowledge were equally valid; the naive assumption that social change was synonymous with a change in individual consciousness; the failure to acknowledge linkages between the dominant school ideologies and knowledge forms that constituted the mainstream culture in the wider society; and, finally, the refusal to acknowledge the material and ideological constraints that operated in schools so as to make the realization of a critical view of the future exceedingly difficult.

Early versions of the "new" sociology of education related power and control to the social construction of school knowledge and culture. Later versions focused primarily on the ways in which various school practices reproduced the logic of the workplace and dominant cultural capital within the capitalist order. Within this framework, the focus of research and analysis became the issue of how power relations outside of the schools penetrated and shaped the organization of knowledge and social practices within them. Power in this instance was connected to what we have previously called the reproductive thesis of schooling. Schools were now portrayed and connected to ideological and material forms of power in the dominant society and were viewed as reproductive in a dual sense. First, schools provided different classes and social groups with the knowledge and skills they needed to occupy their respective places in a labor force stratified by class, race, and gender. Second, schools were also seen as reproductive in a cultural sense, functioning in part to distribute and legitimate forms of knowledge, values, language, and modes of style that produced and sustained dominant cultures and their underlying economic and political interests.

For theorists such as Bowles and Gintis, the reproductive approach took the form of a structuralist analysis.[7] Schools were analyzed as sites that reproduce through the hidden curriculum social relations that corresponded to the relations of dominance and subordination in the workplace. Simply put, schools were portrayed as places that prepare students from different socioeconomic classes for the diverse qualities, skills, and dispositions they will need to occupy highly stratified and class- and gender-specific positions in the labor force. The crucial insight here is that working-class students and minorities learn how to be punctual, how to follow the rules, and how to adjust to the alienating demands of unskilled and degrading work, whereas upper middle- and ruling class students learn how to exercise leadership functions, think creatively, work with a high degree of autonomy, and internalize the individualist-consumer ethos that is the ideological bedrock of capitalist rationality.[8]

This approach is valuable because it makes evident how class and power bear down on classroom social relations. By pointing to the structured silences that permeate much of the classroom pedagogy, it helps to deconstruct the ways in which dominant ideologies are embedded in the often ignored relations that make up the texture of everyday life in schools. It points, for instance, to the way specific ideologies are represented in the arrangement of class space and seating arrangements, to the political use of tracking, to the ideologies that structure the form and content of teacher talk, and to the underlying ideological codes at work in the selection and presentation of classroom instructional material.[9] But this perspective has serious problems. As has been noted in chapter four, this position generally ignores the question of how students and teachers produce forms of resistance or, for that matter, how they mediate school life through the histories, languages, and experiences that constitute their various cultural backgrounds and histories.

Another variation of the "new" sociology of education attempted to come to grips with the exclusive relation between culture and power. In these analyses, the issue of power and control in education are analyzed through the linkages among culture, class, and domination. Rather than holding schools as the neutral arbiter of a common culture and language, this position views schools as sites in which contradictory cultures and social relations are subordinated to the political imperatives of a dominant culture, one that functions as the mediating link between dominant class interests and everyday life. Bourdieu and Passeron, for example, argue that the culture transmitted by the school is related to the various cultures that make up the wider society in that it confirms the culture of the dominant groups while disconfirming the cultures of subordinate groups.[10]

The relationships between power and culture have been explored in the various ways in which different forms of linguistic and cultural competencies, whether they be specific ways of talking, dressing, acting, thinking, or presenting oneself, are accorded a certain privileged value and status in schools.[11] For example, it can be argued that in North American and Australian schools white middle-class linguistic forms, modes of style, and values represent "honored" forms of cultural capital. Those students who represent cultural forms that might rely on "restricted" linguistic codes, working-class or oppositional modes of dress (long hair, earrings, outlandish clothing), who downplay the ethos of individualism, who espouse a form of solidarity, or who reject those forms of academic knowledge that embody particular versions of history, social science, and success at odds with their own cultural experiences and norms, often find themselves excluded from the reward system of schools as well as the larger society. What is important to remember here is that the dominant school culture functions differently not only to legitimate the interests and values of dominant groups, but it also functions to marginalize and disconfirm knowledge forms and experiences that are extremely important to subordinate and oppressed groups. This can be seen in the way in which school curricula often ignore the histories of women, racial minorities, and the working classes. It can also be seen in the way in which school curricula reproduce the division between mental and manual labor by celebrating "academic or theoretical" forms of knowledge over practical subjects. Thus, what this position illustrates is the way in which schools legitimate dominant forms of culture through the hierarchically arranged bodies of knowledge that make up the curriculum as well as the way in which certain forms of linguistic capital and the individual (rather than the collective) appropriation of knowledge is rewarded in schools.

As important as this position is on the relationship among power, culture, and schooling, it also suffers from some serious theoretical flaws, the most important of which is its failure to address how oppositional forms of culture get created, contained, or sustained in schools. At the heart of this theoretical posture is the refusal to focus on how oppositional culture gets produced *rather* than merely reproduced. Moreover, underlying this one-sided treatment of culture is the false notion that students are merely passive in the face of oppressive school practices. Similar to other reproductive theories, power is linked to forms of control that become synonymous with the logic of domination. There is no sense here of how power works in the positive sense as a form of opposition, or even as a form of affirmation for those groups engaged in defining the world and human experiences in terms that move outside of dominant discourses.

Of course, it must be stressed that the "new" sociology of education and the various reproductive models we have discussed in general terms provide us a view of school knowledge, classroom relations, and school culture which are treated as being both problematic and normative. That is, various aspects of school experience are portrayed as social constructions that embody ethical, historical, and political interests. The important message is that the underlying codes that inform the various types of signification that constitute the lived reality of schooling have to be interrogated rather than merely transmitted and passively suffered. This perspective contains a powerful challenge to the traditional emphasis on the management of school knowledge and the equally ideological view that organization of school life is merely a question of administration. It is also important to point out that reproductive accounts have provided a new research agenda by raising traditionally ignored questions about how meaning gets sustained in schools, how teachers and students come to understand their own school experiences, and how knowledge and school culture are implicated in the domination of the mind and the body. And yet, as significant as this research agenda appears when compared to what has been on the historical burner, the question still remains as to whether the possibilities exist for teachers to understand and apply such an agenda to their own daily classroom experiences.

We want to demonstrate at this point that one of the more important contributions provided by reproductive accounts of schooling is a theory and language of critique that has been translated into a number of practical applications. These models of critique are important in a twofold sense. First, they illustrate critical approaches to unraveling the relationship between schools and social control. Second, they constitute a starting point for recognizing the theoretical limitations that underlie this form of criticism and the need to move beyond it in the quest for a more comprehensive critical theory of pedagogy.

We have distinguished three basic approaches that predominate among modes of critique associated with reproductive models of schooling. These include: theories of knowledge forms; theories of knowledge content; and theories of classroom social relations and knowledge appropriation. These are, of course, ideal-typical categories derived for the sake of clarity and analysis.

THEORIES OF KNOWLEDGE FORMS

At the core of this critique is the notion that in recent years new kinds of curriculum packaging have been developed that represent a new form of social control. Carol Buswell among others has argued that the ideology embedded in much of the prepackaged curricula materials now being sold to schools represents a direct assault on the traditional role of the teacher as an intellectual whose function is to conceptualize, design, and implement learning experiences suited to the specificity and needs of a particular classroom experience.[12] By examining the structuring principles that constitute these curricula approaches, it has been argued that they contain a form of rationality that separates conception from execution and thereby reduce teachers to simply carrying out predetermined content and instructional procedures. This is clear in Michael Apple's study of a series of curricula packages designed for teaching science in elementary schools in the United States.[13]

Apple argues that the science curricula he examined embodied forms of technical control that in effect actually promoted a type of deskilling among teachers.[14] That is, by dictating every aspect of the teaching process, these curriculum packages reproduce standardization and control that reduces the teacher to the status of a mere technician implementing ideologies and interests constructed by people external to the actual experiences of his or her classroom and student interests. Apple is worth quoting on this issue:

> Skills that teachers used to need, that were deemed essential to the craft of working with children—such as curriculum deliberation and planning, designing teacher and curricular strategies for specific groups and individuals based on intimate knowledge of these people—are no longer necessary. With the large scale influx of prepackaged material, planning is separated from execution. The planning is done at the level of the production of both the rules for use of the material and the material itself. The execution is carried out by the teacher. In the process, what were previously considered valuable skills slowly atrophy because they are less often required.[15]

The most important aspect of this critique is that it alerts teachers to the interests that underlie the form of curricula materials. Moreover, it links these interests to issues of social control and domination, and in doing so provides teachers with some insight into how the cultural forms that find their way into schools are influenced and shaped by interests in the larger society.

The most dramatic and the most representative instance of the separation of curriculum design and execution is, of course, the ordinary textbook—though, with the introduction of Chris Whittle's "Channel One" into the public schools, the issue of teacher and student deskilling finds a new home in the classroom use of commercial television. Increasingly, colleges and universities are employing these prepackaged materials rather than using monographs, critical essays, or traditional studies in the humanities and social sciences. The textbook purports to be a distillation of the accumulated knowledge of the discipline. Its tone is "objective" just as its style is authoritative. That is, the garden variety textbook provides little, if any debate, concerning different positions on a particular object of knowledge. The seamlessness of the narrative betrays a definite point of view and ideological content. Jean Anyon among others has performed valuable research on the ideological slant of secondary school history texts, and Jean Brenkman has shown the degree of business intervention in what is taught in public schools.

However, these important studies do not exhaust the connection between textbooks and the degradation of teacher work. In most cases, textbooks are accompanied by lesson plans, "work" books, and other materials designed to relieve the teacher of all but the most minimal participation in curriculum formation. In sociology, for example, as with other social sciences, these packages coincide with the increasing tendency of colleges and universities to employ adjunct instructors and teaching assistants to teach the introductory courses, leaving the tenure track faculty to offer more advanced courses. In the major universities, a regular faculty member may lecture once or twice a week to as many as 500 students, while sections of about fifty students are taught by graduate student assistants. In other cases, the past two decades' surplus of academic labor in comparison to employment opportunities and budget cuts has encouraged administrators to hire adjuncts, many of whom already possess Ph.D.s. Presumably, the prepackaged textbook is a control device, not only on the content of what counts as knowledge, but also on the teachers themselves who lose their autonomy because they are required to use these standardized materials.

THEORIES OF KNOWLEDGE CONTENT

Theories of knowledge content represent one of the most traditional forms of critique used by reproductive theorists. In this type of analysis, curriculum materials such as school texts, films, and other forms of representation are examined for the ideologies that underlie specific knowledge claims. An exemplary form of this type of criticism has been developed by Jean Lind-Brenkman in her study of school textbooks produced by many of America's leading industries.[16] Attempting to provide models of critique that reveal the concealed interests in these materials, Brenkman links formal analysis of the material with a sustained interrogation of its content. This takes the form of a series of questions applied to the material under study. The questions themselves reveal the nature of the model of analyses used:

> Who are the authors' sponsors? What are their interests in the issue? Find phrases, sentences. What images of themselves do they wish to present?
>
> Who is the intended audience? What are their interests in the issue? Of what does the author-sponsor wish to persuade them?
>
> What content does the author-sponsor focus on? What is omitted? Are biases or prejudices apparent (such as racism, sexism, ageism)?
>
> What alternative viewpoints or arguments exist that are not mentioned or acknowledged?
>
> What meaning is produced by the interaction of the formal, photo/ sketches, and written content? [17]

The importance of Brenkman's model of critique is that it lays out specific sets of questions that can be used to examine the form and content of the materials under study; furthermore, it demonstrates how such a model can be applied to concrete curricula materials. Not only does this form of analysis alert teachers to the role of industry in promoting dominant class interests (and other interests as well), but it also makes a strong case for teachers to raise questions about how the content of curriculum material might be related to a specific sociopolitical context.

THEORIES OF CLASSROOM SOCIAL RELATIONS

The model of critique exhibited in theories of classroom social relations begins from the assumption that the ideologies and practices that structure all aspects of classroom experiences must be analyzed within a sociopolitical context. At the core of this approach is the notion that a hidden curriculum of meaning functions through classroom social relations to legitimize the position and privileges of specific groups of students. For instance, Jean Anyon in her study of five East Coast elementary schools located in differing social class communities found that students from contrasting social classes were being exposed to different forms of teaching. [18] And, in fact, she documents how students from these various social classes were being exposed to social relations and ideologies that fostered particular relationships to the world of work and capitalist rationality in general.

Through an analysis of the actions, language, and teacher expectations displayed in these classrooms, Anyon records how students in the working-class schools were primarily taught in their math and social studies classes how to follow the rules. As Anyon points out, "Work is often evaluated not according to whether it is right or wrong, but according to whether the children followed the right steps."[19] For students in the middle-class school, work was getting the right answer. Language arts was reduced to mastering the simple grammar needed to function in everyday life, with the questions raised by teachers in these schools almost always designed to simply check on the correctness of the answer rather than to promote any critical understanding of either the questions asked or the answers called for. In what Anyon calls the "Executive Elite Schools," the nature of the pedagogy used changes drastically. These students are exposed to a notion of school work that involves developing their analytical prowess. Social studies and math lessons are designed to promote critical reasoning and challenging intellectual postures regarding the knowledge under examination as well as the answers developed in class. Language arts work focused on developing leadership and management skills in students, as for instance in the case where

> there was a series of assignments in which each child had to be a "student teacher." The child has to plan a lesson in grammar, outlining, punctuation, or other language arts topics and explain the concept to the class. Each child was to prepare a worksheet assignment as well. After each presentation, the teacher and the other children gave a critical appraisal of the "student teacher's" performance.[20]

The importance of this study is that it alerts teachers to the deeper significance of the underlying codes that structure the various forms of social control that characterize these various school settings. What is unique about this form of critique is that it develops categories of analysis that highlight how common sense pedagogical categories often function to both define and reinforce forms of class and gender stratification. In each of the classrooms studied by Anyon students are learning class-specific behavior for both understanding and adapting to the world of work and other aspects of the larger society. Students appear to be developing a potential relationship to different forms of work, including domestic labor, and in doing so they are acquiring a specific form of symbolic capital. The research agenda this suggests for teachers who want to take the notion of the hidden curriculum seriously is pointed to in Anyon's concluding remarks:

> Differing curricular, pedagogical, and pupil evaluation practices emphasize different cognitive and behavioral skills for each social setting and thus contribute to the development in the children of certain potential relationships to physical and symbolic capital, to authority, and to the process of work. School experience, in the . . . schools discussed here, differed qualitatively by social class. These differences may not only contribute to the development

in the children in each social class of certain types of economically significant relationships and not others, but would thereby help to reproduce this system of relations in society. In the contribution to the reproduction of unequal social relations lies a theoretical meaning and social consequence of classroom practice.[21]

A number of other illuminating studies of this sort have shed further theoretical light on how the politics of not naming functions in schools. For example, Dennis Carlson has illustrated how an industrial model of the individual is embodied in the systems logic ideology in the Individualized Instructional Planning curricula currently being adopted by many elementary schools throughout the United States.[22] In his analysis Carlson ably demonstrates how individualized classroom instruction was combined with certain human relations applications to make the routinized and standardized aspects of classroom work more palatable to students. In this case, alienating classroom tasks were supplemented with affectionate prompting of students. Rather than responding to student needs in a meaningful and critical fashion, classroom teachers were taught to recognize and confirm student emotions so as to be able to manipulate them more effectively. In this instance, the affective dimensions of a student-centered pedagogy degenerated into a form of social control that promoted a kind of "happy idiocy."

The modes of analysis that have developed in the various forms of radical pedagogy under analysis have been critically important in challenging conservative and liberal accounts of schooling. As forms of critique, they have provided educators with modes of analysis that are essential to unraveling the ideological interests that structure existing notions of educational theory and practice. This is an important aspect of this literature and cannot be overemphasized. At the same time, it is crucial to point out what is missing from these accounts, especially if the issue of developing a language of possibility and a transformative pedagogy is going to be taken seriously. It is at this point that we will take up the issue of developing a language of possibility for curriculum theory and practice.

DEVELOPING A LANGUAGE OF POSSIBILITY FOR CURRICULUM THEORY

In our view, most exciting critical accounts of schooling fail to provide forms of analyses that move beyond theories of critique to the more difficult task of laying the theoretical basis for transformative modes of curriculum theory and practice. We believe that the basis for such a project would have to be developed around a radically different conception of fundamental categories such as identity, social agency, power, knowledge, and the role of teachers as intellectuals. Some of these we elaborated on

in the beginning of this chapter; now we want to be more specific about
how these categories might provide the basis for a language of possibilities
in curriculum theory and practice.

Power as it is generally dealt with in radical analyses of schooling, as
we have previously mentioned, is defined primarily as a negative force that
works in the interests of domination. Treated as an instance of negation,
power becomes a contaminating force that leaves the imprint of domination or powerlessness on whatever it touches. Thus, social control *becomes*
synonymous with the exercise of domination in schools, while school
knowledge and culture are reduced to serving the interests of privileged
groups. The question of how power works in schools is almost by intellectual default limited to recording how it reproduces relations of domination
and subordinacy through various school practices.

If schools are to be seen as active sites of intervention and struggle in
which the possibilities exist for teachers and students to redefine the nature
of critical learning and practice, then the notion of power will have to be
rescued from its current usage among radical educators. We believe that
power is both a negative and positive force. Its character is dialectical, and
its mode of operation is always more than simply repressive. In actuality,
power is at the root of all forms of behavior in which people say no,
struggle, resist, use oppositional modes of discourse, and fight for a different vision of the future. Michel Foucault's analyses of power and how it
works provides the basis for this perspective and is worth quoting at length:

> If power were never anything but repressive, if it never did anything but to
> say no, do you really think one would be brought to obey it? What makes
> power hold good, what makes it accepted, is simply the fact that it doesn't
> only weigh on us as a force that says no, but that it traverses and produces
> things, it induces pleasure, forms of knowledge, produces discourse. It needs
> to be considered as a productive network which runs through the whole
> social body, much more than as a negative instance whose function is repres-
> sion.[23]

When viewed dialectically, the concept of power is both a positive and
negative force and provides the basis for redefining the nature of social
control and its relationship to schooling. In our view, social control has to
be seen as not just an instance of domination but also as a form of emancipatory practice. That is, a positive notion of social control establishes the
theoretical basis on which to develop the conditions for critical learning
and practice. The notion of power that underscores this positive view of
social control takes as its starting point the empowerment of teachers and
students and the confirmation of their histories and possibilities. At work
here is the view that social control, if it is to serve the interests of freedom,
must be seen as a form of cultural politics, which suggests that schools

should be regarded as sites around which a struggle should be waged in the name of developing a qualitatively better life for all. (Schools, of course, are only one site where this should take place.) As used here, social control speaks to forms of practice necessary for the demanding task of designing curricula that give students an active and critical voice, that give them the skills which are basic for analysis and leadership in the modern world. Doug White sums this up when he argues that one major task of critical educators is to rethink the relationship between the curricula and forms of social life that point to a more desirable future for all people. He writes:

> The curriculum ought to be one which lays the basis for increasing the ability of as many students as possible to become active, participating adults. By active participation I mean that students learn some real skills and knowledge which allow them to take part in adding to the general social good—both materially and spiritually—and also gain the basis for making judgments about undesirable social directions.[24]

The idea of social control that is implied in White's comment is illuminating in that it links the notion of freedom to specific forms of structure and discipline, and in doing so inveighs against those elements of pedagogical tradition that argue for a view of freedom that embraces an unbridled notion of student experience. What is at stake here is that a critical notion of social control cannot elude the tough issue of responsibility, of providing the context and conditions for the development of emancipatory forms of curricula.

Underlying the notion of social control serving emancipatory interests is the important question of how teachers and others can work so as to produce curricula around forms of culture and school knowledge that empower students who traditionally have been excluded from the benefits of a "critical" education. The starting point for such a position would have to begin with Paulo Freire's notion that the form and content of knowledge, as well as the social practices through which it is appropriated, have to be seen as part of an ongoing struggle over what counts as legitimate culture and forms of empowerment.[25] In this case, a critical pedagogy has to take seriously the notion of cultural politics, and it can do this by both legitimating and challenging the cultural experiences that make up the historical and social particulars that constitute the cultural forms and boundaries that give meaning to the lives of students and other learners. To start, teachers would have to develop forms of knowledge and classroom social practices that validate the experiences that students bring to schools. This means confirming such experiences so as to give students an active voice in institutional settings that traditionally attempt to silence them by ignoring their cultural capital. This demands acknowledging the language forms, style of presentation, dispositions, forms of reasoning, and cultural forms that give meaning to student experiences. In other words, the cultural capital of students from subordinate social categories must be related to the curricula teachers develop or mediate, to the questions raised in classes, and to the problems that are posed in such settings, regardless of the disciplines or subject areas being discussed.

Second, cultural politics when defined as a pedagogical category refers to the need to critically engage the experiences that students bring to the school. This means that such experiences in their varied cultural forms have to be interrogated critically so as to recover their strengths and weaknesses. A critical interrogation of the cultural forms that give students an active voice becomes the referent for understanding what students need to learn outside of their experiences. In this case, the pedagogical moment translates into a political process that helps students to begin the process of breaking the chains of domination and subordination as expressed not only in the objective forces that bear down on them daily, but also as they are manifested in the very structure of personalities and needs. One aim of a cultural politics then is to provide students with the skills and courage they will need in order to transform the world according to their own vision. One major precondition for such an aim is that students will have to learn how to critically appropriate the codes and vocabularies of different experiences.[26] In effect, students will have to learn how *not* to be imprisoned by the worst dimensions of their sedimented histories and experiences. For radical educators this means taking academic and other forms of knowledge and subjecting them to the test of how they might become useful in the interest of self-and social determination. This invokes the central question of how the pedagogical principle of cultural politics might invoke some directions in deciding what might be critically useful knowledge.

The concept of really useful knowledge as it developed in nineteenth-century England among radical working-class educational associations has been the subject of a number of historical studies. And any attempt to redefine the concept for existing curriculum theory and practice would do well to begin with some of the important analyses radical educators developed historically. Three main analyses are relevant for our purposes. First, really useful knowledge provided the basis for a critique of dominant forms of knowledge. Second, it strongly valued the development of curricula and pedagogies that begin with the problems and needs of those groups that such education was designed to serve. Third, it demanded knowledge that contributed to strategies for changing all forms of domination while simultaneously pointing to more democratic forms of active community. Richard Johnson has captured the specificity of this kind of knowledge in the following comments.

Really useful knowledge started out from everyday concerns. It consisted of theories and explanations of why most people were poor (in the midst of plenty), and why contemporary society shaped character in the way it did—in aggressive, competitive and uncooperative ways. Radicals sought to break down the distinctions between learning and life, between education and work. . . . Really useful knowledge involved . . . a range of resources for overcoming daily difficulties. It involved self-respect . . . which came from seeing that your oppressions were systematic and were shared. It included practical skills, but not just those wanted by employers. . . . Really useful knowledge was also a means to overcoming difficulties in the long term and more comprehensively. It taught people what social changes were necessary for real social ameliorations to occur. It also created solidarities and raised levels of literacy and general understanding within the movements.[27]

The central message to be derived from this analysis is that at the core of what counts as really useful knowledge is knowledge that draws from popular education, knowledge that challenges and critically appropriates dominant ideologies, and knowledge that points to more human and democratic social relations and cultural forms.

One of the most difficult issues for a new critical theory and practice of school knowledge is the question about the liberal arts, particularly the fate of the canon of literary, historical, and philosophical works in the school curriculum. During the 1960s, radicals mounted a massive assault on this canon, in the name of relevance and the demand for useful knowledge. The novels of George Eliot, Dickens, and Thackeray which had been taught in the old curriculum were either removed by student and activist pressure or relegated to a minor place in the pantheon of school knowledge. Many schools, responding to the new progressivism as well as financial pressure, eliminated language requirements from the high schools and severely restricted social science programs to American history and civics.

There was much to commend the student revolt against the boring and uncritical appropriation of the liberal arts by school officials and the ritualistic ways they were taught. We wish to associate ourselves with that impulse but be disassociated from the results. If students are to be empowered by school experiences, one of the key elements of their education must be that they acquire mastery of language as well as the capacity to think conceptually and critically. Of course, the best method for working through this knowledge is that of "close" reading; the interrogation of texts from the perspective of finding the interests, the historical conditions, and the tacit assumptions that underly them as well as the considerable pleasure to be derived from the reading itself. Teachers would ask students to connect their understanding of *Silas Marner, Middlemarch,* and other novels with contemporary issues such as feminism, sexuality, and the moral foundations of the social order. Similarly, a hermeneutic of Plato's *Symposium* could enrich our understanding of love just as his *Republic* might illuminate our views of politics and human nature.

To be sure, the dialogic method of knowledge acquisition contravenes the pervasive tendency to disempower students and teachers through textbooks and other prepackaged materials. A new regimen of teacher "train-ing" would have to be instituted to replace the "methods" taught in many teachers colleges. Teachers would be required to themselves become intel-lectuals in the technical sense, that is, to attain a degree of mastery over the legacy of high culture as well as assimilate and validate the elements of students' experience, which is intimately bound with popular culture. For us it is not a question of "bringing back" the same old crap in the name of culture. Rather, our intention is to suggest that a critical appro-priation of the literature, history, and philosophy by kids from subordinate groups and classes is a linchpin for overcoming the hierarchies of school knowledge inscribed in the curriculum. The point is not to reproduce high culture; the point is to make these works a part of our popular culture and eventually, on the basis of selection, eliminate their canonical status entirely. What is at stake for us is forcing a reexamination of the interre-lationship between high and popular culture in order to make problematic not only their distinctions but also the different ways in which they secure authority and forms of affective investment.

We would also like to add a fourth category that focuses on knowledge as a force that blocks the development of certain subjectivities and ways of critically experiencing the world. Specifically, we are referring to forms of knowledge that people refuse to address, or, for that matter, refuse even to consider, given the threat such knowledge may pose to their view of the world. Shoshana Felman in her discussion of Jacques Lacan's notion of the unconscious refers to this form of knowledge as a way of thinking about ignorance. She argues that

> Ignorance is no longer simply opposed to knowledge; it is itself a radical condition, an integral part of the very structure of knowledge. . . . Igno-rance, in other words, is not a passive state of absence—a simple lack of information; it is an active dynamic of negation, an active refusal of infor-mation.[28]

This is an important point because it teaches us that ignorance is a form of knowing that resists certain forms of knowledge. Ignorance is, in a sense, a form of knowledge defined by the way it actively resists certain knowl-edge. The pedagogical question that emerges from this type of analysis is what accounts for the elements of repression and forgetting at the core of the dynamic of ignorance; or put another way, what accounts for the con-ditions that posit for individuals or social groups a refusal to know or to learn.

A third aspect of cultural politics we wish to emphasize is the need for radical educators to analyze state and nonstate agencies as important sites involved in the production of dominant culture and ideologies. This would necessitate understanding and working through counter-hegemonic actions to transform the various ways in which the state directly intervenes in developing and implementing educational policy, the most obvious ways being through school attendance laws, the implementation of school legislation, the enforcement of state certification requirements, and the distribution of educational research funds through various government agencies. On another level, it is imperative to understand how corporate influences bear down on the shaping of school policy and curricula development. Such influences can be seen in the promotion of texts and school supplies by corporations, the takeover of publishing houses by such interests, the attempts to reprivatize public schools, promote vouchers and choice, and the growing business-school partnerships being promoted by neo-conservative ideologues, particularly in the United States.[29]

Finally, a cultural politics must include as one of its basic theoretical elements the need to rethink the nature and role of being a teacher. We want to return at this point to the argument we presented in chapter two, that is, that teachers must be seen as intellectuals, as critical theorists who provide the moral and intellectual leadership necessary for developing active forms of community life engaged in the struggle for equality and democracy. In this case, we are referring to teachers who are both scholars and activists, whose sphere of intervention is not just the school but the community at large, and who take as a starting point for their work the political injunction of working collectively with others to create a more decent and humane world. At most, this means that a distinction must be made between radical teachers and educators, with the former working in schools and the latter working within oppositional public spheres so as to make the political more pedagogical and to further promote the goals of a critical socialist democracy. Needless to say, radical teachers should embrace both of these roles since they extend their own political work while simultaneously providing the basis for new alliances and collective struggle.

More specifically, we are arguing that conditions must be developed in and out of public education to foster the development of public and transformative intellectuals—that is, intellectuals who are part of a specific class, group, or movement and who serve to give it coherence and an awareness of its own function in the economic, social, and political fields. In this perspective, intellectuals must be fully aware of their active role in mediating between the dominant culture and everyday life. They must also be aware that their role is decidedly political since they cannot escape from the often contradictory function of either legitimating or resisting dominant forms of ideology and culture (not to mention either accommodating or producing such forms).

We describe teachers as being transformative intellectuals in the sense that they recognize the struggle in which they are involved over what constitutes the distinction between normality and deviance, and over the struggle as to what counts as acceptable knowledge and social practice. Yet, the concept of transformative intellectual does more than suggest the political function in which educators engage. It also lays the theoretical ground for them to examine their own histories, those connections to the past which in part define who they are and how they mediate and function in the world. Equally important, the concept of the transformative intellectual becomes a political referent for educators to take seriously the struggle to eliminate the division between intellectual and manual labor, not only in their own work but also in the society at large. For underlying this logic is a division that separates conception from execution, and that reproduces and consigns various forms of labor and cultural life to modes of drudgery and alienation.

The concept of the transformative intellectual is fundamentally important to viewing curriculum theory as a mode of cultural politics. For if radical educators are going to take seriously the need to develop workable alternatives to the current forms of schooling, they will have to investigate historically the nature of the teaching field itself, as both a moment in the labor process and as a particular cultural form for learning. They will also have to investigate how the teaching field has evolved under conditions where race-, gender-, and class-specific practices have become part and parcel of the teaching profession. This suggests that teachers be prepared not only to produce oppositional forms of knowledge and social practice, but also to struggle and to take risks in fighting against injustices, however deeply ingrained that may be in the schools and other social spheres. At the same time, if the notions of social control and cultural production are to be taken seriously, they will have to be developed within a language of possibility that can raise real hopes, forge new alliances, and point to new forms of social life that appear realizable. As difficult as this task may appear, the stakes are too high not to fight for it. As radical educators begin thinking about pedagogical strategies for the future, they will have to develop some clarity about what kind of curriculum is needed to build a critical socialist democracy. This means redefining the notion of power, cultural politics, really useful knowledge, and a number of other categories mentioned in this chapter. Such a task does not mean debunking existing forms of schooling and educational theory; it means reworking them, contesting the terrains on which they develop, and appropriating from them whatever radical potentialities they might contain.

We would like to shift our theoretical focus at this point and turn to another side of the crisis in public education. We want to analyze the crisis posed to public education by emerging neo-conservative and right-wing ideologues.

NOTES

1. M. Adler, *The Paideia Proposal: An Educational Proposal* (New York: Macmillan Co., 1982); G. H. Bantock, *Culture, Industrialism, and Education* (London: Routledge and Kegan Paul, Ltd., 1968).

2. M. W. Apple, *Education and Power* (Boston: Routledge and Kegan Paul, Ltd., 1982); S. Hall and T. Jefferson, *Resistance Through Rituals* (London: Hutchinson and Co., 1976); P. Bourdieu and J. Passeron, *Reproduction in Education, Society and Culture* (Beverly Hills, Calif.: Sage Publishers, 1977).

3. H. A. Giroux and Roger Simon, "Curriculum Study and Cultural Politics," *Journal of Education* 166:2, 1984, pp. 211–236.

4. M.F.D. Young, ed., *Knowledge and Control* (London: Collier-Macmillan, 1971); G. Whitty, "Sociology and the Problem of Radical Educational Change: Notes Towards a Reconceptualization of the 'New' Sociology of Education," in G. Whitty and M. Young, eds., *Society, State and Schooling* (Sussex, England: Falmer Press, 1977).

5. H. A. Giroux, *Theory and Resistance in Education* (South Hadley, Mass.: Bergin and Garvey, 1983).

6. R. Bates, "New Developments in the New Sociology of Education," *British Journal of Sociology of Education* 1:1 (March 1981), pp. 67–80.

7. S. Bowles, and H. Gintis, *Schooling in Capitalist America* (New York: Basic Books, 1976).

8. R. W. Connell et al., *Making the Difference* (Sydney, Australia: George Allen and Unwin, 1982).

9. K. Wilcox and P. Moriarity, "School and Work: Social Constraints on Educational Opportunity," in J. Benet and K. Kaplan, eds., *Education: Straitjacket or Opportunity* (New York: Transaction Books, 1980); R. A. Mickelson, " The Secondary School's Role in Social Stratification: A Comparison of Beverly Hills High School and Morningside High School," *Journal of Education* 162:4 (Fall 1981), pp. 83–112.

10. Bourdieu and Passeron, op. cit.

11. P. Willis, *Learning to Labor* (New York: Columbia University Press, 1981).

12. C. Buswell, "Pedagogic Change and Social Change," *British Journal of Sociology of Education* 1:3 (October 1980), pp. 293–306.

13. Apple, op. cit.

14. Ibid.

15. Ibid., p. 146.

16. J. L. Brenkman, "Seeing Beyond the Interests of Industry: Teaching Critical Thinking." *Journal of Education* 165:3 (Summer 1983), pp. 283–294.

17. Ibid., pp. 293–294.

18. J. Anyon, "Social Class and the Hidden Curriculum of Work," *Journal of Education* 162:1 (Winter 1980), pp. 67–92; see also, Peter McLaren, *Schooling as a Ritual Performance* (New York: Routledge, 1985).

19. Ibid., p. 72.

20. Ibid., p. 87.

21. Ibid., p. 90.

22. D. Carlson, "Updating Individualism and the Work Ethic: Corporate Logic in the Classroom." *Curriculum Inquiry* 12:2 (1982), pp. 125–160.

23. M. Foucault, *Power and Knowledge: Selected Interviews and Other Writings,* ed. C. Gordon (New York: Pantheon, 1980).

24. D. White. "After the Divided Curriculum," *The Victorian Teacher* (March 1983), pp. 6–7.

25. P. Freire, *Pedagogy of the Oppressed* (New York: Seabury Press, 1970).

26. S. Hall, "Education in Crisis," in A. Wolpe and J. Donald, eds., *Is There Anyone Here from Education* (London: Pluto Press, 1983).

27. R. Johnson, "Educational Politics: The Old and the New," in A. Wolpe and J. Donald, eds., *Is There Anyone Here from Education* (London: Pluto Press, 1983), pp. 11–26.

28. S. Felman, "Psychoanalysis and Education: Teaching Terminable and Interminable," *Yale French Studies* 29:2 (1981), pp. 29–30.

29. E. Berman, "State Hegemony and the Schooling Process," *Journal of Education* 166:3 (Fall 1984), pp. 239–253.

Chapter Seven

The Universities and the Question of Political Correctness

On Sunday, October 28, 1990, the *New York Times* cultural correspondent, Richard Bernstein, reported faculty approval of a new writing program at the University of Texas called Writing on Difference in which students would "base their compositions on a packet of essays on discrimination, affirmative action, and civil rights cases." According to Bernstein, the program earned the praise of many members of the faculty. But a few, like English professor Alan Gribben dissented: "You cannot tell me that students will not be inevitably graded on politically correct thinking in these classes." Shortly after the article appeared, the university administration rejected the new curriculum in response to pressure from some state legislators and internal opponents such as Professor Gribben.

It is odd that the idea of political correctness should reappear in the 1990s, for its genealogy can be traced to another era, a time when a substantial segment of 1960s radicals were engaged in reclaiming a Marxist-Leninist heritage they had previously refused. They formed new "communist" groups, most prominently the Revolutionary Union (later the Revolutionary Communist party) and the October League (later the Communist party of the United States—M-L). Their literature was suffused with evidence of Stalinist orthodoxy, principally of the Maoist variety, and their style of politics parodied the discipline prevalent in revolutionary movements.[1] In practice, to be politically correct meant that one had assimilated many of the crucial markers of left culture, particularly anti-racism, a working-class ethos, and support for Third World revolutions which in the 1960s were breaking out in many parts of the southern part of the globe. In many respects, the groups that sprang up in the wake of the demise of the New Left's democratic radicalism had a penchant for rigid applications of these values. In their struggle to become "truly" revolutionary, in an imagined emulation of earlier radical generations or contemporary revolutionary movements elsewhere, they were frequently given to excesses that resulted in some bizarre attacks on individuals who were labeled politically "incorrect."

According to Bernstein, although currently the phrase "politically correct" is "spoken more with irony and disapproval than with reverence, . . . the term p.c. as it is commonly abbreviated is being heard more and more in debates over what should be taught at the universities." The "what" in question—race, ecology, feminism, what has been called multiculturalism and international relations, especially the north/south conflicts—has defined a sort of unspoken ideology of the university. Needless to say, this did not apply to the University of Texas.

Of course, each of these categories has a content. Bernstein goes on to describe the crucial beliefs associated with p.c. as held by conservative and liberal critics of this unofficial ideology. Among these beliefs, none is more prominent than the view that a "white male power structure" is associated with the core meanings of European civilization. The phrase encompasses a constellation of oppressions, notably of race, gender, and sex, and "Third World." The remarkable aspect of the controversy over politics in the universities is not the ideas themselves. We can point to a long history for the judgment that European civilization itself, and not merely a specific political party or government, or a series of regrettable but broadly held social attitudes is responsible for such injustices as inequality, gender, and race discrimination and colonialism. Many believe that the novelty is that these judgments, either singly or in the form of ideology, are now widely supported among faculty and students, especially in some leading universities. For their purposes, an unlikely alliance of old academic radicals, liberals, and conservatives is charging that a new polyglot "left" has entrenched itself within the university as in no other American institution. In this lexicon, "left" encompasses a broad spectrum ranging from ecologists—many of whom vehemently deny their association with the traditional left—to Marxists, deconstructionists, feminists, and African-American intellectuals, all of whom spend as much energy distinguishing themselves from each other as they are distinct from cultural conservatives.

In fact, in what Francis Fukuyama (1989) termed "the end of history" even before the crumbling of the Berlin Wall serves better as a reference to the already apparent decline of revolutionary communism in favor of the reforms of the Gorbachev era. Hence the reappearance of ideological politics within the United States appears, at first glance, anachronistic.[2] Fukuyama, deputy director of the State Department's policy planning staff and former analyst at the RAND Corporation, writes that the communist demise is evidence of "the triumph of the West," or more specifically "the Western idea." In the past, certain reform movements in the Soviet Union and China were motivated not only by major policy changes but also the "ineluctable spread of consumerist Western Culture" in diverse contexts.[3]

Fukuyama is acutely aware that precisely "culture" and "ideology" were at play in the West's prolonged effort to prevail over competing and alternative historical models. He points to a paradox in the defeat of the Hegelian notion that abstract ideas are worth the risk to life. On the one hand, neither the communist nor the capitalist states are able to avoid ideological categories such as the national interest or, indeed, the liberal or the revolutionary communist "idea." For the nearly three quarters of a century following the Bolshevik Revolution, these were the flags of economic and political struggle between the dominant competing social systems. On the other hand, liberalism seeks to naturalize as universal values its twin ideologies of the market as the best guarantee of freedom and representative democracy as the highest achievement of human communities which is presented as a common sense notion, the violation of which constitutes nothing less than moral turpitude.

For Fukuyama the end of history that will accompany the supremacy of liberal ideas will also witness the triumph of the mundane, that is, the ascendancy of "economic calculation, the endless solving of technical problems . . . and the satisfaction of sophisticated consumer demands. In the post-historical period there will be neither art nor philosophy, just the perpetual caretaking of the museum of human history."[4] The end of ideology, except that of technocracy, will be a "very sad time."

Among Fukuyama's respondents in the symposium which the conservative journal *National Interest* devoted to his article, Irving Kristol struck the one ominous note that may serve to comprehend the odd reappearance of ideological struggle in the early 1990s. "We may have won the Cold War," states Kristol, "which is nice [*sic*] its [*sic*] more than nice, its [*sic*] wonderful. But this means that now the enemy is us, not them." American democracy, he states, is now at risk "with all its problematics—as distinct from mere problems—that fester within such a democracy." As some of these problematics he lists "the longing for community, spirituality, a growing distrust of technology, the confusion of liberty with license."[5]

In retrospect, Kristol, himself an old socialist ideologue who led others of his generation into neo-conservatism, may have proven a more accurate forecaster than Fukuyama, although neither denies the ideological force of liberalism. Fukuyama regards, with some foreboding, the prospect that the time has finally arrived for the fulfillment of the confident predictions, widely held by liberal intellectuals of thirty years ago, that no historical problematics have to be faced, that we are fated to exist in a joyless technological/liberal utopia. But Kristol's adroit focus on the "enemy within" seems to foreshadow the 1990s; he seems to have anticipated the idea that the death of Stalinism would not prefigure the end of ideological struggle per se. His generation, having become part of the constellation that forms established authority, must now face what Lionel Trilling once termed the "adversarial" culture and what they believe to be the new authoritarian threat of the marginals. As we will see below, it may prove more difficult to uproot the reemergence of the adversarial culture than that of the political opposition.

Consequently, while the demise of the "evil empire" was cause for celebration, it was somewhat muted and deferred pending the defeat of the nascent internal opposition that would abuse democratic privilege by cloaking itself in precisely liberal values: diversity, pluralism, and difference—the other side of the quest for universalism in liberal political philosophy. Against the doctrine of centralism, the liberals argue vehemently for politics as a public sphere in which difference, guaranteed by the integrity of the private sphere, is the grist of democratic decision-making. Yet, the meaning of "difference" in liberal discourse is not identical with the postmodern use of the word. As Arthur Schlesinger argued more than forty years ago and has recently repeated almost without missing a stroke of the classical argument, difference in the "democratic way of life" is always subsumed under the universal values of Western culture: reason, the scientific spirit, individual freedom, and representative democracy.[6] These values are not necessarily what contemporary advocates of difference have in mind. According to Schlesinger, then, as now, the condition of American freedom is American unity in the face of the totalitarian threat in all of its various guises.

The row over political correctness has emanated from a strange alliance. Outraged mavens of classical culture like Allan Bloom, whose attacks on progressive education, Marx, Nietzsche, and Heidegger as veritable authors of the decline and fall of the West, and on the 1960s as a period of the wanton quest for pleasure, are already legendary; older and young neo-conservatives grouped around magazines such as *Policy Review*, a journal of the right-wing Heritage Foundation, and *New Criterion*, the neo-conservative champion of high modernism; liberals connected to *Partisan Review* and *The New Republic*, each of which has run a special issue on the political correctness controversy, with a characteristic declaiming unanimity among the contributors; social-democratic periodicals include *Dissent*, whose editorial board is barely distinguishable, in its majority cultural opinions, from *The New Republic* but is quite distinct on issues of social justice. And finally, there is a fragment of older, Marxist-oriented professors like Eugene Genovese and Steven Thernstrom who themselves feel victimized by the young politically correct.

In the burgeoning literature on the subject, the "Thernstrom" narrative reappears with deadening monotony. For some years, Steven Thernstrom and Bernard Bailyn, both prominent Harvard historians, had conducted a course in race relations in American history. Thernstrom read from slavemaster narratives in class and his students promptly accused him of "insensitivity" for this alleged indiscretion. But criticism of these and other classroom practices rapidly escalated into student charges that the professors were "racist."

In despair, the instructors eventually dropped the course, but the student charges still dog Thernstrom. This incident, together with another at Brown in 1990 when the university's administration expelled a white student for publicly engaging in symbolic acts of racist aggression, has become emblematic of the frequently repeated charge that universities are in the grip of "a new McCarthyism of the left." Of course, in a few cases professors have been attacked for expressing the view that African Americans are intellectually inferior to whites. Among these is philosopher Michael Levin whose utterances have provoked student and some faculty protests and led to an investigation by New York's City College administration. Still he has not been restrained in his right to teach or otherwise advocate unpopular views.

Clearly, these instances illustrate the existence of a strain of anti-civil libertarianism among some anti-racist and anti-sexist groups and individuals. Indeed, there is reason for disquiet, especially in the face of the long struggle to realize academic freedom and other facets of civil liberties that libertarians and radicals have waged since the birth of the Republic. The U.S. government, employers, and, more generally, institutional authorities have never passionately defended the right to dissent from established policies and consensual values. In fact, America has a long record of witch-hunts, show trials, political prisoners, and, more recently, an appalling absence of public debate about vital political issues even during national election campaigns. Although this is not the place to rehearse specific features of this illiberalism, we may cite the virtual absence of congressional discussion of the U.S. invasion of Panama, the stifling of public protest after President Bush ordered the bombing of Iraq in January 1990, and earlier cases where official versions of the national interest were the only voices heard in print and visual media. One may recall House Speaker Thomas Foley's (D-Wash.) pithy remark upon the occasion of the Panama incident that "this is no time for complicated debate." In addition, a considerable coterie of professors whose work is perceived to be marginal, if not oppositional, to the mainstream social sciences and humanities, have experienced sharp tenure and promotion battles during this period.

For example, during the 1980s, sociologists Theda Skocpol and Paul Starr (Harvard), literary theorist and critic Linda Brodkey (Pennsylvania), and education theorist Henry Giroux (Boston University) were merely the most publicized of outstanding scholars and intellectuals who suffered from the vindictiveness of the established academic generation that felt threatened by their innovative work. Although these victims by no means shared either the same politics or intellectual orientation, in various ways their work challenged the dominant paradigm of the discipline. Skocpol by her sweeping treatment of the relations of states and revolution and Starr by his magisterial social history of medicine violated the unwritten rule in sociology that junior professors confine their research to modest, discrete studies. In each case, they departed from dominant thinking in their respective fields, especially Skocpol. For their part, Brodkey and Giroux overtly challenged the penchant of educational studies to avoid, at all costs, contemporary social and cultural theory, especially concepts that fall outside the dominant functionalism. Even before he was considered for tenure, Giroux had become one of the more controversial curriculum theorists in education. And Brodkey creatively transgressed many of the rules of composition theory by publishing a text that drew heavily on poststructuralism at a time when many of the leading figures in this field were proclaiming their hostility to the French turn in literary and cultural theory. That each of them landed on his or her feet (they all have tenured positions at leading universities) is a tribute to their considerable talents, despite their obvious violation of the prevailing ideology of the university faculties or administrations that denied them tenure.

Nevertheless, conservatives have been able to take the moral high ground on speech issues chiefly because the left has shown itself to be ambivalent. Bitten by the bug of excessive legalism on the one hand, and a sincere desire to resist increasing racialist violence on the other, people who would immediately protest against restricting a radical's right to demonstrate and protest, including the right to disobey immoral laws, have no clear standard against which to evaluate the potentially repressive effects of liberally motivated sanctions against right-wing political speech such as so-called hate speech. For example, in reaction to the 1984 U.S. Supreme Court's unanimous decision overturning the city of St. Paul, Minnesota's hate speech ordinance, People for the American Way, a liberal advocacy organization, condemned the decision and asserted that the Court had made prosecution of racist acts virtually impossible. This judgment plainly refers not to whether there exists sufficient legal machinery to respond to racist provocations such as cross burnings on public and private property, but to the possibility that many people will interpret the Court's decision to mean that such acts are perfectly legal. Some may take the Court's decision as license, but it is obvious that state and local laws such as those prohibiting criminal trespass cover such acts. On the other hand, specific legislation to ban hate speech is, ironically, in the line of criminal sedition laws that banned the right of radicals to advocate revolution and resistance in times of war. In the St. Paul case, the conservative Supreme Court was on the side of the angels, but many fervent anti-racists find themselves appearing to oppose civil liberties under some conditions.

Another example occurred in the fall of 1992. Caving in to election-year pressures against debating the issue of the link between crime and genetics,

Bernadine Healy, the director of the National Institutes of Health, rescinded a grant to the University of Maryland to hold a conference on the topic. Of course, that a group of researchers would revive the dogma of genetically induced social behavior is entirely appalling. Nevertheless, in a time of conservative ascendancy, it is hardly possible to "ban" what is on the minds of many both in and out of scientific circles. Yet, anti-racist groups succeeded in doing just that. The Bush administration revealed the degree to which it was prepared to abrogate free speech in the wake of tactical considerations.

These instances reveal that it is extremely dangerous for the traditionally victimized to occupy the space of prosecutor as if reverse censorship were justified by illiberal practices. Given its history, it behooves dissenters of the cultural left to become the most vigorous proponents of First Amendment rights. They should be especially vigilant to defend, wherever possible, those on the right whose views, however repugnant, are still within the purview of constitutional guarantees of free speech.

Yet, the dispute over academic freedom and, more broadly, public speech does not entirely encompass the underlying issues in the p.c. debate. Even more rancorous than the issue of speech is the widespread perception held by a new generation of graduate students and younger faculty that many professors currently at the height of their prestige and power are hopelessly tied to antiquated paradigms of knowledge, to an outmoded conception of the university—namely, the university as fount of neutral scholarship—and to a politics curiously insensitive to the discourse connected to "new" social movements (principally feminist, gay and lesbian, African-American, and Latino). The fact is that here the cliché applies: the generations' failure to communicate. A substantial fraction of the senior liberal faculty, joined somewhat cynically by the popular press and the right, reproduces, either unwittingly or deliberately, the generational conflicts of two earlier periods: the 1930s when the young cosmopolitan left-wing intellectuals broke from the cultural and political nationalism that inhered in prevailing traditions; and the 1960s when these erstwhile dissenters, having become the academic intellectual establishment, were confronted by a new generation challenging the nationalism they acquired during the cold war.

In the 1990s those who defend "tradition" have offered comparatively feeble arguments against what may yet be the most serious challenge. In contrast to dissenters in earlier struggles when arguments over knowledge were often displaced and masked within contemporary political "issues" such as the war and student political rights, today's dissenters from the academic mainstream are more prepared, both theoretically and historically, to argue about intellectual traditions themselves. They have focused, in the first place, on curriculum issues within some of the core disciplines of Western culture, especially literature, as well as on some social sciences and philosophy. At stake in the debate is the question of "who speaks for the intellectuals"; it is on this question that the legitimacy of the old hegemonic paradigms may hinge. Although American intellectuals may not enjoy high status in a profoundly anti-intellectual culture, they are important in the formulation of what may be taken as legitimate cultural traditions. They set the standards against which pretenders to legitimacy are evaluated.

The past decade has witnessed a well-orchestrated conservative-led campaign to impose artistic and intellectual censorship by supporting legislation that bans pornography. According to some libertarians, this legislation is written so broadly that it can ban work viewed as pornographic, such as that of photographer Robert Mapplethorpe's, even if it is presented as art. Related but not identical to this issue is the conservatives' espousal of obscenity laws that forbid expletives on television, radio, and print media. Many congressional conservatives such as Senators Jesse Helms (R-N.C.) and Strom Thurmond (R-S.C.) who abjure pornography have also sought to restrict a woman's right to an abortion and have successfully led congressional legislation that has denied poor women access to federal funds for that purpose. They have also sponsored and passed legislation banning flag burning. At the same time, we note (and mourn) the deathly silence by the neo-liberal and neo-conservative journals of opinion on these issues, omissions that we suspect signify a double standard of concern for free speech.

Partly in reaction to the assimilationist Americanization of the old left and to the loss of its radical edge, the 1960s generation, as well as younger intellectuals for whom some aspects of its culture and intellectual proclivities are a model, is in the process of forging a new critical practice that has been inspired by European models, chiefly from Britain and France, but also Germany and Italy. In addition, a substantial segment of U.S. academics has become attracted to postcolonial Third World intellectuals, many of whom have selectively appropriated European theory and criticism to argue against Eurocentric perspectives on primarily cultural and political grounds. The new intellectuals have rejected in a large measure the critique of mass culture emanating from the Frankfurt School, its American counterparts on *Partisan Review,* and the parallel condemnations of cultural conservatives such as Alexis de Tocqueville and Ortega y Gasset. Consequently, to the extent that critical and radical academics have recognized the pertinence of American tradition, it is largely that of the oppressed and the popular, particularly African-American, earlier feminist, and working-class writers, and socialist and anarchist political theorists and agitators. But, perhaps equally important, they have insisted on the parity of aural and visual art forms—music, film, and video— with those of literature.

In this struggle, the insurgents can no longer simply identify themselves as victims, any more than could Galileo and Copernicus who, despite considerable persecution, were clearly ascendant over their tradition-bound critics, or James Joyce whose revolution of the word was, despite censorship, irrepressible. The values of the new intellectual radicals have already begun to permeate mainstream institutions such as the Educational Testing Service, which designs various standardized academic sorting devices including the Scholastic Aptitude Test (SAT) and the Graduate Record Examination (GRE). Knowledge of black and women's literature as well as the traditional canon are now included on these tests.

Many universities, under pressure from younger faculty and students to institute major curricular reforms, are scrambling to hire African-American and Latino faculty in strengthened disciplinary as well as cross-disciplinary programs. At the same time, there has been an expansion of interdisciplinary graduate programs, combining, especially, philosophy, the arts, and literary criticism. Equally galling to conservative critics has been the move of some trade and university publishers to eagerly seek out the work of the radicals and the plethora of new journals and magazines which now crowd the bookstores. *Partisan Review* and *Dissent,* once the leaders of the small liberal political/literary magazines, retain only a fraction of their readership. Their viability depends, to a large extent, on the decades of accumulated library subscriptions and a faithful, but diminishing, old-line readership. However, they have failed to win the allegiance of a substantial group of new readers in the last twenty-five years. Nor are Marxist journals exempt from the judgment that their pages are stale with yesterday's ideas. When they do not betray the quasi-religious penchant of quoting scripture, their attempts to come to grips with current changes are often, sadly, little more than rituals of affirmation of good old things.

Just as the advocates of the new pluralism have made significant inroads in U.S. intellectual life, neo-conservative thought has also shown new vitality, if only by being willing to actively engage the new movements in combat. Today, intellectual conservatism may be distinguished by two ideological positions: the resolute defense of the traditional curriculum—whether classical or modernist—against the postmodern, pluralist turn; and its insistence on "excellence" as a euphemism for protecting the prevailing system of educational inequality against the attacks of blacks, Latinos, and women who were traditionally excluded from postsecondary schooling on meritocratic grounds.

Of course, in his immensely popular best-seller *The Closing of the American Mind,* Allan Bloom makes no effort to hide his contempt for curriculum reform that distances itself from his own version of classical texts. He bitterly castigates the handful of "first-class" private universities for pandering to women, people of color, and radicals who want to study Marx, Nietzsche, and Heidegger rather than Plato and Hegel; or Richard Wright and Zora Neale Hurston rather than Charles Dickens; and whose critical sensibility is formed by their own time rather than by the Greek city-state.

Bloom's rant and that of younger conservatives such as Dinish D'Sousa and Roger Kimball have resonated with many middle-class readers—whether intellectuals or not—who, buffeted by rapidly shifting economic, social, and cultural winds, seek a prophet to rearticulate the old values for which they stand, regardless of whether they have read the philosophical and literary canon that girds the West's claim to be the pinnacle of civilized society. But Bloom's *The Closing of the American Mind* is also a call to action, a manifesto of the defenders of the Faith. It argues, albeit incoherently, that for all intents and purposes, there is little, if any, philosophy after Hegel that cannot be charged with inviting the barbarians through the gates. Bloom goes so far as to claim that, however democratic, the recent efforts to open the doors of the universities to many who were formerly excluded, especially through affirmative action and open admissions, are futile gestures because blacks and other people of color are so overwhelmed by economic and social problems that they could not possibly master a rigorous curriculum. (To which the social justice wing of cultural conservatism adds: the federal and state governments have proven unwilling to provide the remedial services needed for minorities to succeed in colleges.) Therefore, they should be relegated to state institutions for occupational training and a taste of the liberal arts, while the elite, private universities should resist reforms that "dilute" classical education and permit only the best and the brightest to occupy their classroom seats.

Although conservative educators have received a great deal of attention in the past decade and have been able to mobilize the media to disseminate their ideas, they are probably engaged in a rear guard action at the level of the intellectual debate, even as they raise troubling issues concerning the liberties of those who hold unpopular social views. Bloom and his acolytes have made a point of saying nothing new: they are committed to the good old things, since, by definition, the new things are always bad because they are disruptive. For the modernists inspired by the New York Intellectuals who dominated high cultural discourse until the 1960s, the distinctions between liberalism and conservatism are, in the face of the rising intellectual radicalism, increasingly blurred. Some might advocate a different canon from that proposed by Bloom. For example, anti-Stalinist liberal intellectuals, especially writers such as Daniel Bell and Irving Howe whose roots in Marxist thought are apparent even in their most anti-Marxist fulminations, cannot dismiss Marx so easily. It is hard to believe that Howe, who knows the difference between zealous anti-racism and McCarthyism can adopt the cynical views of those on the right who hold similar ideas on the canon. Yet, their differences disappear when confronted with challenges to the ideas of canon itself because, in the end, they share with the conservatives a powerful belief that civilization is on trial, a situation that demands nothing less than extraordinary measures to close ranks. The irony of this alliance is, of course, that Bell and especially Howe were never really integrated into the mainstream of their respective disciplines. Bell's style has more in common with the social and cultural criticism of, say, Edmund Wilson than the scientistic bent of most sociologists. And Howe steadfastly defended the intimate connection between politics and fiction at a time when the New Criticism, which insisted on their disjunction, held sway.

In contrast to the 1930s popular front in which "tolerance" became an anti-fascist keyword, there is no doubt that the targets of the new intellectual movements are as much liberals as the right, for in many respects, particularly on knowledge issues, they have aligned themselves similarly. The university wars have radically realigned ideological positions from their usual moorings around questions of economic justice. For the stakes—what is legitimate intellectual knowledge, who are the knowledge producers, and who can speak for "us"—question and otherwise threaten conventional authorities. The weight of the challenge has been so heavy that sections of university administrations which, at first seemed more open to innovation, have slowly yielded ground to the conservatives.

In one respect, the current struggles within the university reproduce the crisis of the middle class that has marked the larger social canvas. For the entire American ethos is intertwined with the well-being of its representative social category. Just as the ranks of the middle management have been thinned by mergers, consolidations, and acquisitions of smaller international corporations by larger ones, and independent small businesses in virtually all production and service sectors face the most difficult times since the depression, so the professoriate that benefited directly and indirectly from the dramatic expansion of the universities through the early 1970s now faces *both* economic and ideological battering.

The salaries of all but the top stars in the discipline have been virtually frozen since the late 1980s, and working conditions have been progressively deteriorating, not only in the state universities but also in the private schools. Many state and private universities which once, under pressure from the civil rights and feminist movements, opened their doors to "minorities," are now in the process of closing them. The conjuncture of long-term economic stagnation; technological transformations that are beginning to affect intellectual labor as well as manual and clerical work (Columbia recently announced the closing of its library science school, and Yale wants to shut down its engineering school); the fiscal crises afflicting many colleges and universities; and the sharpened cultural struggle in evidence in the 1992 presidential campaign as well as in academic precincts—all these have created severe pressures for the shrinkage of higher education.

For example, the huge state universities of California and New York, once the premier sites of open admissions, have all but announced plans for nontemporary cutbacks in both enrollments and faculty. With state budgets in more or less permanent deficit, educational administrations have collapsed under pressure from political and economic executive authorities to undertake planned shrinkage of their university and college systems. At the same time, major private institutions are repealing their "needs blind" admissions policies, which, until recently, purportedly guaranteed scholarships and living expenses to students regardless of their ability to pay.

These developments are taking place even as the cultural wars have become more bitter and the conservatives perceive themselves to be under siege. Most humiliating, the guardians of Western culture—both the traditionalists and the left anti-communists—have been cut off from the younger faculty and the best students whose minds and hearts have wandered elsewhere. In a sense, their situation is poignant. The older anti-Stalinist generation was unable to experience the 1930s and 1940s as years of upsurge, since their eyes were fixed on the dual defeat they suffered at the hands of Stalinism and the New Deal.[7] Their moment arrived only when the social movements of the communist left and the right ebbed. When they emerged in the 1950s, it was on the side of the established power. Within universities, by the 1960s when a new upsurge emerged, the Hooks, Bells, and Howes *became* the established powers.

Then came the pain of the political youth disaffection just as they arrived in the prestigious chairs. If the immortality of the intellectual resides in the hearts and minds of the succeeding generations who venerate their elders by criticism as much as emulation, these figures could point only to the middle-brow journals for remaining sources of their renown. Sidney Hook lives as the namesake of the National Association of Scholars' annual Freedom Award, but his best works are unread in part because they are a product of his "Marxist" period and have not been reissued. The liberal professoriate stayed in their chairs during the political revolt of the 1960s generation and staunchly defended their newly won academic respectability. Some, such as Seymour Martin Lipset and Lewis Feuer of Berkeley, engaged the student radicals, but most went, figuratively, into hiding.

Once again the political movement ebbed. And the Berlin Wall crumbled, vindicating the *political* choices of anti-Stalinist intellectuals. But, alas, the 1960s were not over. Now the cultural confrontation undermined the intellectual perspicacity of the New York Intellectuals. Postmodernism, the "French turn" in social and cultural theory, multiculturalism, and the neo- and post-Marxist revival have cut the ground from under them. Now they face a new keyword called "cultural studies," which began as an attempt to valorize high culture as an object of legitimate knowledge but has, more recently, proposed a critique of conventional disciplines, and especially their authority to impose an uncontestable canon. For the generations that devoted their lives to rediscovering and remaking America, these trends must be perceived as nothing less than manifestations of disloyalty or, worse, as the coming of a new barbarism.

The cultural politics of the conflict may be expressed in terms of conflicting conceptions of citizenship. Those who have assimilated themselves into American culture have also conflated the idea of freedom with American nationality. Loyalty to the U.S. nation-state is identical with what they mean by democratic citizenship. One may criticize various policies of national or local government or even dissent from major foreign policy objectives of a given administration. But the identity of the United States with what democracy and freedom actually signify has become a precept guiding mainstream intellectuals: their reconciliation with "their" country, signified by an almost universal declaration of noncommunist intellectuals for the "West," has meant that they have merged, politically and culturally, with the values of the dominant groups, even with the myths that have infused American nationality.

In contrast, for the past twenty-five years a minority has tacitly redefined citizenship to mean *cultural citizenship*. For many immigrants and adherents to new social movements, cultural citizenship displaces the notion of class loyalty that, in earlier periods, countered patriotism and nationalism. That is, loyalty to the nation-state, conventionally tied to the meaning of citizenship itself, has shifted to subculture or gender, which is often taken as subculture. In turn, this cultural identity is frequently international as in the case of pan-Africanism or international women's solidarity. In short, cultural citizenship signifies a community of the oppressed and a statement that the nation-state is symbolic of the oppressor.

A strong case has been made, most recently by Jürgen Habermas, that the sufficient condition of democracy is the existence of a "public" of individuals who transcend group interest and, through free access to knowledge and information, as well as their autonomy from the state, are able to participate in both the great and small decisions of the commonweal. In turn, difference is encouraged , not merely tolerated. Beyond divergent opinion within a commonly held series of assumptions, difference should accommodate systemic opposition. The possibility of an articulate, even if minority, opposition to consensual world views may be the basis not only for evaluating the status of "human rights" within a given community but also for determining whether a society can change.

In the universities, liberalism as an idea spans conservative and modern liberal camps and is, indeed, on trial. For the underlying assumption of this doctrine is that Western civilization embodies universal values such as individual freedom. This formulation contains one of the most crucial and explosive contradictions of liberalism: its claim that individuality is the telos of social evolution. Yet, it implies the ineluctability of difference, a characteristic that undermines the universalist claim. Individuality signifies more than the quest for human rights or the celebration of private interest. It has been intertwined with concepts such as democratic vitality, made the condition for the emergence of a "learning society," and is inherent in the very idea of modernity, as the cornerstone of modern liberal thought.

Of the consequences of this philosophy, none stands higher than the idea that through the tolerance of diversity—in thought, culture, and politics—a democracy may thrive, individual aspirations be accommodated, and the "national" interest be served not by pressure to conformity but by free discussion and debate. The trials of liberalism are concentrated in the characteristic claims of the so-called p.c.'s. For, contrary to the earlier dominant alternative position to liberal democracy that there was a revolutionary truth handed down by the "scientific" discoveries of Marxism-Leninism, whether in Moscow or in Beijing, the discourse of multiculturalism (one of the names under which this movement is known) wants nothing more or less than, in the name of pluralism, to place Eastern, African, Latin American, and other nondominant cultures next to European culture. In this way the claims of Western culture to its privileged place on the evolutionary apex of civilizations can be abolished. Similarly, heterosexuality is taken to be only one of several practices that constitute the range of legitimate sexual choices, the others enjoying equal status. It refuses the claim of universal value except that inherent in the ideology of diversity: that individuals have the inherent right to free association and to hold views that run against the current. In a different register, postmodernism has, perhaps most controversially, challenged some of the cherished assumptions of Western values, perhaps most saliently, that science refers unimpeachably to a reality independent of its procedures; and both the ancient and modern belief that all reliable knowledge must be *grounded* in foundational thinking derived from Aristotelian conceptions of logical first principles.

As with oppositional political ideologies, small and otherwise marginal publications and spiritualist, left-wing, nationalist, and feminist movements have with some persistence disseminated their orientations for decades. What is new is that now they demand public representation in the curriculum of mainstream educational institutions at all levels, and they seem to have the popular force to compel consideration by established authorities. Moreover, they want to take their rejection of, and alternatives to, the privileged place traditionally accorded a literary/philosophical canon into the mainstream of U.S. academic and intellectual life.

Subordinate groups argue that the prevailing canon that gives precedence to the works of white males is a matter of convention rather than of human nature and has occupied a majisterial place only since the nineteenth century. At that time, most notably, Matthew Arnold, responding to the rise of contemporary working-class movements and a nascent working-class culture, defined the canon as "the best that has been thought and said" against the claims of this burgeoning social movement that carried with it popular class-based literature. According to the new educational reformers, these conventions are too narrow because they fail to make room for "Third" World, women, African-American, gay and lesbian writers and practitioners of other art forms and alternatives to Western philosophy such as those of the East and Africa. But the challenge to the canon emanates from another direction as well. Since the early 1960s a movement to valorize working-class, black, and Latino popular cultures as aesthetically valid works of art has contested the claim of "high" culture to aesthetic privilege. In the pursuit of what is sometimes known as "cultural studies," which is most often identified with the insistence on the academic legitimacy of popular culture studies, there is a new emphasis on going beyond the disciplines. This development has been dictated as much by the character of its objects as by the diverse credentials of its practitioners.

"Cultural studies" was the name given to the movement in British universities and among disaffected American cultural critics, mostly those outside the academic system, in order to *aesthetically* and *politically* valorize popular culture. Cultural studies signified the refusal of a substantial fraction of a new generation of British and American intellectuals in the late 1950s and 1960s to observe the hierarchy between high culture and the culture, in both the artistic and anthropological sense, of the popular classes, particularly workers, youth, and blacks. While insisting on the cultural value of the "lower" classes, these critics most saliently addressed the ideological basis of distinctions between high and low. In the subsequent decades, as new, emergent discourses developed into social movements, particularly of feminism and race, but also ecology and sexuality, and they found their way into universities, cultural studies became one of the names for what became a virtual revolution in the literary and cultural-theoretical canon. These emergent discourses demanded the inclusion of women's, Third World, and African-American writing, or, alternatively, they claimed the irrelevance of the established canon in literature, philosophy, and criticism. As we have noted, some proponents of cultural studies have even disputed the category of canon itself on the ground that the authority of knowledge has already been radically decentered and that those who insist on it hold on, not as they claim by virtue of the intellectual or moral superiority of their position, but on the basis of sheer power over institutional resources.

The past decade has witnessed an outpouring of critical studies of science and technology which, in the long run, may be the most important aspect of the several challenges to traditional conceptions of legitimate intellectual knowledge. These new social studies of science differ from older work by not focusing chiefly on the social and cultural effects of scientific discovery or the reward systems that accrue from the uses of science for economic and military purposes. Rather, they presuppose that, instead of occupying a privileged place in the knowledge hierarchy owing to the superiority of its methods, the processes of scientific inquiry and their results, like other knowledge, are influenced by the historical context under which they are produced and, for some ethnographers, by the power relationships of the laboratory and within the discipline.[8]

These arguments have been made by historians, sociologists, and philosophers who have extended and revised Thomas Kuhn's celebrated thesis that scientific knowledge is not cumulative to mean that it is situated in its own milieu.[9] For example, feminists such as Donna Haraway, Sandra Harding, and Evelyn Fox Keller have argued that science, like any other knowledge, is "gendered";[10] historian Paul Forman found that the Weimar culture, especially its disillusionment with ideas of determinism and causality, shaped the development of quantum mechanics;[11] and anthropologists Bruno Latour and Steve Woolgar disputed the widely held notion that experiment screened out ideological elements in scientific knowledge.[12] They showed how laboratory life, especially conversations among investigators, produces what is taken as fact. In addition, a growing number of studies have shown that machinery and what is termed "incriptions" are not merely tools of inquiry but are *internally* linked to the results of investigation. In some respects, this more recent work follows Ludvik Fleck's work who, in 1938, showed that the scientific community did not even recognize syphilis until it had affected the middle class. His conclusion, that scientific "facts" are not discovered but are *constructed* from the interests and concerns of scientists acting within a broader social and cultural environment, has become one of the more powerful and recent concerns of social studies of science: to discern the conditions under which knowledge becomes legitimate and hegemonic. The philosophical and ideological implications of what is ordinarily taken as pristine scientific knowledge comprise a new, crucial dimension of efforts by a substantial, though a minority, movement within social scientific disciplines, to question the authority of disciplines they believe hold a privileged place in the pantheon of legitimate intellectual knowledge. What distinguishes this effort from earlier work is the much disputed statement that there are no purely internalist explanations for scientific discovery and that the referent for the content of these discoveries is not only their object but also the context within which they are produced.

But these academic movements do not, in the main, seek to create new disciplines that can stand alongside others. Instead, they have initiated new lines of inquiry that depart from algorithms, methods, and models employed by schools of positivism, historicism, and empiricism which still prevail in both the humanities and the social sciences. In the past two decades, philosophers and social and cultural theorists influenced by Marx and Wittgenstein, by the post-Nietzschean emphasis of French social thought, and by Durkheim's theory that what is called "truth" is socially conditioned, have adopted the perspective that objects of inquiry may be treated as "texts." Investigators trained in all of the social scientific disciplines and history have become interested in language as a constituting element of knowing. Consequently, they borrow the methods of contemporary literary studies—narrative and discourse analysis, semiotics, and ideology-critique—and have exhibited increasing interest in ethnography.

During the past decade, these ideas have circulated with increasing force in U.S. universities, but not without controversy and rancor. One of the difficulties in gaining institutional, as opposed to academic, intellectual legitimacy may consist in the relative distance of cultural studies from the historical successes of social movements outside the university. Proponents have represented their educational ideas primarily in conceptual terms. This strategy has successfully opened up a major debate about the critical function of the university, and the legitimacy of traditional knowledge and its division of labor. It has also resulted in few *permanent* institutional bases for the movement. However, despite relatively little institutional power, the movements of multiculturalism, cultural studies, as well as the older gender, race, and ethnic studies are perceived by their critics as the true "enemy within."

NOTES

1. To be politically correct signified that one adhered to the line of whatever movement claimed to have a morally unimpeachable politics. It rapidly became an ironic comment among those who refused to join the rush toward revolutionary communist politics in the early 1970s. In conversation it usually reminded interlocutors that they were engaging in dubious moralism. Or, if you wished to say something that was iconoclastic, you prefaced your remarks with, "I know this may not be politically correct but . . . ."

2. Francis Fukuyama, "The End of History," *National Interest,* No. 16 (Summer 1989). The Free Press published Fukuyama's book, *The End of History and the Last Man* in 1992.

3. Fukuyama, "The End of History," p. 3.

4. Ibid., p. 18.

5. Irving Kristol, "Comment" in *National Interest,* No. 16 (Summer 1989), p. 28.

6. Arthur Schlesinger, Jr., *The Disuniting of America* (New York: Doubleday, 1992).

7. Jürgen Habermas, *Theory of Communicative Action,* vol. 2 (Boston: Beacon Press, 1987).

8. Here we can give only representative works of an accelerating outpouring. For the best introduction, see Karen Knorr-Cetina and Michael Mulkey, eds., *Science Observed* (London, Beverly Hills, Calif., and New Delhi: Sage Publications, 1983); Michael Mulkey, *Science and the Sociology of Knowledge* (London: George

Allen and Unwin, 1979) ; David Bloor, *Knowledge and Social Imagery* (London: Routledge, 1976).

9. Thomas Kuhn, *The Structure of Scientific Revolutions,* 2d ed. (Chicago: University of Chicago Press, 1969).

10. Sandra Harding, *The Science Question in Feminism* (Ithaca, N.Y.: Cornell University Press, 1986), is clearly the most comprehensive feminist critique of scientific knowledge in the literature. It provides an excellent overview of the argument. See also Evelyn Fox Keller, *Reflections on Gender and Science* (New Haven, Conn.: Yale University Press, 1985); and Helen Longino, *Science as Social Knowledge* (Princeton, N.J.: Princeton University Press, 1990).

11. Paul Forman, "Weimar Culture, Causality, and Quantum Theory, 1918–1927: Adaptation by German Physicists and Mathematicians to a Hostile Intellectual Environment," *Historical Studies in the Physical Sciences,* Third Annual Volume (Philadelphia: University of Pennsylvania Press, 1971). This monograph may be taken as the exemplary work of the study of scientific knowledge as, in part, the outcome of the cultural context within which it is produced. While others have looked at "laboratory life" to find this context, Forman reaches to the complex influences on the intellectuals of art, philosophy, and the cultural consequences of cataclysmic events such as the Great War to discover the roots of knowledge.

12. Bruno Latour and Steve Woolgar, *Laboratory Life* (London and Los Angeles: Sage Publications, 1979); Ludvik Fleck, *The Genesis and Development of a Scientific Fact,* eds. Thomas Kuhn and Robert Merton (Chicago: University of Chicago Press, 1976).

Chapter Eight

Are We Having Fun Yet? Computers and the Future of Work and Play

LOOKING BACK

I (SA) am a volunteer at a small alternative public elementary school in Brooklyn that is using Apple computers and several instructional programs to assist fifth and sixth graders to learn typing and to improve their language skills. My job is to insert the disks and load the software, observe that the programs are being properly used, and help with any problems the kids may have. Four kids at a time come to the computer room, a small, attic-like space on the top floor of this old building. With the exception of beginners, the kids are required only to follow the program's commands, complete a sequence of operation, and either do it all again or return to their classrooms.

The typing program is a multicolored version of the one I used in the seventh grade on the old Underwood manual typewriter provided to us in Junior High School 118 by the New York City Board of Education some forty years ago. Although the typing is now very quiet, the routine is identical—FRF [space] JUJ [space] . . . and so on. The feedback from the program is cuter than my typing teacher's watchful eye and disapproving correcting words, but it is no more exciting. The programs are indexed to the kids' improvement with the higher levels of proficiency needed to copy business letters and disembodied, abstract texts geared to training modern secretaries.

Learning the old skill of typing is undoubtedly useful, and there may be no reason to forsake tried but true methods. It also makes sense to learn typing on a soft keyboard since most writers now use word processors, but there is nothing special about this computer exercise.

The programs for language skills are examples of alternative ways of learning. The old "supply the missing word" and practice drills for vocabulary building that I experienced in my time have been replicated by the programs. And like most of the kids back then, the kids today are appropriately bored—they dutifully perform the commands that appear on the screen with more or less difficulty, but all seem anxious to finish their assignment and leave. While their haste may have something to do with the uninviting ambience, it is also caused by a kind of learning that feels more like work than play.

These exercises are comparable to the early days of any new medium—of cinema, for example, where people filmed stage plays or early TV where people televised radio shows. In other words, while the programmers of these learning "tools" seem to recognize that display graphics can enhance what would otherwise be routine operations and dull images, they also seem to have no sense of the contexts within which their programs are to be used. The cute graphics only serve to underline the degree to which the capacities of the medium are underutilized, and, most significantly, in this concern with display, the users and their specific needs and interests disappear.

Of course, this example may be criticized as the extreme case in which the computer takes on the function of the rote teacher (minus the disciplinarian's disdain). The computer can be used to help students learn physics and math, subjects in which operational competence seems to presuppose (at least in part) familiarity with procedures and categories that resist efforts to eliminate drills. Students can learn at their own pace the aspects of those relatively decontextualized disciplines such as math and physics that require a certain amount of rote learning at the outset. In programs developed by sophisticated computer scientists and educators such as Seymour Papert and Joseph Weizenbaum, play is combined with rigorous, rule-driven algorithms. Under these conditions, learning becomes challenging, an enjoyable activity that helps the student master traditional analytic skills. Nevertheless, as I will show below, the possibilities for playful *self-development* inherent in the technology remain to a large degree unexplored in schools as well as in the workplace.

The ubiquity and power of computers in the contemporary world has provoked considerable debate. For enthusiasts like Papert, Shoshana Zuboff, and many others, the computer is a tool, a term that suggests a neutral social and political content.[1] The versatility of the computer can provide the key to the historic dream that all work, including school work, can become a vehicle of human creativity, that is, a form of play. According to this claim, the computer provides one of the keys to the kingdom of delineated culture. Meanwhile, critics of computers in education—people like Weizenbaum, Hubert and Stuart Dreyfus, and Edmund Sullivan—have warned about the excessiveness and even dangers of the claims made by researchers such as Herbert Simon and his followers, that artificial intelligence (AI) represents a new stage in human dominion over nature and "man."[2]

These critics, most of whom proceed from humanistic assumptions, propose that the human agency is irreplaceable and that computers can do no more or no less than those who create, program, and operate them. Some of these humanists, however, agree with the enthusiasts that the computers can be useful; where they disagree is on the idea that computers can solve most, if not all, of the problems of learning and teaching and constitute nothing less than a panacea for settling educational issues. The humanists want to preserve the traditional idea that technological advances can become a "tool" of freedom from onerous work, but they, too, share the pessimism of the more determined critics of computers: the belief that technology is now the predominant form of life, penetrating not only our social relations but our personalities and culture as well.

A third perspective reverses this sweeping notion that we now live in what may be termed a *technoculture*. If it is true that we have all become "pluggies" in that we are now surrounded by various forms of computer-mediated work, communications, arts, and education, technology has penetrated, metaphorically, our *being*. In contrast to earlier judgments of critics like Herbert Marcuse, Jacques Ellul, and Lewis Mumford[3]—thinkers spawned in the last bourgeois era for whom the advance of electronic media spelled the doom of critical thought and democratic politics (since most of us have been deprived of the capacity for independent judgment by the new communications technologies)—the new theorists of technoculture are postcritical.[4] They believe that, just as it is futile to mourn the passing of the horse and carriage, there are really no alternatives to computer and electronic mediations in everyday life. Technology has become the new form of life; the only issue is how to harness it for playful, erotic, and otherwise self-fulfilling purposes.

This chapter explores the position of professionals in light of postcritical attitudes about computers. It is presented in three sections: first, a model of the professional life that is embedded in my brief description of computer-aided instruction; second, three accounts of the ways in which computer technology is being integrated into the prevailing regime of management-directed production of goods and services; and last, a reconsideration of the problems of educating students for the computer-mediated literate culture of the future.

ON BEING A PROFESSIONAL

The ideology of professionalism is rooted in the belief that some categories of labor possess skills or knowledge that entitle those who possess them to considerable autonomy in the performance of their work.[5] Thus, there is a contrast between the capacity to make independent decisions based on specialized knowledge and the close supervision of most labor, called for by Taylorism, presumably because most manual jobs require little or no training that is not obtained in the workplace. Even skilled labor forms a relatively small part of the total labor process. Meanwhile, the extent of the autonomy enjoyed by a given profession is relative to its status within the larger culture. For example, at least until recently, physicians in the United States were ordinarily subject only to peer review similar to the self-policing of natural scientists, whereas in the former Soviet Union as well as many countries of both Eastern and Western Europe, the state bureaucracy is under the control of political managers who oversee work in the natural and health sciences.

The rapidly changing knowledge needed to perform professional work limits the ability of those physicians, scientists, and engineers (traditionally the most *professional* of our professions) who occupy high administrative positions in their respective bureaucracies to direct professional work. In a climate marked by rapid change in the professional's knowledge base, professionals who can no longer practice their trade are often made managers; their link to emerging knowledge is extremely fragile and, in time, may disappear entirely. One response to this recent trend is to replace such specialist-managers with professional managers in cases where there is no presumption of shared expertise. For this and other reasons, the hierarchical relation between the bench and management is made clearer.

Even in the United States, where state bureaucracy is weakest among the "advanced" industrial societies, this transformation may be traced, in broad outlines, to the increased stratification of most professional services—that is, to the close integration of public and private investment in both goods and services. For example, nearly all basic research in the natural sciences is publicly supported, even if it is frequently administered by nongovernmental organizations. The complexity of the relations between public and private agencies has led to the creation of a new profession of decision-making. Thus, managers, especially those in the health, education, and other public services, must now concern themselves with budgets and other specialized financial issues as well as issues involving the unionization of workers.[6] In such an environment, the administrative task of making decisions is often abstracted from the concrete labor to which they refer.

Although it would be a mistake to overemphasize the degree of collegiality in the older institutions concerned with the production and dissemination of knowledge, the appearance of the knowledge factory at the turn of the twentieth century and its maturation during World War II signaled an important change in the history of science and technology. This change can be traced back to the movement from Pasteur's laboratory, to General Electric's research facility in Schenectady, New York, and Bell Labs in New Jersey, and to the Lawrence-Livermore Labs and comparable facilities in Brookhaven and Oak Ridge, and finally to the massive biotech labs of the University of California at San Diego.[7]

It is perhaps too easy to forget how such large organizations are often inimical to invention and even innovation. Bureaucracies like other social forms regularly take on a life of their own, outliving their original purpose. Consequently, even giant electronic corporations such as IBM, ITT, and ATT have finally grasped the wisdom of financing independent entrepreneurs to develop both hardware and software. Bankrolled by wealthy corporate sponsors, a plethora of tiny companies of two to six employees sprang up headed by former IBM, Microsoft, or DEC hackers. After developing a new wrinkle on a calculating or word processing program, they are typically reintegrated by the corporation as a new division or "team" charged with providing technical assistance to customers using the new product or heading up a new development group. This shift toward allowing hackers (at least temporarily) the greater flexibility of small business operators has been decisive, not only in software development, but also in business systems generally. Yet even this trend gives no indication that real control has ever passed from the hands of the traditional players.

At work here is a system that has developed largely since the end of World War II. Within the regime of the corporate/state bureaucracy, ruled by a professional manager rather than a specialized practitioner, the traditional professions have been increasingly proletarianized, if not with respect to income, then certainly with respect to their subordination. That is, they have tended to lose their right to control the conditions of their own labor, especially to make autonomous decisions based on judgments linked to their credentials and knowledge.[8]

The computerization of whole categories of industrial work has attracted intellectual labor mainly because it seems to provide a scientific and technical, rather than a political, basis for reintegrating design and execution. The widespread introduction of computers into industrial production, administration, and various services seems to extend the tendency associated with the old mechanical/industrial regime's effort to reproduce the "mass worker."[9] This mass worker represents the triumph of Fordism. Through this industrial movement, production and consumption were integrated even as workers were deprived of the smallest vestiges of control they had formerly enjoyed within the labor process before the full implementation of mass, mechanical industrial production.[10]

The new post-Fordist labor process seems to be marked by the integration, and not the separation, of intellectual and manual labor. The logical and temporal sequences within design itself and between design and production have been dramatically foreshortened in those plants that employ Computer-Aided Design and Manufacture (CAD-CAM). Instantaneous communication between once distinct sectors of a plant means that different parties must adapt to and assimilate each other's specific characteristics and problems. At a minimum, the traditional bottlenecks to industrial production are more rapidly widened. At best, CAD-CAM blurs the lines of demarcation between design and execution, so that the shop floor can "participate" in the design process to the extent that management is able or willing to broaden and even democratize power over decision-making so as to include "manual" labor.[11]

In fact, today such distinctions are often blurred (but not entirely obliterated) in most technologically advanced plants. Corporate-sponsored "quality circles," for example, provide an opportunity for nearly the entire workforce to give their views on such matters as the labor process, work conditions, management characteristics, and other shop issues. Yet such "quality circles" also provide enlightened management with the opportunity to coopt union-sponsored protest as well as to train workers under changing conditions that require their participation and, to a certain extent, their independent judgment regarding production decisions.[12] In the United States and Britain, however, many efforts are still being made to impose the old managerial regime on newly "socialized" workers who are themselves capable of managing the entire labor process—that is, among workers whose grasp of the new helped integrate the computer-mediated manufacturing process, gained through their mastery of CAD/CAM.

NARRATIVE 1: A HOPEFUL LOOK

In 1986–89 I (SA) was part of a group of social investigators who observed what happened when CAD was introduced into two large New York public agencies that employed hundreds of engineers and into a similarly large New Jersey state agency.[13] What effects did this innovation have on a group of professional and technical workers as well as on those who, even if not conventionally credentialled, perform professional and technical labor? Specifically, we wanted to know how the character of the work was changed and whether power relations between managers and employees were significantly altered. How did these groups compare with industrial and clerical labor, workers who, in the main, had experienced computerization as an extension of the old industrial culture? Were new work relationships forged among these more highly qualified groups?

Civil, electrical, and mechanical engineers employed by public agencies design a variety of infrastructure installations such as water systems, pumping stations, switch signals for subways, and bridges for trains and autos. Traditionally, nearly all the design work was performed by hand and brain, employing no mechanical equipment other than drafting tools, many of which were as old as engineering itself. CAD and its counterpart, CAM, marked a revolution in the work of these engineers. Now almost all of the painstaking labor of preparing blueprints, a process that used to occupy weeks of work before matters of design innovation could even be considered, is reduced to several hours of work on a computer. After the basic model has been generated on the screen, adjustments and variations can be made quickly online.

Whereas in the old design process mathematical calculations had to be performed one at a time, the CAD program provides the engineer with a menu of mathematical options merely by pressing a key. Since much of the design work of civil engineering is based on standard dimensions, only a small percentage of the work involves special problems of calculation. In the old regime, nearly 90 percent of an engineer's time was spent on drafting and math. These were more or less routine activities that were the necessary preconditions for whatever innovations were required as a result of the special conditions of a project—for example, the limitations of space and terrain in a waste disposal system. CAD sharply reduces the time necessary to generate these routine preconditions and thus allows far more time to be spent on how to take these limiting special conditions into account. But CAD can also do much more. Some CAD programs developed in the past decade are equipped with three dimensions, a feature that partially obviates one of the most crucial components of engineering design, the engineer's ability to visualize the end product. Now the relative literalization of the image removes another major obstacle to the elapsed time of design.

At first the engineers at one of the agencies were delighted to have CAD, because it made their work not only infinitely less tedious, mainly by removing many drawing requirements, but more precise as well without their having to produce a seemingly endless series of distinct drawings. The introduction of computer terminals throughout this agency enhanced the engineers' solidarity by providing them with knowledge that managers did not necessarily possess. In addition, they learned CAD together, and its application, unlike that of drafting, became a collective effort. The managers and engineers, eager to expand CAD so that everyone had access to a terminal, hoped that the new technology would bolster their longstanding complaint against contracting out design work. Here they felt was a technology that made them more versatile and more productive. Many of the agency's managers shared a vision of restoring the reality of a fully competent *public sector* that might use private contractors for specialized jobs but would take full responsibility for all aspects of the design process.

For these employees, the dream of merging work with play seemed to be within their grasp. The actual work process began to resemble a basic science laboratory that facilitated experimenting with different approaches to a given problem. What had formerly been considered routine, manual labor now became truly intellectual work. We observed engineers who delighted in the work regardless of the routine nature of the design problem itself. What counted here was, in the first place, the possibility of gaining, through technology, an edge in their never-ending quest for greater job control. They were learning something new, and it was this learning itself that excited them as much as the possibilities for gaining greater autonomy from managerial bureaucracies whose responsibilities in the past often constrained creative work.

It is still too soon to know whether such hopes can be fully realized in what remain hierarchical organizations, even for qualified professionals and even with the support of creative managers. The work process, after all, is finally subject to the economic and political exigencies and struggles of larger organizations. Even if these engineers are being transformed from relatively highly paid workers to "hackers" (the term denoting people who dedicate themselves to exploring the full potential of personal computers), they are finally not free to determine the product of their labor. In this respect, they are like the important group of systems analysts and programmers described by Steven Levy who were completely oblivious of or indifferent to the larger context of their work—the extensive defense operations at MIT.[14] In this, too, they mirrored the complicity of those scientists who, without reservation, worked for the defense establishment because the Department of Defense was virtually the only source of funds for basic research. Civil engineers are historically also liberated from such considerations, and thus free to turn their relatively routine labor into creative work.

NARRATIVE 2: A TROUBLING LOOK

The outcome for the engineers in the other two public agencies provides a fruitful contrast to this relatively optimistic case. In these other two agencies, management selected a far less versatile CAD program, one lacking three-dimensional capability. Nor was training provided for the entire engineering workforce. The management of these two saw the introduction of CAD strictly as a question of productivity gain: its chief function was to reduce and eventually eliminate drafting and to facilitate the rapid completion of completely routine tasks. The engineers in turn did not respond enthusiastically to the introduction of this limited CAD program or to the prospects of computer technologies in general. Instead, they were suspicious of management's exclusive preoccupation with productivity at their expense, and so issues of job security rose to the fore.

As with the first agency, engineers in these other two organizations were also long concerned with the issue of contracting out. Management, they charged, had reserved the more interesting and complex work for outside contractors; management's response to this charge was that inside employees lacked the necessary expertise. Over the years the amount of work that was farmed out grew steadily, with inside employees relegated to routine assignments and inspecting the finished work of others. These engineers complained that they were really correcting the mistakes of the contractors, while being prevented by political and bureaucratic authorities from fully utilizing the potential of CAD. The interviews with the engineers in these two agencies reveal the extent to which the panopticon, that is, employee surveillance, remains in place, even as technology with truly revolutionary potential is directed to the task of reproducing power—indeed, of further proletarianizing the labor of engineers.

NARRATIVE 3: A REALISTIC LOOK

General Electric's Aircraft engine plant in Cincinnati, Ohio, employs some 2,000 design engineers, divided into several categories: a fairly large number employed in CAD/CAM whose work consists mainly in solving the technical problems of integrating the two functions of quality control of the end product and working closely with managers and workers in the production end; a smaller section employed exclusively on the designs of engine parts using CAD for routine adjustments of fairly well-established products; and, finally, a small, elite corps engaged in basic and applied research on CAD software itself, of which General Electric is a major producer both for its own operations and on a commercial basis. The employment relations manager of the plant told me that much of this research was dedicated to finding ways of making further cuts in the labor force of engineers as well as manual workers. He acknowledged that the productivity savings in drafting made possible by CAD would eventually reduce the number of engineers to one-sixth of its current numbers, a number that could only be balanced by a sixfold increase in defense and commercial orders. When I visited the plant in 1986, half the orders were for civilian aircraft and the other half for military. With pressures for cuts in the military budget mounting in Congress, the company anticipated considerable reductions in the number of drafters and engineers.

Also clear was the severe reduction in the ratio between manual and professional employees. Millions of square feet of space stood relatively empty of living labor, inhabited instead by computer-driven numerical controls sitting inconspicuously atop most of the machine tools and computer-mediated lasers used for boring holes. Whereas in the old regime the floor would have been crammed with people, now only the haunting presence of robots was visible. The few "live" workers, who seemed marginal to the production process, were in fact knowledgeable workers who served not merely as "watchers" in the sense that Marx used the term in the *Grundrisse*. They were constantly making adjustments in the programs, in part by continual communication with the CAD/CAM engineers to whom they offered valuable input used in making design changes. These machinists may have lost some of their older skills, but they were now programmers. They may have missed some of the features of the old industrial regime, but they also enjoyed the considerable range of activities offered in their new work.

Although some machinists and toolmakers stated that they had always interacted with engineers, they also admitted that the new knowledge base that had resulted from the introduction of CAD/CAM had improved the quality of this interaction. The manufacturing side now seemed less subordinate. The distinction between socially constructed intellectual and manual labor ("socially constructed" because all work entails judgment and planning), however, was preserved, in part, by corporate labor relations and union contracts. The managerial and engineering staffs, as part of the company's commitment to preserving the hierarchy of knowledge, shared only a limited quantity of power with the machinists. Although the integration of design and execution had become the official discourse of company managers with whom I talked, hierarchical relations remained (ultimately) in force, especially in the face of a lurking disagreement. There was no mechanism for ironing out differences, and the machinists were frequently obliged to back down, despite their considerable experience in the technical aspects of design, their newly won familiarity with computer programming, and their understanding of production problems.

This GE plant is only one of several that I visited in which the introduction of CAD/CAM revealed the Janus-faced character of technology. The company employed computer-mediated processes to upgrade the qualification of some workers and thus to enable these workers to *participate* in some decisions. At the same time, the company also used the technology to cut costs by reducing labor forces at all levels while retaining operational control, as well as ultimate authority, at the level of top management. Despite the partial breakdown of the pure form of managerial authority characteristic of older assembly and parts plants, the panopticon remained alive and well at GE.

LOOKING FORWARD

Proponents of computer-aided education have advanced several central arguments. Computers, they maintain, can individualize instruction in a way that traditional teaching modes cannot.[15] Computers are also versatile; they can be tutors, as seen in the opening of this chapter, or they can be tools, as they are here in providing an array of editing features even as I compose. They can even be tutees, that is, agents that students themselves (playing the role that Seymour Papert calls epistemologist) instruct by writing programs. As Papert contends, the discipline of writing instructions helps the student learn a metaskill, although his insight is partially vitiated by his adherence to an information-processing model of human thought, one that equates insight into how a computer operates with insight into human intelligence.

Hubert and Stuart Dreyfus, John Broughton, and Edmund Sullivan, among others, have provided powerful critiques of such thinking.[16] For the Dreyfuses, for example, the computer has a valuable, though limited, role to play as a classroom tutor for those subjects that require considerable rote learning. However, they reject the notion that the human mind really follows rules analogous to that of the computer, and thus they reject attempts to apply computers in areas involving context-bound thinking. Here knowledge of the terrain must be obtained more by intuition, memory, and specific knowledge of actors or geography than by mastering logical rules. In learning to program, we come to know only certain Aristotelian rules of thought. We do not learn much about the process of thinking which is intertwined with indeterminate situations in which the governing rules are invented by the actors themselves, modified in the course of interaction and negotiation, and not infrequently even violated in order to accommodate to the specificity of the terrain.

Whatever its physiological and biological presuppositions, the development of thinking is profoundly shaped and frequently altered by a multiplicity of determinations, including choices made by people themselves. Even if psychological and physiological research has established that the brain is a binary organ, with each side the repository of certain functions, such an understanding supplies us with only the general preconditions of thinking. Thus, although we can design a computer that helps us address logical, analytic problems (surely an important part of education), the computer will not be able to anticipate or respond to problems that lie outside its logical ordering, say, to the emotional, cultural, and social context within which the learner lives everyday life. While the computer may be designed to replicate the epistemological foundations of technological thinking that is rule-, rather than context-, driven, it cannot be taken as a model for normative thought. It is an interesting machine, beautifully designed for some, not all, purposes.

The elementary school that uses programs to replicate traditional pedagogies is, consciously or not, wasting the instructional potential of computers. Better to employ peer tutoring in cases where some students need additional assistance in mastering the rote features of some disciplines. Interacting with another person is usually a more pleasant way to learn a routine exercise; besides, the tutor can use insights into the nonlogical problems that the tutee may be experiencing. Here the computer may be employed as a supplement, a practice machine enabling the learner to work alone, but only after the benefits of interaction with an instructor-peer or professional have been acquired.

Papert persuasively argues that certain computer games can teach students problem-solving skills in math and science. Such creative employment of the discoveries of artificial intelligence (AI) has been utilized in schools all over the country. Yet the epistemological and educational claims for these programs demonstrate the severe limitations of computer-aided instruction as well. They presuppose a theory of thinking that reduces the brain to a calculating instrument, one whose characteristics may be described and measured with the same precision as a bridge or water distribution system.

Here in the image of the computer program is the basis for the mechanistic world view of molecular biology. The course of an individual's life, like circuits of a computer chip, are inscribed in DNA, the substance that constitutes the genetic material of life. This determinism, which continues the great tradition of genetic science and challenges the largely indeterminate character of evolution theory, evokes the image of the body as a type of machine, an image that has dominated biological thought since the sixteenth century. Vitalism arose in the nineteenth century to oppose this reductionism and proposed, instead, a teleonomic model of the organism.[17] According to this model, from the smallest level of cell to the body as a whole, *purpose* is seen as part of the process of reproduction and decay. Most importantly, although the mechanists obliterated the distinction between mind and body by reducing mind to the brain and the nervous system, that is, by reducing human consciousness to the variations and combinations of atoms and molecules, cells, ganglia, and receptors, the vitalists insisted on a place for spirit, although they used the biological parlance of teleonomic language to disguise the term's idealist origins.

Between mechanism and vitalism, a third group has insisted on treating thinking as a dialectically complex process involving both the internal relations of the organism to itself as well as to its environment and the external relations to the larger economic, political, and cultural milieu.[18] Such an approach holds that the life process in all its aspects bears on how we think. Each of us is shaped by a biophysiological situation, just as each of us is an actor who shapes the multiple aspects of our own thought—modes of communication, discourse, ideology—forms of knowledge that constitute the life-world in which we are all ensconced.

Learning, as seen in this third approach, is not exclusively or even principally a matter of acquiring logically constructed, decontextualized systems of knowledge. Instead, it is a matter of being able to test on a selective basis the appropriateness of fixed knowledge in concrete situations. Only in reflecting on such tests do we ever acquire new knowledge. The student working with a computer on programming or in the pursuit of traditional material is not truly participating in education, as a tutor or a tutee. In either case, as John Broughton has shown, the student is obliged to surrender control over his or her education to the deterministic algorithms of the computer program. Such a student must submit to an externally determined order of knowledge, regardless of how playfully it is taught. Indeed, even the language of computer terminology, with terms such as "command" and "menu ," indicate the degree to which self-management of the learning process is constrained by heteronomy. The binary structure of the computer's yes-and-no questions provides few opportunities for "maybe"; Turing's logic inevitably reduces choices to an Aristotelian imperative.[19]

To be sure, attempts have been made to reach beyond such limitations, as in the playfulness of computer-mediated hypertext. Logging printed texts of all kinds on the computer allows the reader literally to construct a text without observing any linear order. What such a practice reveals is the degree to which readers can produce, and not merely imbibe, texts. Thus, this crucial claim of reader response theory in literary criticism is now given material substance in the indeterminacy of a hypertext. Armed with a bountiful hard disk on which a "classic" novel, poem, or play has been transcribed, the reader is free to become the producer of a new text by juxtaposing words, sentences, and paragraphs, creating new narratives and images, and scrambling the symbolic order of the "original" author, revealing hidden dimensions of the work of art or the treatise that had otherwise been statically enframed.

The implications of such a practice are quite revolutionary. We seem to be entering an era when irony and its companion skepticism are no longer incidental rhetorical devices. Hypertext may become a form of *techne*, in Heidegger's usage, but beneath this new kind of text lies a larger will to playfulness.[20] In a time when we generally admit that the past can be recaptured only from the perspective of a present that is characterized by its own doubts concerning the possibility of any form of self-knowledge, the invocation of the sacred texts of Western culture on the computer monitor no longer enframes our culture. The enframing that does occur makes the opposite point—that what we had thought of as permanent is really only contingent, that high and popular culture are ineluctably intertwined with technology. The assertions that the reader is the author and that the text is a system of signs whose meaning possesses no fixed center have moved beyond the pretty formulations of a literary critic to become, at least tendentiously, our new historical situation.

Some claim that when reading becomes nearly identical with writing—that is, when reading is no longer a putatively passive activity but instead an intervention, an act of transformation—the problem of literacy may no longer possess existential significance. Just as work can become play for those who are empowered to remain at the controls, so art will no longer be, properly speaking, the work of specialists ("artists"), but will be broadly dispersed throughout the technoculture. This transformation applies not only to language but also to images that can now be reproduced without the painstaking preparation of art school or its equivalent in endless years of practice. Such computer-generated images bear the same relation to painting that the mass-produced automobile bears to the hand-built car.

In this regard, Walter Benjamin's meditation on the fate of art work after lithography and photography also applies to the age of the computerized text.[21] The aura has by no means disappeared; throngs of people crowd into museums to view authentic paintings in the latest Matisse, Picasso, or Van Gogh retrospective, and dealers and collectors offer millions of dollars to possess just one of them. Yet too often the significance of going to a museum is encapsulated in being there rather than in our relation to the *meaning* of the work of art, in any of the possible connotations of that phrase. Museum statistics have become a sociological category that has little to do with the aesthetics of presence.[22]

So too with the technoculture's appropriation of literary works. The reader can now deconstruct the work even before reading it in a continuous manner, a practice some would recoil at, not only on grounds of bourgeois taste, but also as an educational and a political issue. After all, might it not be the case that those who ignore history, literary or otherwise, are doomed to relive it, or worse, are just plain doomed?

Under such circumstances, some believe that books will become objets d'art, museum pieces whose survival is a measure only of the reluctance of a conservative publishing industry to develop new markets. As repositories of fixed knowledge, even if subject to interpretations and variations, books would no longer act as cultural gatekeepers. The unfulfilled promise of hypertext is that it abolishes all forms of intellectual authority, revealing in the process that "standards" are socially produced, usually in behalf of the claims of the powerful to act as legatees of culture. In other words, what hypertext promises to expose is the authoritarian character of taste; it is a weapon of the powerless in the struggle for control over the signifiers of culture.

In this context, hypertext is at once a reading of the past and a production of the future in the present. The question is, By whom and for what? For those who object to Benjamin's withering critique of high culture, it is enough to recall that he was among its most dazzling products. Given his understanding of culture as a discourse on power, Benjamin saw the mechanical reproduction of art as an important element in the effort to transform power relations. In effect, he felt that capitalism's development of the means of mass reproduction of art, a corollary of its compulsion to revolutionize the means of production, also signaled its loss of control.

The technoculture, notwithstanding its appropriation by capital as the condition of its growth, is, in all its forms, inherently destabilizing to the regime that gave it birth—the result of dispersal of knowledge by the technology that separates it, at least in part, from power. Or, to be more optimistic, power and knowledge shift away from centers where the new technologies can be easily assimilated into the old cultural and industrial order. The judgments of such writers as Andre Gorz, that the technical experts are merely an adjunct to the capitalist order (largely because they have lost their critical capacity), need to be reversed. Although the traditional intellectual had a wide ideological influence in dominating ethical and cultural discourses, even when politically at the margins of power, the manager nevertheless remained the key intellectual of the industrial order. To the degree that scientific and technical intelligence was merged with management through its final separation from manual labor in the nineteenth and early twentieth centuries, capital could regard resistance in the workplace as a large, albeit manageable, problem existing within rather than outside of the social order.

Since the Second World War, we have witnessed a massive growth of the technical intelligentsia far beyond the traditional professions. The real work of this stratum in the labor system has been to eliminate labor, a development that has produced such massive disruptions in the social and political order that capitalism has had to devise artificial ways of maintaining social discipline through all sorts of useless employment and education. Many capitalist economies today can offer only part-time work for tens of millions of workers, many of whom have experienced sharp reductions in their standard of living.

Meanwhile, technoculture has transformed the nature of information and knowledge beyond the workplace. The growing skepticism of the underlying populations of all countries concerning their economic and political systems is not the result of ignorance but of the countersurveillance techniques of mass communications and computerization. Even though such events as the Iran-Contra investigation in the mid-1980s were "botched" by a political system lacking political will and the Reagan and Bush administrations succeeded in concealing the Savings and Loan scandal for months, their eventual exposure has accelerated the anti-political tendency of the majority. To understand electoral politics profoundly is to despise and shun them, even where there is no alternative. One of the hallmarks of the panopticon, the one-way mirror, has been smashed, but its result is not to strengthen the democratic tendencies of liberal culture. Rather, in the steadily diminishing voter participation rates in elections (with the marginal exception of the 1992 presidential election), we can observe the formation of a new oligarchy of the involved who, in turn, fear the entropic effects of what is commonly called political "apathy."

Thus, despite truly herculean efforts to quarantine technoculture in trivial pursuits and to confine its applications to entirely conventional areas, its corrosive, anti-authoritarian effects persist. Technological determinists are wrong in thinking that industrial societies can safely contain these effects. One of the inherent features of the microchip is presaged in Marshall McLuhan's nimble phrase "the global village." Prevailing powers have always been able to evoke and reproduce the exotic, the esoteric. In a computer-mediated world, even the subaltern has lost the aura of otherness. With the emergence of dialogics and the philosophy of difference, we now have the promise that communication can overcome all barriers, even though the spurious quest for universal truth seems as common today as it ever was.

Which brings us full circle to the promise of technology. Contrary to some claims, the computer is most valuable not so much in fostering scientific/technical learning, but in radically transforming the character of the humanities and social sciences. Its radical futurity lies not chiefly in its uses for transmitting past knowledge—in Sartre's terms for (re)producing the practico-inert. When confronted with knowledge as the "always already," kids imbued with the postmodern condition (experienced as joissance as much as suffering), students often charge that they are being burdened by schools with "old " learning. Where some view the past as representing a particular view of the civilized society (the absence of which marks the individual and group as somehow "deprived"), young people from both dominant and subaltern cultural backgrounds emphatically reject characterizations of their culture as inferior.

As we argued in the chapter on political correctness (chapter seven), the so-called culture wars are being waged over who has the power to confer cultural legitimacy, a power that is linked to but not subordinate to system considerations. That is, insofar as culture, including schooling, is relatively autonomous and is not entirely subject to the configurations of power in other arenas such as the economy and the state, issues such as curriculum, pedagogy, and the technologies of learning may be treated as discourses in their own right. Although it is not surprising that computer-aided teaching and learning would arise in the wake of the technoculture and the shape of its deployment might resemble the reductionism characteristic of its assimilation into prevailing managerial ideologies, there is still remove from counter-hegemonies.

For example, we could argue that the computer's versatility subverts the deadness of the past and is an effective way of selectively recovering social and historical memory. Thus, history may no longer be conceived in the model of approved tradition but as a terrain as much as a treasure of *counter-memories,* an opportunity to store narratives of resistance on disks written by "learners" as well as by traditional historians. At the same time, in contrast to the physical book that must be subject to processes of industrial production, autobiographies and other stories inscribed in the computer's memory may be transmitted via e-mail to a vast, unseen network of readers who can, in turn, comment, reply, and supply their own stories.

Thus does the computer begin to valorize Benjamin's assertion that mass reproducibility constitutes a democratic promise rather than an authoritarian scourge as many critics have claimed. However, whether the computer emancipates or subordinates is not, as technological determinism would have it, given. On the one hand, computer-mediated labor tends to liberate all but a relatively small coterie from the waged workplace. If the fantastic productivity gains were shared according to an egalitarian ideology of distributive justice, computers would become the vehicle for a kind of play/work in which the full development of the individual now liberated for much of the day/week from paid labor was, at least putatively, embodied. Or, the computer realizes Jeremy Bentham's panopticon on a scale unimagined by the philosopher.

The path computer-aided education should take is entirely a political question. As much as we may ruminate on the possibilities for genuine, noninstrumental learning suggested by the personal computer, its deployment inheres not in its chip and keyboard but in its discursive position in the larger framework of social production and distribution of knowledge. In this connection, the computer as a fundamental technology of life-long learning should not be construed in the prevailing mode: If we are destined to have seven careers in a typical working life, we have no alternative but to exceed our initial credentials. This argument, however valid, misses the point: the role of the computer as a force for empowerment depends on freeing education from its recent rational-purposive context, wage labor. In this case, education becomes a way to disseminate counter-hegemonic culture, and computers are no longer subsumed under a regime of cost accounting.

NOTES

1. Seymour Papert, *Mindstorms: Children, Computers, and Powerful Ideas* (New York: Basic Books, 1980).

2. For example, see Edmund Sullivan, "Computers, Culture, and Educational Futures: A Critical Appraisal." *Interchange* 14 (3) (1986), pp. 17–36.

3. Jacques Ellul, *The Technological Society* (New York: Vintage Books, 1964).

4. Of course, the prototypical expression of this position can be found in Herbert Marcuse, *One Dimensional Man* (Boston: Beacon Press, 1964).

5. This issue is taken up in Stanley Aronowitz, *The Politics of Identity* (New York: Routledge, 1992), esp. chapter 5.

6. See ibid., chapter 6.

7. See Bruno Latour, *Science in Action* (Cambridge, Mass.: Harvard University Press, 1986).

8. This issue is addressed in Shoshana Zuboff, *In the Age of the Smart Machine: The Future of the Smart Machine* (New York: Basic Books, 1988).

9. See Richard Edwards, *Contested Terrain: The Transformation of the American Workplace* (New York: Basic Books, 1979).

10. Stuart Hall, "Brave New World," *Socialist Review* 91 (1) (January/March 1991), pp. 57–64. See also a variety of essays on post-Fordism in Stuart Hall and Martin Jacques, eds., *New Times* (London: Verso Press, 1989) .

11. See Stanley Aronowitz, *Science as Power* (Minneapolis: University of Minnesota Press, 1988), esp. Part 1.

12. See Zuboff, op. cit.

13. This is discussed in Aronowitz, *The Politics of Identity,* op. cit.; see chapter 5.

14. Steven Levy, *The Hackers* (New York: Anchor Press/Doubleday, 1984).

15. For an analysis of this position, see C. Paul Olson, "Who Computes?" in David Livingstone et al., eds. *Critical Pedagogy and Cultural Power* (Westport, Conn.: Bergin and Garvey, 1987), pp. 179–204.

16. See Sullivan, op. cit.

17. This is taken up in Stanley Aronowitz, *Science as Power,* op. cit.

18. See John Broughton, *Computers In Education* (New York: Teachers College Press, 1989).

19. See Stanley Aronowitz, "Working Class Culture in the Electronic Age," in *The Politics of Identity,* op. cit., pp. 193–209.

20. Aronowitz, *Science as Power,* op. cit.

21. Walter Benjamin, "The Work of Art in the Age of Mechanical Reproduction," *Illuminations,* ed. Hannah Arendt (New York: Schocken Books, 1969), pp. 217–252.

22. This issue is discussed in Ivan Karp and Steven D. Lavine, eds. *Exhibiting Cultures: The Poetics and Politics of Museum Display* (Washington, D.C.: Smithsonian Institution, 1991).

Chapter Nine

Multiculturalism under Siege in the Reagan/Bush Era

Within the last decade questions of identity and culture have been mobilized within a largely authoritarian populism aimed at containing the possibilities of a multiracial and multicultural democracy. Whiteness as the representation of all that is good, human, and civilized has been called into question by a legacy of decolonization, the rise of new social movements, and an explosion of theoretical discourses aimed at displacing the values and practices of Eurocentrism. Unfortunately, the debate over multiculturalism and its implication for schooling and educational reform has been dominated by neo-conservative intellectuals and public servants under the financial backing of conservative foundations and the power of right-wing government sponsorship. We want to recontextualize the debate on multiculturalism in order to reappropriate its democratic and utopian possibilities as part of a progressive educational agenda.

The notion of multiculturalism that we will develop, though highly tentative and overly schematic in its implications, highlights some considerations not only of the stories we tell as educators but also those stories that we sometimes refuse to hear. Our strategy is to offer a new language in order to help people to raise fresh questions and to address those issues often dismissed from the dominant discourse. The test of this language is whether it helps us as educators and cultural workers to name the specifics of our own worlds with an enunciative energy that generates new forms of practice. Because we don't know the specifics of schooling in those places where this language might be taken up, we do not presuppose that it can be applied outside of those problems whose cogency derives from the particularity of the sites in which they emerge. Hence, it is a collective project that we will have to work out together as part of a broader effort to reform schools and public life.

MULTICULTURALISM, IDENTITY, AND THE
WAGES OF WHITENESS

> Let me begin by saying that we are living through a very dangerous time.
> . . . We are in a revolutionary situation, no matter how unpopular that
> word has become in this country. The society in which we live is desperately
> menaced, not by [the cold war] but from within. So any citizen of this coun-
> try who figures himself as responsible—and particularly those of you who
> deal with the minds and hearts of young people—must be prepared to "go
> for broke." Or to put it another way, you must understand that in the at-
> tempt to correct so many generations of bad faith and cruelty, when it is
> operating not only in the classroom but in society, you will meet the most
> fantastic, the most brutal, and the most determined resistance. There is no
> point in pretending that this won't happen. The obligation of anyone who
> thinks of him or herself as responsible is to examine society and try to change
> it and to fight it—at no matter what risk. This is the only hope society has.
> This is the only way societies change.[1]

We read Baldwin's declaration less as a prescription for cynicism and
powerlessness than as an expression of hope, a desire, as Roger Simon has
put it, "constituted in the need to imagine an alternative human world and
to imagine it in a way that enables one to act in the present as if this
alternative had already begun to emerge."[2] Baldwin's words are moving
because he confers a sense of moral and political responsibility on teachers
by presupposing that they are critical agents who can move between theory and practice in order to take risks, refine their visions, and make a
difference for both their students and the world in which they live. We
want to take up Baldwin's challenge for teachers to "go for broke." In
doing so, we want to address some questions relevant to the debate that is
increasingly being waged around the relationship between multiculturalism
and difference. In this context, we want to focus particularly on what it
means for dominant groups to confront their own space of privilege and
power, while simultaneously addressing the needs of those groups who
traditionally have been excluded from the dominant discourses of schooling and public life.

Our argument addresses multiculturalism as a politics of representation
and a pedagogical practice that is concerned not only with how social
agents write and are written by culture but also with how they struggle to
change it. In this case, multiculturalism is not only about learning simply
how to read, write, or produce culture differently; it also focuses on the
importance of acknowledging that meanings are not fixed. To be literate
is to undertake a dialogue with the multiple languages, discourses, and
texts of others who speak from different histories, locations, and experiences.

But multiculturalism is about more than negotiating and translating the terrain of cultural and semiotic differences. It is also a rupturing practice that engages questions regarding who narrates, for what audience, in what institutional setting, and with what purpose in mind. Put another way, it raises the haunting postcolonial question regarding who speaks, for whom, and under what conditions. Defined in these terms, multiculturalism makes visible how oppressive and dominating practices mediate between the margins and centers of power. Refashioned more critically as a notion of insurgent multiculturalism, it points to pedagogical relations that map difference under conditions of inequality while simultaneously recognizing agency in others. Within this context, multiculturalism points to performative competencies and social practices that are aimed at transforming the material relations of domination and abolishing oppressive regimes of signification.

As part of a broader politics of difference and democracy, multiculturalism points, at the very least, to three important considerations. First, it draws attention to the historically and socially constructed strengths and limitations of those places and borders that we inherit and that frame our discourses and social relations. It raises questions at the very borders of our historical and disciplinary existence.

Second, it is a form of ethical address that highlights how teachers and students construct relationships between themselves and others. It delineates the boundaries of difference and analyzes how power is inscribed differently on the body, culture, history, space, land, and psyche. It points to and makes problematic the conditions of travel among teachers and students between different cultural worlds. Furthermore, it offers a critique of those approaches to multiculturalism defined in monolithic terms that erase power, multiplicity, and diversity, while at the same time sustaining borders of privilege and domination.

Third, insurgent multiculturalism calls into question those spaces and locations that diverse cultural workers and intellectuals inhabit as they seek to secure authority through specific ways of reading or misreading their relationship with the world and others.

An insurgent multiculturalism highlights how differences in power and privilege mediate who speaks, under what conditions, and for whom. In this sense, insurgent multiculturalism raises the question of whether people are speaking within or outside a privileged space, and whether such spaces provide the conditions for different groups to listen to each other differently in order to address how the racial economies of privilege and power work in this society.

In the aftermath of the Los Angeles uprising in 1992, educators need to rethink the politics of multiculturalism as part of a broader attempt to understand how issues regarding national identity, culture, and ethnicity can be rewritten in order to enable dominant groups to examine, acknowledge, and unlearn their own privilege. In part, this demands an approach to multiculturalism that not only addresses "the context of massive black [Latino, Asian, and Caribbean] unemployment, overcrowded schools, a lack of recreation facilities, dilapidated housing and racist policing,"[3] but also makes a concerted attempt to view most racism in this country "not as an issue of black lawlessness but primarily as an expression of white 'supremacy.'"[4] More specifically, a critical multiculturalism must shift attention away from an exclusive focus on subordinate groups—especially since such an approach tends to highlight their deficits—to one that examines how racism in its various forms is produced historically, semiotically, and institutionally at various levels of society.

In opposition to a quaint liberalism, multiculturalism means more than simply acknowledging differences and analyzing stereotypes. More fundamentally, it means understanding, engaging, and transforming the diverse histories, cultural narratives, representations, and institutions that produce racism and other forms of discrimination. As bell hooks points out, white people have for too long imagined that they are invisible to black people. Not only does whiteness in this formulation cease to mark the locations of its own privileges, but also it reinforces relations in which blacks become invisible in terms of how they name, see, experience, and bear the pain and terror of whiteness. Hooks makes this point succinctly:

> In white supremacist society, white people can "safely" imagine that they are invisible to black people since the power they have historically asserted, and even now collectively assert over black people, accorded them the right to control the black gaze. . . . [And yet] to name that whiteness in the black imagination is often a representation of terror. One must face written histories that erase and deny, that reinvent the past to make the present vision of racial harmony and pluralism more plausible. To bear the burden of memory one must willingly journey to places long uninhabited, searching the debris of history for traces of the unforgettable, all knowledge of which has been suppressed.[5]

In the aftermath of the recent Los Angeles uprising, many educational commentators have ruled out any discussion of the relationship between race and class and how they are manifested within networks of hierarchy and subordination both within and outside of the schools. This particular silence, when coupled with the popular perception that the Los Angeles disturbances can be explained by pointing to those involved as simply thugs, looters, and criminals, makes it clear why the multicultural peril is often seen as a black threat. It also suggests what such a belief shares with the traditionalist's view of the "other" as a disruptive outsider. In this scenario, multiculturalism becomes the source of the problem.

In the following pages, we discuss the necessity of creating a border pedagogy as a basis for a new vocabulary of educational leadership. Such a pedagogy allows students and others to move between cultures and to travel within zones of cultural difference. At stake is the need to develop a discourse that challenges the boundaries of cultural and racial difference as sites of exclusion and discrimination while, simultaneously, rewriting the script of cultural difference. This project is part of a broader attempt to provide new spaces for expanding and deepening the imperatives of a multicultural and multiracial democracy.

In short, we want to confront what it means to treat schools and other public sites as border institutions in which teachers, students, and others learn to think and imagine otherwise in order to act otherwise.[6] It is within such institutions engaged in daily acts of cultural translation and negotiation that students and teachers are offered the opportunity to become border crossers. They are thus enabled to recognize that schooling is really an introduction to how culture is organized, demonstrating who is authorized to speak about particular forms of culture, what culture is considered acceptable and worth of valorization or, conversely, invalid and unworthy of public esteem. Drawing in part on Homi Bhabha, we propose that schools, in part, need to be understood as sites engaged in the "strategic activity of 'authorizing,' agency" and of exercising authority in order "to articulate and regulate incommensurable meanings and identities."[7] Within this perspective, leadership is removed from its exclusive emphasis on management. Instead, it is defined as a form of political and ethical address that weighs cultural differences against the implications they have for practices that disclose rather than mystify, democratize culture rather than shut it down, and provide the conditions for all people to believe they can take risks and change existing power relations.

After the fires went out in Los Angeles, the Bush administration once again reneged on its responsibility to address the problems and demands of democratic public life. In the face of escalating poverty, increasing racism, growing unemployment among minorities, and the inability of a growing number of Americans to receive adequate health care or education, the Bush administration invoked a wooden morality coupled with a disdain for public life by cynically blaming the nation's ills on the legislation of the Great Society, TV sitcom characters such as Murphy Brown, and the alleged breakdown of family values. Within this scenario, poverty is caused by the poverty of values, racism is seen as a "black" problem (lawlessness), and social decay can be rectified by shoring up the family and the logic and social relations of the alleged free market.

The Bush administration's response to the Los Angeles riots exemplifies the calcuated blindness characteristic of the Reagan/Bush eras. Abandoning its responsibility for political and moral leadership, the federal government reduced its intervention in public life to waging war against Iraq, using taxpayers' money to bail out corrupt bankers, and slashing legislation that would benefit the poor, the homeless, and the disadvantaged.

There is a tragic irony at work when a government can raise $500 billion to bail out the thrift banks and $50 billion to fight a war in Iraq (put in perspective the combined costs of these adventures exceeds the cost of World War II, including veterans' benefits), while at the same time it cuts back food stamp and school lunch programs in a country in which nearly one out of every four children under six lives in poverty.

But there is more at stake here than simply the failure of moral and political leadership. The breadth and depth of democratic relations are being rolled back at all levels of national and daily life. This is seen, for example, in the growing disparity between the rich and the poor, the on-going attacks by the government and courts on civil rights and the welfare system, and the proliferating incidents of racial harassment and violence on college and public school sites. In this connection, we are obliged to call attention to the complicity of a sector of the liberal establishment in this campaign. A surge of recent books and articles by academics have charted a new approach to the welfare state, according to which the poor are themselves held morally accountable for their condition. Consequently, in Mead's discourse, the state may help find a route out of poverty by requiring welfare recipients to work as a condition of receiving public as-sistance. While retaining some of the precepts of the welfare state, Kaus asks us to accept inequality as a permanent feature of public life, while others in the Clinton administration urge the government to deal with eco-nomic deprivation through trickle-down policies such as investment tax credits.

The retreat from democracy and, especially its fundamental presupposi-tion, a political commitment to equality, are also evident in the absence of serious talk about how we as a nation might educate existing and future generations of students in the practices of moral compassion, critical agency, and public service. The discourse of leadership appears to be trapped in a terminology in which a good society is described through indices that mea-sure profit margins and the Dow Jones Average. Missing in this vocabulary is a way of nourishing and sustaining a popular perception of democracy as something that requires constant struggle within public arenas such as the schools and other sites that embody the promise of a multiracial and multicultural democracy.

This current assault on democratic public life has taken a new turn in the last few years. At one level, American conservatives have engaged in a long-term project of discrediting and dismantling those institutions, ideol-ogies, and practices that are judged incompatible with the basic ideology of the marketplace. In this instance, a diverse alliance of conservatives and neo-liberals has launched a full-fledged and unswerving campaign to trans-form the principles of individualism, choice, and the competitive ethic into state policy. Parallel to this attempt has been the effort to reprivatize and deregulate schools, health care, the welfare system, and other public services and institutions. The extent to which conservatives have gone to promote this project, one that Stuart Hall has rightly called "regressive modernization,"[8] can be seen in President Bush's suggestion in 1992 that Los Angeles sell its international airport to private investors in order to use some of the revenue to rebuild south central L.A.[9] In this perspective, the imperatives of privatization and the profit margin become more important than issues of human suffering and social justice. Of course, this suggestion should not be surprising given the radical rightist assault on all aspects of the public sphere that has been waged during the last decade.

The attempt to rewrite the terms of discourse regarding the meaning and value of public life can be seen in the emergence of a new breed of intellectuals, largely backed by conservative think tanks such as the Madison Group, the Hoover Institute, the Heritage Foundation, and a host of other conservative foundations.[10] With access to enormous cultural resources infused by massive financial backing from the Olin, Scaife, and Smith Richardson foundations, right-wing think tanks have mounted mammoth public campaigns to promote their cultural revolution. Many of the major right-wing intellectuals who have helped to shape popular discourse about educational reform in the last decade have received extensive aid from the conservative foundations. These include intellectuals such as Diane Ravitch, a neo-liberal who has allied herself with the right, Chester Finn, Dinish D'Souza, William Bennett, and Allan Bloom, all of whom have targeted public schools and higher education as two principal spheres of struggle over issues of content, privatization, choice, and difference.[11] In order to understand their model of leadership, it is important to examine how some of their underlying ideological concerns relate to the broader issues of democracy, race, and public accountability.

For many conservatives, the possibility of cultural democracy has become dangerous at the current historical conjuncture for a number of reasons. First, it encourages a critique of those relations that trap people in networks of hierarchy and exploitation. That is, it provides a normative referent for recognizing and assessing competing political vocabularies, the visions of the future they presuppose, and the social identities and practices they both produce and legitimate. By subordinating the discourse of management and efficiency to moral and ethical considerations, a critical discourse of democracy keeps alive the importance of democratic values and how they can be institutionalized into practices that animate rather than restrict the discourse of justice, equality, and community. Clearly, such a position poses a challenge to right-wing educators whose celebration of choice and the logic of the marketplace abstracts freedom from equality and the imperatives of citizenship from its historical grounding in the public institutions of modern society.

In fact, many conservatives such as Lynn Cheney, William Bennett, Chris Whittle, and Diane Ravitch have been quite aggressive in rewriting the discourse of citizenship *not* as the practice of social responsibility but as a privatized act of altruism, self-help, or philanthropy. It is crucial to recognize that, within this ideology of privatization, the disquieting, disrupting, interrupting difficulties of sexism, youth unemployment, AIDS, and other social problems, and how they bear down on schools, are either ignored or summarily dismissed as individual problems caused, in part, by the people who are victimized by them. Of course, not only does this position ignore the necessity for social criticism in a democratic society, but it also erases the moral and political obligation of institutions to recognize their complicity in both creating such problems and eradicating them. In this scenario, we end up with a vision of leadership in which individuals act in comparative isolation and without any sense of public accountability. This is why many right-wing educators praise the virtues of the competition and choice but rarely talk about how money and power, when unevenly distributed, influence "whether people have the means or the capacity" to make or act on choices that inform their daily lives.[12]

Jonathan Kozol is instructive here in recounting the story of how President Bush told a group of parents in 1990 in a desperately poor school district in New Jersey that " 'A society that worships money is a society in peril.' [Kozol responds by asking] Why didn't he say that to the folks in Bloomfield Hills, Michigan or in Great Neck, Long Island? What is the message?"[13] The message, of course, is that power, wealth, and privilege have no bearing on the choices that different groups make, especially if those groups are rich and powerful. Choice in this case serves to rewrite the discourse of freedom within a limited conception of individual needs and desires. What disappears from this view of leadership is the willingness to recognize that the fundamental issues of citizenship, democracy, and public life can neither be understood nor addressed solely within the restricted language of the marketplace or choice. Choice and the market are not the sole conditions of freedom, nor are they adequate to constituting political subjects within the broader discourses of justice, equality, and community. In fact, no understanding of community, citizenship, or public culture is possible without a shared conception of social justice. Yet it is precisely the notion of social justice that is missing in mainstream school reforms.

Robert Bellah and his associates have also argued that Americans need a new vocabulary for talking about the problem and future of schooling. They write: "Money and power are necessary as means, but they are not the proper measures of a good society and a good world. We need to talk about our problems and our future with a richer vocabulary than the indices that measure markets and defense systems alone."[14]

We live at a time when 45 percent of all minority children live in poverty, while the dropout rate among minority students has attained truly alarming proportions, reaching as high as 70 percent in some major urban areas. These problems are compounded by an unemployment rate among black youth that is currently 38.4 percent. In the face of these problems, conservatives are aggressively attempting to enact choice legislation that would divert funds away from the public schools to private schools.

Claiming that these problems can be solved by raising test scores, promoting choice, developing a national curriculum, and creating a uniform standard of national literacy is a one-stop, but authoritarian, program that, if implemented, would simply put more burdens on the victims of social injustice. But this is where the discourse of critical democracy becomes subversive: it makes visible the political and normative considerations that frame such reforms. It also analyzes how the discourse of excessive individualism and competitiveness serves to make social inequality invisible, and it promotes an indifference to human misery and exploitation. Moreover, it suggests that the language of excellence and individualism, when abstracted from considerations of equality and social justice, serves to restrict rather than animate the possibilities of democratic public life.

It is becoming increasingly clear that democracy has become a subversive category to those who would subordinate public institutions to the laws of the marketplace and treat cultural difference as the enemy of Western civilization. In part, this is exemplified in a recent article in *Education Week* in which Chester Finn attempts to provide a rationale for the privatization of schools and other public institutions. He argues that the concept of public no longer merits either the attention or the support of the American people. Couched in the bad versus good rhetoric of simplistic binarisms, Finn dismisses public education by asserting that all institutions that attempt to serve the public as a matter of service rather than profit are doomed to fail (i.e., public transportation, public bathrooms, public health, etc.). Like his conservative colleague, Allan Bloom, Finn argues that he would rather have " 'you' send your kid to Princeton."[15] Of course, the ubiquitous "you" in this sentence speaks for everyone, while failing to mark its own location of privilege. What kind of politics and notion of choice informs the assumption that all parents occupy an equal ground in being able to send their kids to an Ivy League school?

More is revealed here than an offensive elitism (not to mention racism). Lacking any sense of specificity and refusing to address how money and power provide the very conditions for exercising choice, Finn uses choice as a code word to suggest that those who are suffering the most in this society simply lack either the intelligence, character, individual initiative, or competitive spirit to pick themselves up and make a successful go of their lives. These are strange words coming from intellectuals who receive massive financial funding from some of the most aggressive, ideologically conservative foundations in the United States.

Another reason why democracy is so threatening to many conservatives is that it provides a rationale for constructing public spheres in which dif-

ferent groups can reclaim their identities and histories as part of an attempt to exercise power and control over their lives, while simultaneously
attempting to take part in the political system as true participants rather
than as mere consumers.[16] In this context, democracy highlights how cultural difference can be addressed in relation to wider questions of politics,
power, membership, participation, and social responsibility. This perspective flies in the face of the historic program of assimilationism to which
conservative intellectuals are cathected. Their hostility to a cultural politics
of difference is rooted in the tradition that elevates American national culture—its language, its literature, and its system of moral values—to the
status of universality.

Most importantly, numerous groups that have been profoundly underrepresented in the social and cultural narratives of the dominant culture
have begun to redefine the relationship between culture and politics in
order to deepen and extend the basis for a radical democratic society. In
this sense, the promise of a critical democracy has mobilized many subordinate groups to question how cultural identity and representation are being
defined within existing social, cultural, and political institutions. Central
to such concerns are questions regarding how the schools and other institutions are actually responding to the changing conditions of a society that
will no longer have a white majority by the year 2056.[17]

It is difficult to imagine what is either unpatriotic or threatening about
subordinate groups attempting to raise questions such as: "Whose experiences, histories, knowledge, and arts are represented in our educational
and cultural institutions? How fully, on whose terms, and with what degree of ongoing, institutionalized participation and power?"[18] Nor in a
democratic society should subordinate groups attempting to fashion a pedagogy and politics of inclusion and cultural democracy be derisively labeled as "particularistic" because they have raised serious questions regarding either how the public school curriculum works to secure particular
forms of cultural authority, or how the dynamics of cultural power works
to silence and marginalize specific groups of students. This emerging critique of schools and other cultural institutions is based on the assumption
that intolerance, structured inequality, and social injustice, not cultural differences, are the enemy of democracy, as E. D. Hirsch and others have
argued.[19]

Rather than engage the growing insistence of more and more groups in
this country to define themselves around the specificity of class, gender,
race, ethnicity, or sexual orientation, traditionalists have committed themselves to simply resisting these developments. While traditionalists rightly
recognize that the struggle over the form and context of public school
curriculum is fueled, in part, by anxiety about the issue of national identity, they attack this issue from a largely defensive posture. In doing so,
they lack any understanding of how the curriculum itself is implicated in

producing relations of inequality, domination, and oppression. When critical multiculturalists criticize how the curriculum through a process of exclusion and inclusion gives some groups precedence over others, such critics are summarily dismissed as being political, partisan, and radically anti-American.[20]

Central to the traditionalist view of multiculturalism is a steadfast refusal to rethink the source of "moral truth" in light of the expanding social, cultural, and political diversity that has come to characterize American life. As new antagonisms have emerged over the purpose and meaning of schooling, curriculum, and the nature of American democracy, traditionalists have reasserted their allegiance to a foundation of moral truth based on an orthodoxy that, according to James Davison Hunter, represents

> a commitment on the part of [its] adherents to an external, definable, and transcendent authority. Such an objective and transcendent authority defines, at least in the abstract, a consistent, unchangeable measure of value, purpose, goodness, and identity, both personal and collective. It tells us what is good, what is true, and how we should live, and who we are. It is an authority that is sufficient for all time.[21]

In treating national history in fixed and narrow terms, traditionalists relinquish one of the most important defining principles of any democracy. That is, they ignore the necessity of a democratic society to rejuvenate itself by constantly reexamining the strengths and limits of its traditions. In the absence of a critical encounter with the past and a recognition of the importance of cultural diversity, multiculturalism becomes acceptable only if it is reduced to a pedagogy of reverence and transmission rather than a pedagogical practice that puts people in dialogue with each other as part of a broader attempt to fashion a renewed interest in cultural democracy and the creation of engaged and critical citizens.[22] Bhikhu Parekh rightly argues that such a stance defines what he calls demagogic multiculturalism. For Parekh, the traditionalists' refusal of cultural hybridity and difference in favor of the fixity of identity and culture promotes a dangerous type of fundamentalism. He writes:

> When a group feels besieged and afraid of losing its past in exchange for a nebulous future, it lacks the courage to critically reinterpret its fundamental principles, lest it opens the door to "excessive" reinterpretation. It then turns its fundamentals into fundamentalism, it declares them inviolate and reduces them to a neat and easily enforceable package of beliefs and rituals.[23]

Parekh's fear of demagogic multiculturalism represents a pedagogical problem as much as it does a political one. The political issue is exempli-

fied in the traditionalists' view that critical multiculturalism with its assertion of multiple identities and diverse cultural traditions represents a threat
to democracy. The fatal political transgression committed here lies in the
suggestion that social criticism itself is fundamentally at odds with democratic life. Indeed, this is more than mere rhetoric; it is a challenge to the
very basic principles that inform a democratic society. Pedagogically, demagogic multiculturalism renders any debate about the relationship between democracy and cultural difference moot. By operating out of suffo-
cating binarism that pits "us" against "them," traditionalists end all
possibility for dialogue, education, understanding, and negotiation. In other
words, such a position offers no language for contending with cultures
whose boundaries cross over into diverse spheres that are both fluid and
saturated with power. How this type of fundamentalism will specifically
impact the schools can be seen in the increased calls for censorship in the
schools as well as in the bleaching of the curriculum to exclude or under-
represent the voices and histories of various subordinate groups. What is
at stake here is not simply the balkanization of history and national identity, but the attempt to critically recover the diverse narratives of struggle
and possibility that have for better or worse defined this country's engage-
ment with democracy.

Central to the ongoing debates over multiculturalism and the curriculum
is the recognition that curriculum has been increasingly linked to an emerging
politics of cultural difference. This new politics has raised a number of
serious questions about the conditions and forms of authority produced
and secured within public schools. More specifically, at the public school
level, the curriculum has become a contested terrain centering on questions
of representation and the related battle over self-definition and identity.
But in spite of the dismissal of multiculturalism and the politics of cultural
difference, the conflict over the curriculum cannot be understood merely
as an educational problem in the narrow sense of the term. Nor can it be
dismissed as the ranting of discontented minorities and radical educators.
On the contrary, what is at stake in the debate over multiculturalism and
curriculum are crucial issues regarding the meaning and purpose of public
life, national identity, and cultural democracy. Renato Rosaldo is on target
in arguing that "These days questions of culture seem to touch a nerve
because they quite quickly become anguished questions of identity."[24]

Two issues are often overlooked in current public discussions of multiculturalism. First, there are the systemic, economic, political, and social
conditions that contribute to the domination of many subordinate groups.
Second, too little attention is paid to the diverse struggles subordinate groups
undertake through the development of counternarratives that make them
the subject rather than the object of history.

We are not suggesting that multiculturalism can be defined in essentialist
terms. In fact, in contrast to the notion that multiculturalism is simply

dangerous to American society and its public schools, as some traditionalists contend, we would argue that multiculturalism is a complex term
that can be defined through a variety of ideological constructs.[25] In fact,
educators need a definition of multiculturalism that offers schools the possibility to become places where students and teachers can become border
crossers engaged in critical and ethical reflection about what it means to
bring a wider variety of cultures into dialogue with each other. But if the
concept of multiculturalism is to become useful as a pedagogical concept,
it must be redefined outside of a sectarian traditionalism. Educators should
reject any form of multiculturalism in which differences are registered and
equally affirmed but at the expense of understanding how such differences
both emerge and are related to networks and hierarchies of power, privilege, and domination. Moreover, in opposition to the liberal emphasis on
individual diversity, a critical multiculturalism must also address issues regarding group differences and how power relations function to structure
racial and ethnic identities. Furthermore, cultural differences cannot be
merely affirmed in order to be assimilated into a common culture or po-
liced through economic, political, and social spheres that restrict full citizenship to dominant groups. If multiculturalism is to be linked to a renewed interest in expanding the principles of democracy to wider spheres
of application, it must be defined in pedagogical and political terms that
embrace it as a referent and practice for civic courage, critical citizenship,
and democratic struggle. Parekh offers a definition that appears to avoid
both a superficial pluralism and a notion of multiculturalism that is structured in dominance. He writes:

> Multiculturalism doesn't simply mean numerical plurality of different cul-
> tures, but rather a community which is creating, guaranteeing, encouraging
> spaces within which different communities are able to grow at their own
> pace. At the same time it meant creating a public space in which these com-
> munities are able to interact, enrich the existing culture and create a new
> consensual culture in which they recognize reflections of their own identity.[26]

Multiculturalism like any other articulating term is multi-accentual, and
it takes on a different meaning when situated in a more critical perspective.
A critical multiculturalism represents an ideology and set of pedagogical
practices that offers a powerful critique and challenge to the racist, patriarchal, and sexist principles embedded in American society and schooling.
Within this discourse, the curriculum is viewed as a hierarchical and rep-
resentational system that selectively produces knowledge, identities, desires, and values. The notion that curriculum represents knowledge that is
objective, value free, and beneficial to all students is forcefully challenged
as it becomes clear that those who benefit from public schooling are generally white, middle-class students whose histories, experiences, language,

and knowledge largely conform to dominant cultural codes and practices. Moreover, critical multiculturalism performs a theoretical service by addressing curriculum as a form of cultural politics that demands linking the production and legitimation of classroom knowledge, social identities, and values to considerations of power.

In what follows, we want to suggest some general elements that might characterize a critical multicultural curriculum. First, a multicultural curriculum must be informed by a new language in which issues of identity and cultural difference become central to educating students to life in a democratic society. That is, we need a language of politics and pedagogy that is able to speak to cultural differences not as something to be tolerated but as essential to expanding the discourse and practice of democratic life. Multiculturalism is not just an ideological construct; it also refers to the fact that within sixty years people of color will be the numerical majority in the United States. Thus, educators need to develop a vision and curriculum in which multiculturalism and democracy become mutually reinforcing categories. Manning Marable has spoken eloquently to this issue. His definition of a multicultural democracy offers important insights for reworking democracy as a pedagogical and cultural practice necessary for what John Dewey once called the creation of an articulate public.

> Multicultural political democracy means that this country was not built by and for only one group—Western Europeans; that our country does not have only one language—English; or only one religion—Christianity; or only one economic philosophy—corporate capitalism. Multicultural democracy means that the leadership within our society should reflect the richness, colors and diversity expressed in the lives of all of our people. Multicultural democracy demands new types of power-sharing and the re-allocation of resources necessary to great economic and social development for those who have been systematically excluded and denied.[27]

Second, as part of an attempt to develop a multicultural and multiracial society consistent with the principles of a democratic society, educators must recognize that men and women of color are disproportionately underrepresented in the cultural and public institutions of this country. Pedagogically, this suggests that a multicultural curriculum must provide students with the skills to analyze how various audio, visual, and print texts fashion social identities over time, and how these representations serve to reinforce, challenge, or rewrite dominant moral and political vocabularies that promote stereotypes that degrade people by depriving them of their history, culture, and identity.[28]

This should not suggest that such a pedagogy should concentrate solely on how meanings produce particular stereotypes and the uses to which they are put. Nor should a multicultural politics of representation focus exclusively on recovering and reconstituting the history of subordinate groups. Although such approaches are essential to giving up the quest for a pure historical tradition, it is imperative that a multicultural curriculum also focus on dominant, white institutions and histories in order to interrogate them in terms of both their injustices and their contributions to humanity.

Of course, more is at stake here than avoiding the romanticizing of minority voices or including Western traditions in the curriculum. In this sense multiculturalism concerns making whiteness visible as a racial category. That is, it points to the necessity of providing students who have been constructed as "white" with the cultural memories that enable them to recognize that their own identities are the product of historical and social events and that class identities are obliterated by racial constructs. In part, this approach to multiculturalism as a cultural politics provides "white" students with self-definitions on which they can recognize whether they are speaking from within or outside privileged spaces. It also allows them to see how power works within and across differences to legitimate some voices and dismantle others.

Bob Suzuki further extends the pedagogical importance of making whiteness visible as an ethnic category. In teaching a course on racism to college students, he discovered that the ethnic experiences and histories of many white students had been erased. By helping them to recover and interrogate their own histories, he found that the white students "could relate more empathetically to the problems of people of color and become more open to understanding their experiences and perspectives."[29] We would further extend Suzuki's important point by arguing that, as crucial as it is to get white students to listen emphatically to students of color, it is also important that they understand that multiculturalism is also about understanding how dominant institutions provide the context of massive black unemployment, segregated schools, racist violence, and run-down housing. Multiculturalism means not just analyzing stereotypes but also showing how institutions produce racism and other forms of discrimination.

Third, a multicultural curriculum must address the matter of articulating a relationship between unity and difference which moves beyond simplistic binarisms. That is, rather than defining multiculturalism against unity or simply for difference, educators must develop a unity-in-difference position in which new forms of democratic representation, participation, and citizenship provide a forum for creating unity without denying the particular, multiple, and the specific. In this instance, the interrelationships of different cultures and identities become borderlands, sites of crossing, negotiation, translation, and dialogue. Underlying this notion of border pedagogy is neither the logic of assimilation (the melting pot) nor the imperative to create cultural hierarchies, but the attempt to expand the possibilities for different groups to enter into dialogue so that they will further understand the richness of their differences and the value of their commonalities. Jeffrey Weeks speaks to this issue well: "We may not be able to find, indeed we should not seek, a single way of life that would satisfy us all. That does not mean we cannot agree on common political ends: the construction of what can best be described as 'a community of communities', to achieve a maximum political unity without denying difference."[30]

Fourth, a critical multiculturalism must challenge the task of merely representing cultural differences in the curriculum. It must also educate students to the necessity of linking a justice of multiplicity to struggles over real material conditions that structure everyday life. In part, this means understanding how structural imbalances in power produce real limits on the capacity of subordinate groups to exercise a sense of agency and struggle. It also means analyzing specific class, race, gender, and other issues as social problems rooted in material and institutional factors that produce specific forms of inequality and oppression. This would necessitate a multicultural curriculum that produces a language that deals with social problems in historical and relational terms, and uncovers how the dynamics of power work to promote domination within both the school and the wider society.

Fifth, a multicultural curriculum must not simply be imposed on a community and school. It is imperative that as a power-sensitive discourse a multicultural curriculum refigures relations between the school, teachers, students, and the wider community. In this case, schools must be willing to draw on community resources and include members of the community in making fundamental decisions about what is taught, who is hired, and how the school can become an integral part of the society it serves. Teachers need to be educated to be border crossers, to explore zones of cultural difference by moving in and out of the resources, histories, and narratives that provide different students with a sense of identity, place, and possibility.[31] This does not suggest that educators become tourists traveling to exotic lands. On the contrary, it points to the need for them to enter into negotiation and dialogue on issues of nationality, difference, and identity so that they will be able to fashion a more ethical and democratic set of pedagogical relations between themselves and their students. At the same time, they will thereby allow students to speak, listen, and learn differently within pedagogical spaces that are safe, affirming, questioning, and enabling. In this case, a curriculum for a multicultural and multiracial society provides the conditions for students to think and act otherwise, to imagine beyond the given, and to critically embrace their identities as a source of agency and possibility.

NOTES

1. James Baldwin, "A Talk to Teachers," in Rick Simonson and Scott Walker, eds., *Multicultural Literacy: Opening the American Mind* (St. Paul, Minn.: Graywolf Press, 1988), p. 3.

2. Roger I. Simon, *Teaching Against the Grain* (Westport, Conn.: Bergin and Garvey, 1992), p. 4.

3. Alan O'Connor, "Just Plain Home Cookin," *Borderlines,* Nos. 20/21 (Winter 1991), p. 58.

4. Marcia Tucker, " 'Who's on First?' Issues of Cultural Equity in Today's Museums," in Carol Becker et al., eds., *Different Voices* (New York: Association of Art Museum Directors, 1992), p. 11.

5. bell hooks, *Black Looks: Race and Representation* (Boston: South End Press, 1992), pp. 168, 172.

6. The notion of imagining otherwise in order to act otherwise is taken from: Richard Kearney, *The Wake of Imagination* (Minneapolis; University of Minnesota Press, 1988), p. 370.

7. "The Postcolonial Critic: Homi K. Bhabha," Interviewed by David Bennett and Terry Collits, *Arena,* No. 96 (1991), pp. 50–51.

8. Stuart Hall, "And Not a Shot Fired," *Marxism Today* (December 1991), p. 10.

9. Larry D. Hatfield and Dexter Waugh, "Right Wing's Smart Bombs," *The San Francisco Examiner* (May 24, 1992), p. A–10.

10. For a brief but informative view of right-wing think tanks, see Lawrence Soley, "Right Thinking Conservative Think Tanks," *Dissent* (Summer 1991), pp. 418–420. For a history of these groups, see Russ Bellant, *Old Nazis, the New Right, and the Republican Party* (Boston: South End Press, 1991).

11. For the connection between right-wing foundations and a number of prominent educators such as Diane Ravitch, Chester Finn, Charlotte Crabtree, Allan Bloom, and others, see Dexter Waugh and Larry D. Hatfield, "Rightist Groups Pushing School Reforms," *The San Francisco Examiner* (May 28, 1992), p. A18.

12. Stuart Hall and David Held, "Citizens and Citizenship," in Stuart Hall and Martin Jacques, eds., *New Times: Changing Face of Politics in the 1990s* (London: Verso, 1990), p. 178.

13. Jonathan Kozol, "If We Want to Change Our Schools," unpublished speech given to the Commonwealth Club in San Francisco, 1992, pp. 1–2.

14. Robert N. Bellah et al. "Breaking the Tyranny of the Market," *Tikkun* 6: 4 (1991), p. 90.

15. Chester E. Finn, Jr., "Does Public Mean Good?" *Education Week* 11:21 (February 12, 1992), p. 30.

16. On the relationship between democracy and cultural difference, see Henry A. Giroux, *Border Crossings* (New York: Routledge, 1992) and Henry A. Giroux, *Living Dangerously: Multiculturalism and the Politics of Difference* (New York: Peter Lang Publishers, 1993).

17. Manning Marable, *Black America* (Westfield, N.J.: Open Media, 1992), p. 13.

18. James Clifford, "Museums in the Borderlands," in Carol Becker, et al., eds., *Different Voices* (New York: Association of Art Museum Directors, 1992), p. 119.

19. E. D. Hirsch, Jr., *Cultural Literacy: What Every American Needs to Know* (Boston: Houghton Mifflin, 1987).

20. Such pronouncements have become commonplace among traditionalists such as Lynne V. Cheney, John Silber, William J. Bennett, Chester E. Finn, and Allan Bloom. See, for example, Carolyn J. Mooney, "Scholars Decry Campus Hostility to Western Culture at a Time When More Nations Embrace Its Values," *The Chronicle of Higher Education* (January 30, 1991), pp. A15–A16.

21. James Davison Hunter, *Culture Wars: The Struggle to Define America* (New York: Basic Books, 1991), p. 44.

22. I have paraphrased this insight from: Gregory Jay, "The End of American Literature: Toward a Multicultural Practice," *College English* (March 1991), p. 266.

23. Bhikhu Parekh, "Identities on Parade: A Conversation," *Marxism Today* (June 1989), p. 3.

24. Renato Rosaldo, *Culture and Truth* (Boston: Beacon Press, 1989).

25. For an analysis of the history and varied meanings of multicultural education, see Christine E. Sleeter, ed., *Empowerment Through Multicultural Education* (Albany, N.Y.: SUNY Press, 1991); Cameron McCarthy, *Race and Curriculum* (Philadelphia: Falmer Press, 1990). Also see Peter Erickson, "What Multiculturalism Means," *Transition* No. 55 (1992), pp. 105–114.

26. Bhikhu Parekh, "Identities on Parade: A Conversation," *Marxism Today* (June 1989), p. 4.

27. Manning Marable, *Black America: Multicultural Democracy in the Age of Clarence Thomas and David Duke* (Westfield, N.J.: Open Media, 1992), p. 13.

28. On this issue, see ibid.

29. Bob Suzuki, "Unity with Diversity: Easier Said Than Done," *Liberal Education* (February 1991), p. 34.

30. Jeffrey Weeks, "The Value of Difference," in Jonathan Rutherford, ed., *Identity, Community, Culture, Difference* (London: Lawrence and Wishart, 1990), p. 98.

31. The issue of border pedagogy and border crossings is taken up in Henry A. Giroux, *Border Crossings: Cultural Workers and the Politics of Education* (New York: Routledge, 1992).

Chapter Ten

Education and the Crisis in Public Philosophy

In the current debate around the crisis in education and the role that federal policy should play in resolving it, U.S. society may be facing a dilemma that calls into question its very foundation as a democratic nation.

There are hints of the magnitude of the crisis in the language of the recent reports on public education and in the current assault on public education that has been waged by the Reagan/Bush administrations.[1] In the words of the National Commission on Excellence in Education, we are a "nation at risk" because of the poor quality of our educational system. Similarly, the Carnegie Foundation report argues that "the teaching profession is in crisis in this country," and the National Task Force on Education for Economic Growth claims that "a real emergency is upon us." Needless to say, the nature and extent of the crisis in public education and its relationship to the wider society are the objects of national debate. This debate is important not only because it focuses attention on the declining quality of our schools and economy, but also because it brings into view a "new" public philosophy, one that, in our estimation, is as problematic as the crisis that it attempts to define and resolve.[2]

Two fundamental questions must be brought into this debate. First, does this new public philosophy, which has defined the parameters of the existing crisis and the varied recommendations to resolve it, adequately name the nature of the crisis? Second, does this philosophy itself represent as much of a threat to our nation as the problems it has identified? These are crucial issues because any attempt to define what form a federal policy in education might take will be contingent on understanding how such a policy has been made, what interests it represents, and, ultimately, how it defines the nature of the problems it attempts to address.

In our view, the debate about the reality and promise of U.S. education should be analyzed not only on the strengths of its stated assumptions but also on the nature of its structured silences, that is, those issues which it has chosen to ignore or deemphasize. Such an analysis is valuable because it provides the opportunity to examine the basis of the public philosophy that has strongly influenced the language of the debate and the issues it has chosen to legitimate.

What is most striking in the current debate is the relationship that is being drawn between the state of the U.S. economy, with its lagging domestic performance and its shrinking preeminence in the international marketplace, and the failure of the schools to educate students to meet the economic needs of the dominant society. In some cases it is argued that schools are in fact responsible for this crisis; in other instances more restrained voices have claimed that, although schools may not have caused the economic crisis, they can ameliorate it by promoting excellence and educational leadership. These and other voices share a discourse that defines economic rationality as the model of public reason. This discourse is evident, for instance, in the National Commission on Excellence report when it measures educational success against the need to maintain "the slim competitive edge we still retain in world markets"; this form of logic is also evident in the claim of the Economic Growth Task Force that public schools "are not doing an adequate job of education for today's requirements in the workplace, much less tomorrow's."[3]

The important issue here is that economic rationality becomes both the referent and the ideal for change. Within the context of this rationality, business and educational leaders argue for specific forms of knowledge that are deemed important for our schools and the future of our society. For instance, different types of knowledge are measured against the benefits they provide to national security and technological growth. Thus, science, math, and forms of knowledge associated with high technology occupy a high-status position in this model. Furthermore, as an ideal, this model of economic rationality becomes the basis for new relationships between the schools and the economic sector. John Casteen, the former secretary of education for Virginia, expresses the spirit of this position in his call for each state to bring "together the corporate sector and the schools to define common goals, to articulate statements of standards for schools, and to pool resources to achieve the goals."[4]

As we have stated throughout this book, within the boundaries of this discourse, schools become important only to the degree that they can provide the forms of knowledge, skills, and social practices necessary to produce the labor force for an increasingly complex, technological economy. Moreover, the solutions for school reform that have emerged from the current debate are strongly shaped by the technocratic and instrumental logic that informs this model of economic reason. Thus, proposed solutions are both political and technical in nature and include on the one hand, such recommendations as extending the school day, raising teacher salaries, and enforcing school discipline. More recently, reforms initiated by the business community include linking choice to privatization, promoting voucher plans, and creating corporate-financed schools in order to shape the students necessary for the "New World Order." Even when there is an appeal for excellence, it is often defined less in terms of a substantive call for developing higher order forms of critical reasoning and civic behavior than in terms of procedural demands for more stringent modes of competency testing and evaluation.

In our judgment, the new public philosophy, with its celebration of economic and technocratic reason, begins with the wrong problems; furthermore, it misrepresents the problems it endorses and, in doing so, advocates the wrong solutions. The current economic crisis this country faces has not been caused by public education, though the economic crisis has had a significant effect on the problems schools are experiencing. High unemployment, declining productivity, inflation, and the persistence of vast inequalities in wealth and power in this country have little to do with the absence of school-related skills. In addition to poor planning and bad investment policies, the economy has undergone a major shift from dependence on its traditional agricultural and manufacturing base to reliance on high technology and service industries. As a result, the number of jobs requiring middle-level skills has been gradually decreasing. This has not only produced high unemployment levels, but it also points to the growing polarization of future job opportunities.[5]

The implications of this polarization for schools are at odds with the urgent demands by educational and economic leaders that the country implement a massive educational program to train students for the high technology job revolution. The irony of this recommendation becomes clear in the most recent study by the Bureau of Labor Statistics which indicates that the bulk of jobs that will be available in the next ten years will be in low-level service industries that require very little skill, and that a relatively small proportion of jobs will be available in the high technology fields.[6] Educating a labor force with skills for which there will be few jobs available, while simultaneously ignoring the growth of a market that demands fewer and fewer intellectual skills, raises fundamental questions about the nature of the economy itself and the ideologies that legitimate it.

Needless to say, the quality of schooling has been deeply affected by the crisis in the economy, and this is evident in the financial stress that plagues many school systems. In many of our major cities, "inflation, plant closings, and unemployment [have left] communities with fewer economic resources to tax."[7] This shrinking tax base has contributed to massive teacher layoffs, the closing of schools, the growing shortage of curriculum materials, and the elimination of many school programs. If there is a crisis in the quality of education in this country, it has been exacerbated by these trends—trends for which education is not responsible. But there are other problems that must be highlighted. Schools, for many students, particularly those from the lowest socioeconomic level of society, offer few opportunities for self and social empowerment. For these students, schooling is a place that disconfirms rather than confirms their histories, experiences, and dreams. In part, this alienation is expressed in the high rate of student absenteeism and school violence, and in the refusal of many students to take seriously the academic demands and social practices of schools. It is alarming to note, for instance, the estimation that on any one day in New York City 50 percent of the high school students are absent from school.[8]

It is important to point out that many of these problems are social and political in nature and cannot be understood solely within the framework proposed by the new public philosophy. These are problems that need explanations and solutions other than those that presently dominate the debate on education. But it is one thing to argue that this philosophy has misrepresented the crisis in education and proposed inadequate solutions; it is another issue altogether to claim that it actually contributes to that crisis. It is to this point that we will now turn.

In our judgment, the new public philosophy fails not only in its analysis of U.S. schools and the nature of the existing crisis, but also in its inability to provide a vision that takes seriously the kind of thoughtful participation in sociopolitical life that is expected from citizens in a democratic society. Moreover, this version of public philosophy places undue emphasis on specific cognitive and technical outcomes. This emphasis represents an ideology that undermines the importance of promoting in this society the development of critical public spheres where the capacity for learning is *not* reduced to economic or technical considerations. Put another way, the new public philosophy undermines the development of public spaces where people can learn and practice the skills of democratic participation in the wider political, social, and cultural processes that structure American society.[9] What is being stressed here moves far beyond the so-called "new consensus" demand to teach students how to become functionally literate or how to master minimal competencies and basic skills. In actuality, the logic underlying that public philosophy centers around support for a marriage between public schools and the business community on the one hand, and a dizzying celebration of testing, sorting procedures, and the mastery of technical and specialized skills on the other. What all its divergent intellectual strands have in common is a theoretical indifference to providing students with the knowledge and skills necessary for a broad understanding of the sociopolitical processes at work in this country.

It is our contention that the new public philosophy abdicates its responsibility to insure that public schools can function to enable students "to experience a meaningful sense of personal and political liberty and to live a moral life, that is, a life lived in accordance with moral rules and principles." [10] Moreover, this abdication reinforces the developing crisis in moral and civic courage that our nation currently faces. This issue points, in fact, to a very different crisis from that being emphasized in the current debate, one that centers around not only the failure of the United States to broaden its conception of the proper role of the citizen in a democratic society, but also its failure to promote an ethic of civic responsibility that holds in check those privatized and narrow interests that constantly threaten the public good. That is, the risk our society confronts involves in part the failure to take seriously the need to develop a public policy informed by the principles of critical literacy and civic courage, issues that should be at the core of any debate regarding educational policy at the local, state, and federal levels. [11]

Underlying the new philosophy's commitment to reordering public education is a set of assumptions that are profoundly conservative in nature and detrimental in purpose to viewing schools as institutions that provide a noble public service. Offering little or no critique of how existing social, political, and economic institutions may contribute to the reproduction of deep inequalities in this society, the new philosophy is generally silent about how schools might be influenced by such institutions in reproducing larger structural inequalities. In effect, what is missing here is any understanding of how power, ideology, and politics work on and in schools so as to undermine the basic values of community and democracy. For instance, there is no room in this discourse for understanding how the quest for excellence might be undermined by the realities of social class, privilege, and other powerful socioeconomic forces that pull schools in the opposite direction; or for comprehending those school practices that systematically promote failure among certain segments of our nation's youth, particularly working-class and minority youth; or, finally, for understanding that many of the problems schools face are, in part, political, cultural, and economic in nature and transcend the limited focus on individual achievement and success. Furthermore, within this model of rationality public education is defined primarily through a struggle for economic success and individual mobility. These are not entirely negative goals, but an undue emphasis on them suggests that economics are more important to our nation and schools than our commitment to democratic principles. [12] Such a view is not only wrong, but it also provides the philosophical basis for launching an assault on the relevance of *any* public sphere dedicated to goals other than those which merely defend narrow models of technical reason and economic needs.

What is at issue is the importance of recognizing that the new public philosophy represents an ideology that does not contain an adequate rationale for defending schools, or any other public sphere committed to performing a democratic public service. That is, such a philosophy does not hold an adequate justification for linking schools to a mission that promotes a civic consciousness, one that encourages the development of an active citizenry and public participation on the basis of moral and ethical principles, as opposed to forms of participation tied merely to economic self-sufficiency and self-interest. The new philosophy is tied largely to assumptions that view schools as means to increasing individual achievement and promoting industrial needs. Such a view makes it difficult to defend public education in political and ethical terms. In fact, it lends support to programs aimed at severely reducing funding and dismantling public education.

The economic and privatized interests on which the new philosophy defends itself do not offer a challenge to the government's call for tuition tax credits, educational vouchers, reduction of federal funding for education, or elimination of the Department of Education. Its model of economic reason cannot generate a discourse that defends programs as a public service tied to improving democratic traditions. A critique of Bush's policies would have to begin on very different terms and principles. It would have to defend schools as public spheres responsible for developing an indispensable public service to the nation. Such a view would point to the value of schools as institutions designed to awaken the moral, political, and civic responsibilities of its youth. This would demand an altogether different public philosophy, one that would point to very different problems in public education, advocate different solutions, and provide a different rationale for federal policymaking in education.

The fundamental question that has haunted many educational and political critics is, "What principles do we use to reconstruct U.S. schools on the basis of democratic values?" Some critics have avoided the question by arguing that schools are merely the pawns of corporate capital, while others have argued that schools should become an extension of such interests. In both cases, it is claimed that schools do not serve the public interest. But neither the determinism and cynicism of liberal critics nor the relatively individualistic tendencies celebrated by their more conservative counterparts provides a program for reconstructing schools around the notion of the public good. An alternative form of public philosophy needs to fill this theoretical void and provide the basis for developing a constructive federal policy on education. Such a philosophy would take as its starting point not the particularities of individual interests or forms of achievement, but the relationship of schools to the demands of active forms of community life. An alternative public philosophy would begin by recognizing the relationship between the public sphere and the state, on the one hand, and the notion of learning and citizenship, on the other.[13]

The public sphere, in our view, refers to those arenas of social life such as church associations, trade unions, social movements, and voluntary associations, where dialogue and critique provide for the cultivation of democratic sentiments and habits. It is in this sphere that people create the conditions not only where they can explore and talk about their needs, but also where democratic traditions function to mediate the role of government action. In the public sphere, forms of civic courage are nourished and displayed, and the state becomes an object of critical inquiry rather than veneration. In this case, civic courage represents a form of political and ethical scrutiny that defines citizenship not as a function of the state but as a quality that permeates all of social life, a quality that speaks to forms of critical literacy and social empowerment aimed at developing democratic and just communities. The principles that inform the role of state and federal policy within this context are organized around a public philosophy dedicated to the creation of an educated citizenry capable of exercising political and ethical leadership in the public sphere.

The notion of active citizenship is not limited to the conservative policy of making a choice between private and public education. On the contrary, it points to developing educational policies outside an elite pattern of politics proposed by experts and government officials. But the notion of active citizenship also simultaneously endorses educational policies designed to strengthen public education by securing financial assistance from the federal government, while qualifying such aid by ensuring that the federal government is not able to control the programs it supports. In this case, the federal government is providing a service rather than exercising a form of centralized control.[14]

The notion of being able to think critically on the basis of informed judgment and to develop a respect for democratic forms of self- and social empowerment represents the basis for organizing school programs around the principles of critical literacy and civic courage. In other words, schools should be seen as institutions that prepare people for democracy. They should promote the acquisition of a critical culture and social practices that allow students and others to view society with an analytical eye. Michael Katz summarizes how the ideal of using critical thinking to develop an educated citizenry might be used to shape school policy. He argues:

> First, it would provide a general basis for determining whether schooling policy and practice is seriously taking account of the value of critical thinking. The environments of schools characterized by a commitment to this value would be alive with the spirit of critical dialogue between teachers and students and among the students themselves. Various and diverse forms of intellectual inquiry, moreover, would be evident. Students in this environment would expect to receive serious and constructive intellectual criticism on their work so that they would be able to internalize the standards for making reasoned intellectual appraisals of their own thinking and that of other people. On the other hand, schools that clearly did not take the value of critical thinking seriously might be ones that were dominated by rote memorization, routine drill, and passive, unquestioning acceptance of every-

thing said by the teachers or written in the textbooks. Such schools would discourage students from questioning their teachers and expressing divergent views.[15]

Underlying this form of alternative public philosophy is a view at odds with the notion that schools should merely promote industrial needs and public sector interests. Pedagogy for training in the limited economic and technical sense does not constitute the basis for the discourse of freedom. The dominant public philosophy, with its economic model of reason and its celebration of privatized sensibilities, not only presents a limited view of learning but also represents a threat to all forms of discourse that take seriously the politics of possibility.

If the crisis in schooling is to be addressed adequately, we will need to construct a public philosophy that points to new approaches for the education of existing and future teachers. At the core of such an approach would be a commitment to developing forms of knowledge, pedagogy, evaluation, and research that promote critical literacy and civic courage. From this starting point federal education policy would use its financial and political resources to promote absolute commitment to public schools as sites of learning, of social interaction, and of human emancipation. Within this theoretical context can be developed policy recommendations that encourage research and education that view teachers as intellectuals and moral leaders rather than mere technicians; students as critical thinkers and active citizens rather than simply future participants in the industrial-military order; and schools as centers of critical literacy and civic courage rather than merely training sites for occupational positions in the corporate order.

NOTES

1. See, for instance, the National Commission on Excellence in Education, *A Nation at Risk: The Imperative for Educational Reform* (Washington, D.C.: U.S. Department of Education, 1983); Task Force on Education for Economic Growth, *Action for Excellence: A Comprehensive Plan to Improve Our Nation's Schools* (Denver: Education Commission of the States, 1983); the College Entrance Examination Board, *Academic Preparation for College* (New York: College Entrance Examination Board, 1983); Twentieth Century Fund Task Force on Federal Elementary and Secondary Education Policy, *Making the Grade* (New York: Twentieth Century Fund, 1983); Carnegie Corporation of New York, *Education and Economic Progress: Toward a National Educational Policy* (New York: Carnegie Corp., 1983).

2. The notion of "new" public philosophy as it is used in this chapter comes from the work of Sheldon S. Wolin; see his "The New Public Philosophy," *Democracy* 1 (1981), pp. 23–26. Another excellent source is James M. Giarelli, "Education and Democratic Citizenship: Toward a New Public Philosophy," paper

presented at the National Council for Social Studies Annual Meeting, Boston, November 24, 1982.

Representative examples of the "new" public philosophy are found throughout the October 1983 issue of *Educational Leadership* and in the September 1983 issue of *Phi Delta Kappan*. One problematic aspect of the new public philosophy is its indifference to alternative views of schooling. This can be seen in the views of one of its major spokespersons, Chester Finn, when he writes: "I am hard pressed to imagine how anyone could *disagree* [italic in original] with the Excellence Commission's curriculum recommendations or, for that matter, with the commission's other diagnoses, proposals, and suggestions," in "How Could Anyone Disagree?" *Educational Leadership* 41 (1983), p. 28. For one of the most cogent disagreements with the National Commission on Excellence in Education findings, see the report, *Our Children at Risk: An Inquiry into the Current Reality of American Public Education* (New York: National Coalition of Advocates for Students, 1983). A more general critique of the new public philosophy is found in *Education for a Democratic Future* (St. Louis, Mo.: Public Information Network, 1985); a critique of England's version of the new public philosophy is found in Ann Marie Wolpe and James Donald, eds., *Is There Anyone Here from Education: Education After Thatcher* (London: Pluto Press, 1983).

3. The National Commission on Excellence in Education, p. 7; Task Force on Education for Economic Growth, p. 32.

4. Statement of Casteen in press release of the Education Commission of the States Task Force on Education for Economic Growth, Washington, D.C., May 12, 1983.

5. An analysis of this issue is found in Stanley Aronowitz, *Working Class Hero: A New Strategy for Labor* (New York: Pilgrim Press, 1983); Manual Castells, *The Economic Crisis and American Society* (Princeton, N.J.: Princeton University Press, 1980); and Paul Weckstein, "Democratic Economic Development Is the Key to Future Quality Education," *Phi Delta Kappan* 64 (1983), pp. 420–423.

6. Figures from the Bureau of Labor Statistics on occupations producing the most new jobs appeared in William Serrin, "High Tech Is No Jobs Panacea, Experts Say," *New York Times*, September 18, 1983, pp. 1, 28.

7. Weckstein, op. cit., p. 420.

8. Robert B. Everhart, "Introduction," in *The Public School Monopoly*, ed. Robert B. Everhart (Cambridge, Mass.: Ballinger Press, 1982), p. 3. For an excellent extended analysis of this issue, see W. Norton Grubb and Marvin Lazerson, *Broken Promises: How Americans Fail Their Children* (New York: Basic Books, 1982). For a stinging indictment of inner city schools, see Jonathan Kozol, *Savage Inequalities* (New York: Crown, 1991).

9. The ideology of technocratic rationality and the importance of oppositional public spheres is discussed at great length in Henry A. Giroux, *Theory and Resistance: A Pedagogy for the Opposition* (South Hadley, Mass.: Bergin and Garvey, 1983).

10. Michael Katz, "Critical Literacy: A Conception of Education as a Moral Right and Social Ideal," in *The Public School Monopoly*, p. 209.

11. Recent eloquent expressions of this position include ibid.; James M. Giarelli, "The Public, the State, and the Civic Education of Teachers" and Michael W. Apple, "Politicizing 'Civic Values' in Education," both in *Civic Learning in Teacher*

Education, ed. Ayers Bagley (Minneapolis, Minn.: Society of Professors of Education Monograph Series, 1983); and Jonathan Kozol, *Prisoners of Silence: Breaking the Bonds of Adult Illiteracy in the United States* (New York: Continuum, 1980).

12. A glaring example of this is found in Harold L. Hodgkinson's argument that the higher education community needs to take seriously the possibility for minority youth to go to some form of higher education. The rationale for such a concern is based on what he calls sheer middle-class self-interest, as illustrated in his comment: "The dependency of middle-class white Americans on the success of minorities in school and at work is just beginning. Ninety percent of the work force in 1990 is already at work today, and close to half of the remainder will be minorities. Retiring white workers will find themselves increasingly dependent on a work force heavily composed of minorities *to pay their Social Security trust funds* [italics added]," in "College Students in the 1990s: A Demographic Portrait," *Education Digest* 48 (November 1983), p. 29.

13. A cogent discussion of these issues is found in Ralph Miliband, "State Power and Class Interest," *New Left Review* 138 (1983), pp. 57–68; Joel Spring, "The Evolving Political Structure of American Schooling," in *The Public School Monopoly,* pp. 77–105; George Armstrong Kelly, "Who Needs a Theory of Citizenship," *Daedalus* 108 (Fall 1979), pp. 21–36.

14. This position is further outlined in Arthur Wise, *Legislated Learning* (Berkeley: University of California Press, 1979), pp. 203–212. A variety of ideological positions on this issue are found in "Rethinking the Federal Role in Education," a special issue of the *Harvard Educational Review* 52 (1982), pp. 371–593.

15. Katz, in *The Public School Monopoly,* p. 209; see also Harvey Siegel, "Critical Thinking as an Educational Ideal," *Educational Forum* 45 (1980), pp. 7–23.

Chapter Eleven

Schooling and the Future: Revitalizing Public Education

As the United States moves into the twenty-first century, it faces a dual crisis in public education. Both aspects of the crisis have been discussed in this book. The first is apparent in the rise of the new right and its economic and ideological attacks on the schools.[1] The second centers on the failure of radical educators to match neo-conservative politics with a corresponding set of visions and strategies.[2] We believe that both crises offer critical educators the opportunity to rethink the nature and purpose of public education and to raise ambitions, desires, and real hope for those who wish to take the issue of educational struggle and social justice seriously in the future. But for such hopes to become realizable, we have argued the need to assess the failures of left educational thinking in the past decade, and the reasons for the success of neo-conservative educational policy and the "authoritarian populism" on which it has been able to construct a broad national consensus. We will first analyze the nature and ideology of neo-conservative discourse on public education, and how it has challenged some of the basic assumptions of radical educational theory. We will conclude by briefly summarizing some of the elements of a critical educational theory that need to be addressed in the future.

The most obvious aspect of the crisis in public education and the response it is engendering from neo-conservatives is in the discourse they use to describe the role schools should play in American society. They no longer celebrate schools as democratizing institutions. On the contrary, as we have mentioned throughout this book and as the recent spate of commission reports illustrates, they view schools within the narrow parameters of human capital theory.[3] Simply stated, conservatives argue that the traditional arm's length relationship between schools and business be dismantled for the purpose of overhauling schools in order to align them more closely with short- and long-term business and corporate interests. For the most part, they have successfully imposed their ideology on school administrators, parents, and the public.

The turn toward public education as a citadel of corporate ideology, of course, comes at a specific historical conjuncture in the United States. For many, this conjuncture is both characterized and understood as an expression of the capitalist economic recession. This explanation is only partly true, because it fails to comprehend the popularity of neo-conservative discourse on public education as part of both a struggle and response to a political and ideological crisis the nation currently faces. In other words, neo-conservatives have not appeared out of thin air; they are part of a varied set of historical traditions that have congealed into a particular political and ideological force at this time in history. And in doing so they have realigned and reshaped the political nature of their discourse and the ideological configurations that inform it. Moreover, neo-conservatives seem to make convincing sense to an American public that is both worried and intimidated by the changes the country has gone through since the 1960s. At issue here is the paradox of how groups that so blatantly favor the rich, the upper classes, and the logic of unbridled individualism can so effectively mobilize the needs and desires of subordinate and oppressed groups such as the working classes.

Neo-conservative discourse about public schooling not only taps into a wide range of discontents, but it also takes a strong position on important educational issues such as standards, values, and school discipline. In mobilizing existing public discontent, it combines two aspects of conservative philosophy so as to add a powerful element of popular cultural appeal to its theoretical discourse. In diverse ways, it embraces elements of community and localism in its support of the family, patriarchal authority, and religion. Similarly, these aspects of traditional conservative philosophy are combined successfully with the tenets of classical liberalism, with its stress on individualism, competition, and personal effort and reward.

Around the pro-family issue, for example, an important strain of neo-conservative discourse examines a whole range of issues related to the nature of the current economic and moral crisis as they define it, and how it can be challenged. In this case, the family is seen as a "natural" entity that is "God given" and allegedly exists beyond the bounds of history. Defined as the center of morality and order, the nuclear family is celebrated as the locus of civilization, community, and social control. As the primary unit of society, it is appealed to as a moral and political referent from which to mobilize and wage a constant struggle against its "enemies." Allen Hunter is worth quoting on this issue:

> A great many issues are . . . combined in the defense of the family. In this way family imagery acts as a "condensation symbol," and—like the "pro-

family coalition"—is used to draw together a wide range of distinct issues and to give them a positive image. Enemies are lumped together too. Feminists, youth culture and drugs, black music, homosexuals, abortion, pornography, liberal educators, liberal divorce laws, contraception, and a melange of other phenomena, are all assimilated to a common feature: they are destructive of the family, and along with it the society.[4]

Neo-conservative discourse also fuels its celebration of the family with the ideology of individualism. While, at first glance, the ideology of militant individualism may appear to be at odds with neo-conservative support of the family and community, it is actually displaced to another sphere of society in that it is used as an ideological prop to wage an attack against the state and other forms of bureaucratic intervention. In this case, the notions of mobility, liberty, and freedom are linked to the ability of individuals to cast their fate to the competitive dynamics of the marketplace. In contrast, it is argued that state and government intervention block this possibility and in doing so undermine the virtues of hard work and self-sufficiency, while simultaneously eroding the economic well-being and spiritual and patriarchal privacy necessary to maintain family life.

What is interesting about neo-conservative ideology is that it takes seriously the way in which the state and other institutions, including schools, either intrude into people's lives or, through the arrogance of administrative policy, function to exclude them from participating in vital issues that affect their experiences on a daily level. Needless to say, in many respects working-class people and others respond positively to anti-statist ideologies because they encounter state policy and social practices less as a beneficiary than as a demeaning and powerful bureaucratic imposition into their lives. On the other hand, many people have expressed an ambivalence about public education that neo-conservatives have capitalized on and redefined in their own interests.

For many people, schools occupy an important but paradoxical place between their daily experiences and their dreams of the future. In one sense, public education has represented one of the few possibilities for social and economic mobility. On the other hand, because of the many problems plaguing schools systems, whether they be school violence, absenteeism, falling "standards," or the shrinking of economic resources, popular concern has shifted from the traditional emphasis on gaining access to public education to a concern for shaping and controlling school policy. Neo-conservative ideology has been politically adroit in addressing these concerns, but it does so in a way that represents "them within a logic or discourse which pulls them systematically into line with policies and class strategies of the right."[5]

In capitalizing on popular sentiments and discontents, neo-conservative discourse has conveniently argued for educational policies that promote traditional values, cultural uniformity, and conservative forms of authority and discipline. Rather than denying the role of schools in promoting values, neo-conservatives have argued that moral regulation should become a central dimension of the curriculum. Consequently, school curriculum has become a major focus of popular contestation and a site for a kind of competitive struggle. This becomes evident with right-wing arguments for the inclusion of religious practices, the banning of subversive books and areas of study, the fight against multicultural curricula, and a renewed involvement in forms of schooling that display an instrumental enterprise in developing curricula that enshrine goals and values that support the ideology of business pragmatism. In addition, as neo-conservative policy promotes cutbacks in financial aid to public schools along with other forms of social service, it creates a new labor force of unpaid women, whom it argues belong in the home. At the same time, neo-conservatives strongly support voluntary work to be done by mothers in the face of cuts among the ranks of teachers and ancillary staff.[6] In this case the attack on public education is buttressed by a discriminatory policy against women.

What this all adds up to is starkly revealed in the way neo-conservative ideology separates public education from the discourse of self-empowerment and collective freedom. That is, rather than confronting the inequalities and real failures of public education, neo-conservative policy, such as that espoused by the Reagan/Bush administration's, views public education within a model of reason that celebrates narrow economic concerns, private interests, and strongly conservative values. For instance, the ideology underlying the Bush position strongly celebrates the free enterprise logic of consumer choice and economic self-sufficiency; the organizing ethos that structures this position is based on the dubious policy of giving the public a choice between public and private forms of education. The principles being espoused here are self-interest and individual mobility, principles heavily weighted in favor of those groups who exercise an inordinate amount of power and influence in a society characterized by deep racial, gender, and class inequalities. Furthermore, what is being systematically rejected in this proposal is any commitment to defending schools as sites that have a fundamental connection to the idea of civic responsibility and human emancipation. In other words, within this discourse there is no room for viewing schools as public places where students and others can learn and practice the skills for democratic participation necessary for a critical understanding of the wider political, social, and cultural processes that structure American society.

It is instructive to note that the neo-conservative discourse currently dominating the debate on education in the United States has partly strengthened its position by linking the crises in everyday life with the failures of public education. What is particularly interesting here is that conservative coalitions have been able to intervene into popular concerns about schooling around a number of ideological issues in a way that has rendered radical educators almost invisible in the current debate. We believe that this says less about the credibility of neo-conservative ideology than it does about the theoretical failure of radical educators to take seriously the social and historical particularities of people's lives. In our view, radical educational criticism has for too long focused on either the question of who has access to public education or on providing often despairing accounts of how schools reproduce through the overt and hidden curricula the varied inequalities that characterize the dominant society. It is important to reemphasize that, although these educators have provided important insights into how schools work, they have often fallen far short of what is theoretically needed to develop a more comprehensive and critical theory of schooling. For the last decade, radical accounts of schooling have focused too heavily on critiques of schooling, while failing to provide the more difficult theoretical task of laying the groundwork for alternative modes of educational theory and practice.

As we stressed in chapter six, the one-sided nature of radical educational theory is evident in the way in which it has treated the notions of power, social control, and popular struggle. In other words, power in these accounts has often been defined primarily as a negative force that works in the interest of domination. Treated as an instance of negation, power took on the characteristic of a contaminating force that left the imprint of either domination or powerlessness on whatever it touched. Consequently, the notion of social control became synonymous with the exercise of domination in schools, and the question of how schools could become the site for the production of new forms of opposing knowledge and social practices was largely ignored. It is clear, for example, that there has been a fundamental confusion around what constituted freedom within the discourse of radical pedagogy. This point is best seen in the underlying assumption in most radical pedagogy that school discipline, authority, and academic standards are representative of coercive impositions that limited the development of the natural emotional and intellectual abilities of students. Thus, freedom became synonymous with demystifying and eliminating the ideological and material restraints imposed by schools so students could discover their real abilities and possibilities for learning. In other words, freedom is defined as the absence of control and the student is presented as the embodiment of an individuality that has to mature as part of a natural developmental process. What is lost in this account is the understanding that education always functions in complex ways: either a positive or negative force to produce the very conditions under which individuality is constituted. Freedom is not removed from power, or from the issues of authority, standards, and discipline within schools. In fact, it is linked directly to the issue of how it both informs and emerges from those daily conditions in schools that help to produce students who are critically literate and socially responsible. Valerie Walkerdine cogently makes this point in her claim that "what educators need to understand is how that condition which we call individuality is formed within apparatuses of social regulation, including education."[7]

Radical educational theory provided many insightful criticisms about the socially constructed nature of the school curriculum, but at the same time it failed to take seriously what was implied in such a judgment. That is, school curriculum is not simply a social construction. It is also an historical expression of both past struggles over what constituted political and cultural authority, and the forms of ethical, intellectual, and moral regulation implied in specific forms of school authority. With few exceptions, radical educational theorists gave little attention to the positive side of school life, that is, to those dimensions of schooling that reached deep into the concerns of everyday experience. Neglected in this case were questions such as what constituted critical knowledge, or how identity, language, and culture should be developed as part of a critical pedagogy. More specifically, what was ignored was the fundamental issue of how to create a language of possibility that would provide the basis for developing a positive notion of social control and responsibility from which to build and defend democratic conceptions of school organization, classroom relations, and organized bodies of school knowledge.

In this connection, we need only consult the example cited in the first chapter of the shameful appropriation by conservative educators of the issue of educational quality. Like many of his colleagues, Chester Finn has virtually nothing concrete to say about the content of the slogan "excellence." Its mere repetition constitutes a code signifying that only conservatives can offer a language of possibility.

On the other hand, we have the rich traditions of progressive education and some strains in European Marxism to draw on for an alternative that addresses curriculum quality. Recall that Gramsci called for broad-scale mastery of language as a foundation for personal and social autonomy and specified that he meant Latin, Greek, and philosophy as core languages that put students in touch with the history of Western civilization. Similarly, in the early days of the Bolshevik Revolution, Leon Trotsky advocated a curriculum that would ask students to appropriate the literary and philosophical traditions of bourgeois culture. Finally, the history of the labor movement in this country and in Europe is replete with examples of workers' education efforts that went far beyond the confines of grievances, wage bargaining, and other practices of the trade unions. Unions have provided literacy for foreign-born members, courses in history, literature, and philosophy, and, in recent times, they have assisted members to acquire new skills required by the job market.

The United States does not require philosophy or broad language mastery in its secondary schools. To a large extent, computer "literacy" has replaced the traditional demand for intellectual mastery, and this reflects a trend that the poet Joseph Brodsky has identified as the predominance of "numbers" in our curriculum. The American public philosophy has always disparaged rigor, and when the official flags are raised for learning, this move generally reflects a sense of urgency brought on by a new "crisis."

Just as Sputnik generated our last educational renaissance, so the Japanese talent for inexpensive cars and electronic gadgets has spurred our new concern. But lest we believe that conservatives mean to genuinely upgrade our schools, we need only consult the new vocationalism and Eurocentrism that inform their search for excellence. If there are any among the neo-conservatives who would demand of schools what ruling classes once meant by education, or the labor movement during its insurgent years, radicals should clap their hands. We do not deny that learning the skills associated with many occupations can contribute to serious learning. With Dewey we are persuaded that learning can take place *through* occupations, but the point is not to learn a narrow skill which is likely to become obsolete in the near future; we contend that only a multifaceted education can enable students to achieve the autonomy and creativity that a democratic society needs. Learning is a way to power and gratification, but neo-conservatives have no program for empowerment, only for providing human capital able to make American business viable once more in the world market.

We need to stress, once again, that schools need to be seen as active sites of interventions and struggle. But in order to take seriously the notion that schools contain possibilities for redefining the nature of critical learning and practice, educators must rescue the status of curriculum politics and production from its disparaged history. In the past, curriculum studies has been relegated to the margins of educational theory and practice while educational administration and psychology dominated the field. Under these circumstances, the management, administration, and control of knowledge subsumed the significance and importance of critical learning. Similarly, schools were no longer analyzed within a discourse of possibility as much as they were relegated to the imperatives of systems management and the rigors of educational testing and selection.

In our view, curriculum can no longer be considered of secondary interest. It must become the center of what schools are about, which in the insights provided by Gramsci, Dewey, and Freire point to schools as public spheres dedicated to forms of learning that promote critical citizenship, civic courage, and training of organic intellectuals, and sites for learning about the principles of a multicultural and multiracial democracy.

But for curriculum theory and practice to become the center of school life, then the relationship between power and social control will have to be redefined. Power will have to be viewed as both a negative and positive force, as something that works both on and through people. Its character will have to be viewed as dialectical, its mode of operation as both en-abling and constraining. This view of power has significant implications for redefining the relationship between social control and schooling.

It is important to view social control as having both positive and nega-tive possibilities. That is, when linked to interests that promote self- and social empowerment, the construct of social control provides the theoreti-cal starting point on which to establish the conditions for critical learning and practice. Similarly, the notion of power that underscores this position begins with the assumption that if social control is to serve the interests of freedom it must function so as to empower teachers and students. As used in this context, social control speaks to the forms of practice necessary for the demanding task of designing curricula that give students an active and critical voice, providing them with the skills that are basic for analysis and leadership in the modern world.

But we use the notion of social control in a way that speaks also to something more fundamental. We link the notion of freedom to forms of social structure and discipline that would be essential in creating and or-dering new criteria for the development of the principles needed to pro-mote curricula that embody emancipatory interests. It is important to stress here that a critical notion of social control cannot elude the tough issue of responsibility, of providing the context and conditions for the development of emancipatory forms of schooling.

Connected to this notion of social control is the need for radical educa-tors to take seriously the relationship between schooling and, what we call, cultural power. Traditionally, school culture has operated primarily within a logic that defends it as part of the fabric of high culture. The teacher's job was to transmit this culture to students in the hope that it would offset those cultural forms reproduced on the terrains of popular culture and subordinate class experience. Left educators countered this view of culture by arguing that high culture was itself developed out of the fabric of dom-ination and mystification and as such had to be rejected. As part of an oppositional educational task, the culture of oppressed groups had to be rescued and re-presented so as to offset the worst dimensions of dominant culture. The key notion here was that radical educators had to work with the experience of oppressed groups. As insightful as this concept was in both criticizing dominant culture and giving a voice to subordinate cul-tures (the working class, blacks, women, etc.), it failed to develop curricula forms for dealing with both dominant and subordinate cultures. In other words, it failed to take seriously the need not only to work with subordi-nate cultures, but also to work on them. Thus, "to work on them" meant not just to confirm subordinate cultural experiences, but also to interro-gate them critically so as to recover their strengths as well as weaknesses. Similarly, if the notion of cultural power is to provide the theoretical basis for forms of critical pedagogy, it has to become a referent for examining what students and others need to learn outside of their own experiences. This points to the need to redefine the role of knowledge within the contexts of cultural and curriculum studies.

A critical pedagogy, then, would focus on the study of curriculum not merely as a matter of self-cultivation or the mimicry of specific forms of language and knowledge. On the contrary, it would stress forms of learning and knowledge aimed at providing a critical understanding of how social reality works; it would focus on how certain dimensions of such a reality are sustained; it would focus on the nature of its formative processes; and it would also focus on how those aspects of it that are related to the logic of domination can be changed. Stuart Hall provides a more specific idea of the kind of skills this type of critical pedagogy would involve. He writes:

> It is the skills which are basic, now, to a class which means to lead, not simply to serve, the modern world. They are the basic, general skills of analysis and conceptualization, of concepts and ideas and principles rather than of specific and outdated "contents," of abstraction and generalization and categorization, at whatever level it is possible to teach them.[8]

Similarly, this approach to critical pedagogy would be based on a dialectical notion of what counts as really useful knowledge and school practice in the building of an emancipatory curriculum. It would be developed around knowledge forms that challenge and critically appropriate dominant ideologies, rather than simply rejecting them outright. It would also take the historical and social particularities of students' experiences as a starting point for developing a critical classroom pedagogy. That is, it would begin with popular experiences so as to make them meaningful in order to engage them critically. As radical educators begin thinking about pedagogical strategies for the future, they will have to develop some clarity about what kind of curriculum is needed to build a critical democracy. This means redefining the notion of power, school culture, and really useful knowledge. Such a task does not mean debunking existing forms of schooling and educational theory. Rather, it means reworking them, contesting the terrains on which they develop, and building on them the democratic possibilities inherent both in schools and in the visions that guide our actions.

We also want to stress that the anchoring of transformative intellectuals in ongoing political organizations and oppositional public spheres that are part of the discourse about power has become increasingly difficult but, at the same time, is all the more important to fight for. For one thing, the American left has been primarily read out of the dominant political discourse for the first time in this century. What organizations do exist on the left are in extreme disarray. So the call for transformative intellectuals and the development of democratic public spheres takes on the appearance of a utopian demand. And yet, we admit with Ernst Bloch and others that without a vision of the future there is no possibility for collective transformation in the present. Of course, such a vision is all the more difficult since American progressivism has lost its bearing since the end of the sixties, in part, because of the offensive by neo-conservatives and the crisis of the world left. However, those who refuse to act as if there were no possibilities remain doomed to reproduce themselves as isolated intellectuals, whether they be of the critical or accommodating type. Like Freire and Gramsci, we believe that politics is a pedagogical activity. And, as we have stressed throughout this book, to the extent that our pedagogy is self-critical and self-conscious we engage in politics, but such a politics needs more than the discourse of critique; it also needs the discourse of possibility.

What we have suggested in this chapter points to the need to infuse educational theory and practice with a vision of the future, one that is matched, hopefully, by the willingness of educators, parents, and others to struggle and take risks. The nature of such a task may seem impossible at times, but the stakes are too high to ignore such a challenge. Underlying such a struggle is a ringing call to take seriously the lives of our children. In this sense, what we have advocated is a political and pedagogical movement that speaks to life, to future generations; it is a call that chooses life and takes as its first principle the value and possibilities inherent in human struggles.

NOTES

1. For a detailed analysis of this issue, see chapter nine in this book.

2. See our detailed critical analyses of the limits of Marxist discourse on radical educational theory in chapter five.

3. See also the insightful remarks of Charles A. Tesconi, Jr., "Additive Reform and the Retreat from Purpose," *Educational Studies* 15 (Spring 1984), pp. 1–10.

4. Allen Hunter, "In the Wings: New Right Ideology and Organization," *Radical America* 15 (1981), p. 129.

5. Stuart Hall, "Moving Right," *Socialist Review* 11 (January–February 1982), p. 128.

6. Miriam David, "Nice Girls Say No," *New Internationalist* (March 1984), p. 26; "Teaching and Preaching Sexual Morality: The New Right's Anti-Feminism in Britain and the U.S.A.," *Journal of Education* 166 (March 1984), pp. 63–76.

7. Valerie Walkerdine, "It's Only Natural: Rethinking Child-Centered Pedagogy," in *Is There Anyone Here From Education?*, eds. Ann Marie Wolpe and James Donald (London: Pluto Press, 1983), p. 87.

8. Stuart Hall, "Education in Crisis," in op. cit., p. 6.

Selected Bibliography

Since many of the conservative and liberal sources cited in this book are well known, we want to provide a selected bibliography of sources that are directly and indirectly related to radical educational discourse and practice. In some cases, these works are either relatively unknown or generally ignored in mainstream educational writings and reviews.

Abel, E. K. 1984. *Terminal Degrees: The Job Crisis in Higher Education.* New York: Praeger Publishing.

Adorno, T. W. 1973. *Negative Dialectics.* New York: Seabury Press.

Adorno, T. W. and M. Horkheimer. 1972. *Dialectic of Enlightenment,* trans. John Cumming. New York: Seabury Press.

Althusser, L. 1969. *For Marx.* New York: Vintage Books.

————. 1970. *Reading "Capital."* London: New Left Books.

————. 1971. "Ideology and the Ideological State Apparatuses." In *Lenin and Philosophy, and Other Essays,* trans. Ben Brewster. New York: Monthly Review Press.

Anyon, J. 1979. "Ideology and United States History Textbooks." *Harvard Educational Review* 49: 361–386.

————. 1980. "Social Class and the Hidden Curriculum of Work." *Journal of Education* 162, no. 2: 67–92.

————. 1981. "Social Class and School Knowledge." *Curriculum Inquiry* 11, no. 1: 3–42.

Apple, M. 1982a. *Education and Power.* Boston: Routledge and Kegan Paul.

————. 1984. "The Political Economy of Text Publishing." *Educational Theory* 43, no. 4: 307–319.

————, ed. 1982b. *Cultural and Economic Reproduction in Education.* Boston: Routledge and Kegan Paul.

———— and L. Weiss, eds. 1983. *Ideology and Practice in Schooling.* Philadelphia: Temple University Press.

Aronowitz, S. 1973. *False Promises*. New York: McGraw-Hill.

————. 1977. "Marx, Braverman, and the Logic of Capital." *Insurgent Sociologist* 8, nos. 2, 3: 126–146.

————. 1981. *The Crisis in Historical Materialism: Class, Politics, and Culture in Marxist Theory*. New York: J. F. Bergin Publishers, Inc.

————. 1983a. *Working Class Hero*. New York: Pilgrim Press.

————. 1983b. "Socialism and Beyond." *Socialist Review* 13, no. 3: 7–42.

————. 1990. *Science as Power*. Minneapolis: University of Minnesota Press.

————. 1992. *The Politics of Identity*. New York: Routledge.

————. 1993. *Roll over Beethoven*. Middletown, Conn.: Wesleyan University Press.

Baron, S., D. Finn, N. Grant, M. Green, and R. Johnson. 1981. *Unpopular Education*. London: Hutchinson and Co.

Barret, M. 1980. *Women's Oppression Today*. London: Verso Books.

Bates, R. 1983. *Educational Administration and the Management of Knowledge*. Geelong, Australia: Deakin University Press.

Barton, L. and S. Walker. 1981a. *Schools, Teachers and Teaching*. Philadelphia: Falmer Press.

————. 1981b. *Rethinking Curriculum Studies: A Radical Approach*. New York: John Wiley and Sons.

————. 1983a. *Race, Class, and Gender*. Philadelphia: Falmer Press.

————. 1983b. *Gender, Class and Education*. Philadelphia: Falmer Press.

————. 1984. *Social Crisis and Educational Research*. London: Croom-Helm.

Baudelot, C. and R. Establet. 1971. *L'Ecole Capitaliste en France*. Paris: Francois Maspero.

Benet, J. and A. K. Daniels, eds. 1980. *Education: Straitjacket or Opportunity*. New Brunswick, N.J.: Transaction Books.

Bennett, T., G. Martin, C. Mercer, and J. Woollacott. 1981. *Culture, Ideology and Social Process*. London: Open University Press.

Bennett, T., B. Waites, and G. Martin. 1982. *Popular Culture: Past and Present*. London: Open University Press.

Berlak, A. and H. Berlak. 1981. *Dilemmas of Schooling: Teaching and Social Change*. New York: Methuen.

Berman, E. 1984. "State Hegemony and the Schooling Process," *Journal of Education* 166, no 3: 239–253.

Bisseret, N. 1979. *Education, Class Language, and Ideology*. Boston: Routledge and Kegan Paul.

Boggs, C. 1979. "Marxism and the Role of Intellectuals." *New Political Science* 1, nos. 2, 3: 7–23.

Borman, K. and J. Spring. 1984. *Schools in Central Cities*. New York: Longman Publishing.

Bourdieu, P. and J. C. Passeron. 1977a. *Reproduction in Education, Society, and Culture*. Beverly Hills, Calif.: Sage.

Bourdieu, P. 1977b. *Outline of Theory and Practice*. Cambridge: Cambridge University Press.

Bourdieu, P. 1984. *Distinction: A Social Critique of the Judgement of Taste*. Cambridge, Mass.: Harvard University Press.

Bowles, S. and Gintis, H. 1976. *Schooling in Capitalist America*. New York: Basic Books.

Braverman, H. 1974. *Labor and Monopoly Capital*. New York: Monthly Review Press.

Bredo, E. and W. Feinberg, 1982. *Knowledge & Values in Social and Educational Research*. Philadelphia: Temple University Press.

Brenkman, J. L. 1983. "Seeing Beyond the Interests of Industry: Teaching Critical Thinking." *Journal of Education* 165, no. 3: 283–294.

Buswell, C. 1980. "Pedagogic Change and Social Change." *British Journal of Sociology of Education* 1, no. 3: 293–306.

Carlson, D. 1982. "Updating Individualism and the Work Ethic: Corporate Logic in the Classroom." *Curriculum Inquiry* 12, no. 2: 125–160.

Carnoy, M. 1984. *The State and Political Theory*. Princeton, N.J.: Princeton University Press.

Cherryholmes, C. 1983. "Knowledge, Power, and Discourse in Social Studies Education." *Journal of Education* 165, no. 4: 341–358.

Cohen, J. 1982. *Class and Civil Society: The Limits of Marxian Critical Theory*. Amherst: University of Massachusetts Press.

Connell, R. W., et al. 1982. *Making the Difference*. Sydney, Australia: George Allen and Unwin.

Connell, R. W. 1983. *Which Way Is Up?: Essays on Class, Sex, and Culture*. Sydney, Australia: George Allen and Unwin.

Corrigan, P. 1981. "On Moral Regulation: Some Preliminary Remarks." *Sociological Review* 29, no. 2: 313– 337.

Dallmayr, F. 1984. *Language and Politics*. South Bend, Ind.: Notre Dame University Press.

David, M. 1980. *The State, The Family, and Education*. Boston: Routledge and Kegan Paul.

Dewey, J. 1966. *Education and Democracy*. New York: Free Press.

Derrida, J. 1977. *Of Grammatology*. Baltimore: Johns Hopkins University Press.

Dorfman, A. 1983. *The Empire's Old Clothes*. New York: Pantheon.

Eagleton, T. 1983. *Literary Theory*. Minneapolis: University of Minnesota Press.

Everhart, R. 1983. *Reading, Writing and Resistance*. Boston: Routledge and Kegan Paul.

Felman, S. 1981. "Psychoanalysis and Education: Teaching Terminable and Interminable." *Yale French Studies* 29, no. 2: 313–337.

Feinberg, W. 1983. *Understanding Education*. New York: Oxford University Press.

Foucault, M. 1972. *The Archeology of Knowledge and the Discourse of Language*. New York: Harper and Row.

———. 1977. *Discipline and Punish*. New York: Pantheon.

———. 1980. *Power and Knowledge: Selected Interviews and Other Writings*, ed. C. Gordon. New York: Pantheon.

———. 1980. *The History of Sexuality*. New York: Vintage.

Frankenstein, M. 1983. "Critical Mathematics Education: An Application of Paulo Freire's Epistemology." *Journal of Education* 165, no. 4: 315–340.

Freire, P. 1973. *Pedagogy of the Oppressed*. New York: Seabury Press.

———. 1977. *Education for Critical Consciousness*. New York: Seabury Press.

———. 1978. *Pedagogy in Process*. New York: Seabury Press.

———. 1985. *The Politics of Education*. South Hadley, Mass.: Bergin and Garvey Publishers.

Giarelli, J. 1984. "A Public Philosophical Perspective on Teacher Education Reform." *Journal of Thought* 19, no. 4: 3–13.

Giddens, A. 1979. *Central Problems in Social Theory.* Berkeley: University of California Press.

Giroux, H. 1981. *Ideology, Culture and the Process of Schooling.* Philadelphia: Temple University Press.

———. 1983. *Theory and Resistance in Education.* South Hadley, Mass.: Bergin and Garvey Publishers.

———, et al., eds. 1981. *Curriculum and Instruction.* Berkeley, Calif.: McCutchan Publishing.

——— and R. Simon. 1984. "Curriculum Study and Cultural Politics." *Journal of Education* 166, no. 3: 226–238.

——— and D. Purpel, eds. 1983. *The Hidden Curriculum and Moral Education.* Berkeley, Calif.: McCutchan Publishing.

———. 1988. *Schooling and the Struggle for Public Life.* Minneapolis: University of Minnesota Press.

———. 1988. *Teachers as Intellectuals.* Westport, Conn.: Bergin and Garvey.

———. 1989. *Popular Culture, Schooling and Everyday Life* [with Roger Simon]. Westport, Conn.: Bergin and Garvey.

———. 1991. *Postmodern Education* [with Stanley Aronowitz]. Minneapolis: University of Minnesota Press.

———. 1992. *Border Crossings.* New York: Routledge.

———. 1993. *Living Dangerously: Multiculturalism and the Politics of Difference.* New York: Peter Lang Publishers, 1993.

Goodman, G. 1979. *Choosing Sides.* New York: Schocken Books.

Gramsci, A. 1971. *Selections from Prison Notebooks,* ed. and trans. Quinten Hoare and Geoffrey Smith. New York: International Publishers.

Greene, M. 1978. *Landscapes of Learning.* New York: Teachers College Press.

Habermas, J. 1983. *The Theory of Communicative Action,* Volume 1. Boston: Beacon Press.

Hall, S. 1983. "Education in Crisis." In *Is There Anyone Here from Education,* eds. A. Wolpe and J. Donald. London: Pluto Press.

——— and T. Jefferson, 1976. *Resistance Through Ritual.* London: Hutchinson.

Heller, A. 1985. *Everyday Life.* Boston: Routledge and Kegan Paul.

Henriques, J., et al. 1984. *Changing the Subject: Psychology, Social Regulation, and Subjectivity.* New York: Methuen.

Johnson, R. 1984. "Educational Politics: The Old and the New." In *Is There Anyone Here from Education,* eds. A. Wolpe and J. Donald. London: Pluto Press.

———. 1984. "What Is Cultural Studies." Mimeo. Birmingham, England: Centre for Contemporary Cultural Studies.

Kohl, H. 1984. *Growing Minds: On Becoming a Teacher.* New York: Harper and Row.

Kozol, J. 1985. *Illiterate America.* New York: Doubleday and Co.

Livingstone, D. 1983. *Class Ideologies and Educational Futures.* Philadelphia: Falmer Press.

Lundgren, U. 1983. *Between Hope and Happening: Text and Context in Curriculum.* Geelong, Australia: Deakin University Press.

Macedo, D. 1983. "The Politics of an Emancipatory Literacy in Cape Verde." *Journal of Education* 165, no. 1: 99–112.

McClaren, P. 1980. *Cries from the Corridor*. New York: Methuen.

———. 1985. *Schooling as a Ritual Performance*. Boston: Routledge and Kegan Paul.

Olson, C. P. 1983. "Inequality Remade: The Theory of Correspondence and the Context of French Immersion in Northern Ontario." *Journal of Education* 165, no. 1: 75–98.

Popkewitz, T. 1984. *Paradigm and Ideology in Educational Research*. Philadelphia: Falmer Press.

——— and B. R. Tabachnick, eds. 1981. *The Study of Schooling*. New York: Praeger Press.

———, et al. 1982. *The Myth of Educational Reform*. Madison: University of Wisconsin Press.

Rossi-Landi, F. 1983. *Language as Work and Trade*. South Hadley, Mass.: Bergin and Garvey.

Shapiro, S. 1984. "Choosing our Educational Legacy: Disempowerment or Emancipation." *Issues in Education* 2, no. 1: 11–22.

Simon, R. 1983. "But Who Will Let You Do It? Counter-Hegemonic Possibilities for Work Education." *Journal of Education* 165, no. 3: 235–256.

Sullivan, E. 1984. *A Critical Psychology: Interpretation of the Personal World*. New York: Plenum.

White, D. 1983. "After the Divide Curriculum." *The Victorian Teacher* (March 1983), pp. 6–7.

Whitty, G. and M. Young. 1977. *Society, State and Schooling*. Philadelphia: Falmer Press.

Willis, P. 1981. *Learning to Labor*. New York: Columbia University Press.

Wolpe, A. M. and J. Donald, eds. 1984. *Is There Anyone Here from Education*. London: Pluto Press.

Index